JOYCE CAROL OATES

GARLAND REFERENCE LIBRARY
OF THE HUMANITIES
(Vol. 509)

JOYCE CAROL OATES
An Annotated Bibliography

Francine Lercangée
with a Preface and annotations
by Bruce F. Michelson

GARLAND PUBLISHING, INC. • NEW YORK & LONDON
1986

Library of Congress Cataloging-in-Publication Data

Lercangée, Francine.
Joyce Carol Oates : an annotated bibliography.

(Garland reference library of the humanities ;
v. 509)
Includes indexes.
1. Oates, Joyce Carol, 1938–   —Bibliography.
I. Title.   II. Series.
Z8639.4.L47   1986   016.813'54   84-48022
[PS3565.A8]
ISBN 0-8240-8908-1 (alk. paper)

Printed on acid-free, 250-year-life paper
Manufactured in the United States of America

CONTENTS

Contents

III. Indexes

FOREWORD

This is the first attempt to compile a comprehensive, partly annotated bibliography of the writings by and about Joyce Carol Oates. The period extends from 1963 to August 1985.

The bibliography is divided into two major sections:
I. Primary sources
II. Secondary sources.

Section I contains all the works written by Joyce Carol Oates. The material is organized alphabetically except as concerns the criticism in part 7 which, owing to its very nature, is arranged chronologically.

Section II is arranged chronologically by year. Within each year, entries are first arranged chronologically, then alphabetically by the title of the periodicals. Each item is entered according to the following information when pertinent and available: author's name, title of article, name of periodical, volume, number, season, month, date, page(s). Although some articles were published anonymously, authorship was verified for all of them.

In case of reprints, the expression "repr. in" (reprinted in) only refers to publication in a subsequent year; if a reprinted item appeared in the same year as the first edition, the term "and in" was used.

Entries are identified by numbers in the order of presentation; cross-references guide the researcher whenever necessary.

In the course of time, periodicals may change their own presentation; specific characteristics may therefore disappear from our references which may, as a consequence appear incomplete but are strictly accurate.

ix

In part 7 of Section I and part 3 of Section II, most entries carry annotations. When the content of an article, particularly a short article, is clear from the title, there is no annotation.

Part 4 of Section II contains not only reviews but also review-essays specifically concerned with a particular item in Oates's writing. The subject may be a novel, a volume of collected short stories or poetry or a single poem or short story; its identification number is mentioned for the sake of clarity. These essays are arbitrarily gathered in this chapter and not in the one on "criticism on Joyce Carol Oates"; their length makes them easy to spot.

Several short stories by Joyce Carol Oates were reworked into chapters of novels; they do not appear in Section I part 2 as "reprinted" because in their later guise they were altered sometimes only slightly but at other times so significantly as to constitute a new piece.

The list of articles in languages other than English does not claim to be comprehensive. It is included only to increase the usefulness of this checklist.

Significant material relevant to Joyce Carol Oates constitutes this bibliography exclusively; only printed material was retained.

An index of keywords and proper names has been included as well as a subject index concerning the critical writings by Joyce Carol Oates.

Such then is the nature of this bibliography: perhaps not perfect but complete enough to be useful for some time.

Francine Lercangée
Center for American Studies
Brussels, January 1986

PREFACE

Bibliographies--even annotated ones--of living authors are very much a matter of bouncing along in a turbulent wake. With Joyce Carol Oates still working at the peak of her power, and with critical response only beginning to take shape, no grand overview, no serene, solid vantage point rises up from the headings, subheadings, and lists. Rarely indeed can such a compilation, worked up, as it were, in the very thick of the action, amount to more than a tally of what has gone on up to the end of some arbitrarily-chosen month or year, in this case, August of 1985. But given its timeliness, and the extraordinary qualities of the author concerned, the bibliography which Francine Lercangée has conceived and completed with great skill, could actually make a difference in the open-ended discussions it reviews, and be something beyond a directory to what one American author, still young and overwhelmingly prolific, has poured into print in twenty-odd years of an ongoing literary career, and of the stir which that outpouring has begun to cause. Millions of people have read a little Joyce Carol Oates; there may be many thousands who have read substantially more--but which Oates they consequently "know" can vary dramatically, depending on which Joyce Carol Oates they have read. In her case, unlike that of almost any other major contemporary writer, the impressions one could gather even from frequent encounters--a novel here, a batch of short stories there, essays, poems, reviews by her in this journal or that--can truly mislead one about what she thinks, what she knows, and what, as an artist and a critic, she has so urgently set out to do. To go deeply into an Updike, or a Mailer, or a Bellow, or a Lessing, may be essentially a matter of detailing an aesthetic or psychological portrait which a little reading has brought into passable focus; but to read thoroughly in Joyce Carol Oates is to abandon one conception after another of who she really is.

For the past twenty years, Oates has been furiously busy in every corner of the literary scene. Crisscrossing the path of the common reader like the White Rabbit, she has scattered her way with novels, short stories, poetry, plays, scholarly criticism, quick reviews, sketches, interviews; she publishes in *Critical Inquiry*, *Mademoiselle*, *The Hudson Review*, *The New Republic*, *Shenandoah*, *TV Guide*, world-class journals, pulp magazines, back-porch quarterlies and local newspapers; somehow she also finds time to teach at Princeton and to co-edit *The Ontario Review*. She can seem therefore to be racing off in all directions at once. Anyone who reads contemporary American literature can catch sight of her frequently, yet it can be very hard to tell where she is going. Her intellectual course has never been easy to plot, and her purpose can therefore seem as obscure and crazy as anything that goes on down in Alice's rabbithole. The novels, about a score of them now, and the masses of shorter fiction include out-and-out gothics, breezy social satires, portentous, naturalistic sagas, unassuming love stories, elaborately-restyled classical tragedies and variations on Medieval ballads, compendious meditations on the detective story; meanwhile the essays and reviews continue to appear. Out of sheer bewilderment, perhaps, too, out of envy (think of it: all these thick, best-selling novels, ten short story collections, nine books of poetry, plays, three books of criticism and enough other writings to put whole workshops of authors to shame, all before Oates turned forty !), one might take refuge with her detractors, who equate the sheer bulk of her output with a lack of care and genuine seriousness. There is no question that glimpsed superficially, the Oates phenomenon can seem like a headlong run towards nothing, the career like a self-dissipating welter of talk about everything. But in reviewing all this work from the perspective which a bibliography requires, a very different idea of Joyce Carol Oates comes clear. Simply the lists and annotations of the volume itself suggest this: that Oates is engaged in a quest which encompasses all this activity and which is genuinely worthy of admiration, that she has not only written a great deal more than most of her peers, but written with an extraordinary cogency, literacy, and thoughtfulness. The formal and moral challenges with which, as a novelist, short-story writer, and essayist, she continues to contend place her on the true intellectual and aesthetic leading edge of American fiction, and the questions which have engaged her for twenty years are the most complex, most mordant ones we face, concerning as they do the idea and the future of literature and American life. Not long ago, Oates wrote in the New York *Times* of a gathering at which she and a few good friends tried the comic, wistful game of composing epitaphs for one another: she reports that the one she took to heart for herself was, "She certainly tried." Perhaps this volume can suggest not only how hard but how thoughtfully, and with what intense and constant purpose Joyce Carol Oates has tried.

These are high ambitions indeed for a bibliography. The next few pages expand on thoughts that have occurred in putting it together, about a career still unfolding and a critical response as yet in its childhood. They are ruminations brought on by the project, about why Oates matters, about what kinds of questions have yet to be asked, or must continue to be asked, in order to pay a major writer the kind of attention she deserves.

To begin with, labels for Joyce Carol Oates apparently ought to be given up as hopeless, for the evidence to date suggests that they have done almost nothing to make sense of her as an artist, not even as rough, ground-level classifications to build from in describing what it is that Oates does. In her particular case, labels seem actually to have thwarted understanding, opening straight into a jumble of large-scale paradoxes, and bolstering in too many minds the idea that Oates is a literary gadabout rather than a deliberate artist and a careful, independent thinker. A tour of some of the rubrics that have been tried repeatedly on Oates will make the point. Spoken of regularly as our "champion gothicist," her most famous novel to date, *them*, is hailed not as gothic but as solidly naturalistic fiction; further, she insists on reading consummate gothic novels in subversive ways. *Wuthering Heights* for Oates is not a foray into mystery and emotional extremism, but a positively wholesome story about a very ungothic universe, and the inevitable return of peace and balance and harmony to the Yorkshire moors. But to group her with the realists instead is to have to account for a prodigious heap of allegories, ghost stories and surrealistic interludes. If one makes her out as an experimental formalist--a moment ago I implied something of the sort--then she seems hardly a loyal and well-mannered member of the club, attacking as she does most of today's academically-sanctioned "experimental" fiction as the predictable, vacuous parroting of the likes of Kafka, Borges, Barthelme, or some other style several decades safe, and--like a reactionary--warning her public that fiction which abandons characterization and plot risks losing its bloodline to the heart of the artistic impulse. If she qualifies as a feminist, she also rates as one of our most eloquent defenders of D.H. Lawrence; in an age of isms, she writes with disturbing catholicity of taste about writers as diverse as Henry Fielding, Oscar Wilde, Samuel Beckett, Ivy Compton-Burnett, Henry James, William Shakespeare, Thomas Mann, Saul Bellow, Jane Austen, Vladimir Nabokov. These paradoxes are not sophistry: self-evident in the fiction and the critical prose, they defy any notion that Oates's blaze of words is somehow kept up by burning the same ideological fuel over and over.

Oates's often-wonderful essays on other artists, in fact, help especially in moving us beyond the basic perception that she is by habit a free-ranging questioner rather than an enforcer of aesthetic codes. More strongly perhaps than the fiction itself, they collectively show how central to her thinking is the problem of identity, the question of how to define it, or at least locate it, of its resilience and volatility, of how it can be validly explored and challenged in a work of literature. The nature of the self, its genuineness, its vulnerabilities, its possible reinvention: Oates's abiding concern--almost an obsession--with this all-important modern issue has drawn her to the writers she has valued most and written about best: Lawrence, Joyce, Kafka, Conrad, Jung, Mann, Dostoyevsky, O'Connor, Ionesco, the old balladeers, writers who manage both to affirm and to challenge unsettlingly some idea about individuality, about human nature. Conversely, reductive, trendy thinking about the myths and realities of the self bring down her most devastating blows as a reviewer. How deep the concern runs is clear from a look back through the published criticism, which predates the important fiction. Back in her years as "J. Oates Smith," a young Master's candidate in literature, she was writing that the beguiling comic-seriousness of Fielding grows out of his enduring suspicion that the social masquerade roots deeper into us than we like to believe, that who we "truly" are is always in his fiction a puzzling matter. In the swarm of essays that have followed, Oates has come back again and again to the question with increasing profundity, erudition, and force. Many of the high points of her work as a critic owe their special value to one key perception: that at the center of the work of a truly major writer--James, Lawrence, Dostoyevsky, Conrad--there are disturbing questions about human nature, acutely modern anxieties which outface any schematic theorizing of their own time or ours. For Oates, the Henry James who apparently matters most is the James of *The Golden Bowl*, who can bear the possibility that his own most meticulously-realized characters, including his heroine, can save themselves only by losing themselves in prescribed social roles. Along the same line, the power she praises in the anti-feminist Lawrence is that he can both champion and assault the mysteries of the human heart, can portray passion—which Oates herself has often affirmed as virtually equivalent to character—as both vital and lethal to one's individuality. Writers apparently matter, or fail to matter, to Oates depending in great part on the intensity of their own thinking about identity, not ultimately on what stand they take in the controversy: in a literature which can do no greater service than to pose intelligent questions, we need Beckett and Ionesco as much as we need Joyce.

In some unfriendly circles Oates has established a reputation as a latter-day, suburban Cassandra, thundering and preaching in her fiction about the impending collapse of our culture, even delighting in a catastrophe which may have already begun. Unquestionably she shows a prophetic side, especially in the novels, and when the stories warn that our cities are burning and that our suburbs are reducing us all to murderous money-grubbers, one can freely take these pronouncements with the usual American amusement or indifference. Our time hardly lacks for gloomy amateur historicists, and our fiction doesn't have a distinguished record of forecasting social developments. If Oates is in any sense a true Cassandra, a prophet we need for some reason to take more seriously, it is because her own most important social ideas grow out of this same concern with identity. Again it is the problem of the self, of its nature and its future, which vitalizes the fiction and provides the real center of expertise for her large-scale observations of contemporary America. Some of her most idiosyncratic assertions, which out of context have caused a great deal of misunderstanding, have to do with the immense, fundamental change she sees underway, the impending death of the conception of individuality that has held sway in the West since the Renaissance, and the collapse of any number of cultural and psychological habits based on it. Not only has Oates absorbed too much, meditated too long, and commented too successfully on the subject to be dismissed offhand; her open-ended, undoctrinaire thinking stands by itself, in a wilderness of Postmodern theorizing, in its will not only to understand the issue in all of its dimensions and subtleties, but also to write fiction about it without reducing or mechanizing either the problem or the art. The crisis of modern identity turns up over and over, as a controlling idea in the criticism, as a major theme in the fiction and a reason for much of its success—and perhaps as the heart of the major artistic dilemma that Joyce Carol Oates is now facing.

Beyond the haunted houses, the rapists, killers, suicidal, dangerous lovers, and buried crimes which populate the fiction, the larger, more genuine suspense that Oates can conjure up often has to do with a kind of destructive transcendence of the self, observed with an admixture of yearning and horror reminiscent at times of Poe. An adolescent girl whose life is a pattern of shopping malls and drive-ins and the most banal aspirations awakens not merely to the Demon Lover and violent death, but for an instant to the emptiness of herself, and how some faceless passive archetypal victim has waited beneath the habits of mind she thought of as someone named Connie. In the interwoven stories of *All the Good People I've Left Behind*, bright, promising, lucky young people fight not just against mediocrity and middle age, but against a long slow deterioration into academic and suburban clichés--and most of them lose. The latest generation of Wendalls, Maureen and Jules, may be too intelligent and dynamic as characters to qualify as wholly naturalistic; their growing-up however is a hardening, a grim becoming of the world they behold. Nathan Vickery in *Son of the Morning* moves utterly beyond the world he knows, into his "God-trance" of perfect, blessed indifference, sublime and frightening in the inhumanity he has apparently achieved.

There is a danger in tracing such patterns, of course, beyond implying falsely that fiction with ambitious themes is by nature important or successful. In this particular case they tend to blur the very considerable artistic problem implicit in the theme itself. She is concerned not merely with characters but with the *idea* of character, and challenges, in vigorously Postmodern fashion, the assumption that individuality, as we cherish it, is consequential, strong and transcendent in familiar Renaissance or Romantic ways. Oates collides not merely with a crucial Western tradition but with a basic idea of storytelling, an idea born of those same depths. What her novels and short stories have tested in various ways, ever since *With Shuddering Fall*, is whether fiction can work as something more than one of those emptily-clever experiments she decries. She searches to determine if this idea of character is fundamentally transformed, in the light of what contemporary psychology, linguistics, philosophy, and history seem to be telling the world about human nature.

Like her successes, Oates's failures are born of this enterprise. *Angel of Light*, for example, attempts to propel two young middle-class Washingtonians, the son and daughter of a dead and possibly-murdered bureaucrat, into a re-enactment of the Orestia--a design which proves much too schematic to make a good novel. Again the thin surface-layers of the self erode; again the sub-surface archetypes emerge and the ancient drama is played out, but it all unfolds in tawdry and mechanistic fashion: the new suburban Orestes and Electra have neither the motive for passion nor the psychological or rhetorical fire to make the retelling worthwhile. The more recent *Mysteries of Winterthurn*, a parodic rhapsody on overheated American gothics and detective stories, centers on a young sleuth and a suitably-mysterious Harrassed Female: the main object of the book seems to be old-fashioned literary satire; but beyond the question of whether Charles Brockden Brown and Shirley Jackson merit eight hundred pages of friendly parody, the essential fault is apparently that the hero and his imprisoned lady are both too "universal," too generic and diaphanous, to carry the weight of these tales.

While this bibliography demonstrates that Oates needs no further drubbing by reviewers for past mistakes, it also makes it clear that she deserves a good deal more credit for the kind of mistakes she dares to make. How much easier it might be to write self-professed "anti-novels," to find some half-believable half-truth about the contemporary self--that we are all linguistic constructs, for example, or walking television sets--and simply work it to exhaustion. However, Oates shows uncommon intellectual honesty and courage in trying to see steadily all sides of the case, and as an artist she tries to dwell where so many of us now live: in the difficult terrain between, say, a Robbe-Grillet, who avows that contemporary fiction must contemplate above all its own undoing and that meaning, characters, and even authorial presences are throwback deceptions; and a Walter Ong, who holds that literature is nothing if not a human encounter, that there is a timeless, incurable urgency, philosophically valid or otherwise, that fiction be about selves, and by nature a communion of selves: characters, authors, readers.

In the past few years, Oates has frequently spoken harshly about the state of reviewing in America, and it is easy to imagine that some of her anger is provoked by presumptions that the difficult stance she tries to maintain is in any sense easy or compromised, or that her fiction is not a gamble with a great deal at stake. In the past few months, Oates has struck back most fiercely at her critics on the issue of violence itself. Having endured for years, in lecture halls and review columns all over the world, an insinuating question about the gore and brutality that do run through her stories, she has lately tried both to answer it summarily and to glare it down. Calling the question "insulting," "sexist," and "always stupid," she dignifies it with no more reply than that the world itself is now a nightmare of violence and that she intends to write about the world as it is and may become. Her point about the question and her answer to it, make sense as far as they go, yet the issue raised by it cannot, should not be so easily brushed off. That the question is a sexist gambit doesn't make much sense: Mailer, Updike, Kesey, Sam Peckinpah, and any number of other male writers and film-makers have had to talk about it again and again, though bullying audiences who wouldn't dare heckle a two-hundred pound Ken Kesey will perhaps rail more freely at a diminutive and ordinarily soft-spoken woman. The stupidity of the question has to do with its phrasing: The issue is not why Oates's work is violent, but why it is violent in its own special ways: why the catastrophes in her stories come with their own peculiar cadence and tone, why they play such a central role in structuring the fiction and in transforming the lives of characters. There are, actually, many questions here, which need to be sorted out and asked patiently and specifically. Why, for example, does killing or being killed seem to constitute, for an array of her characters of assorted temperaments and stations of life, the ultimate act of self-realization ? Why are they made out to be nothing until they pick up a gun or a knife, or compose themselves as they await the blow ? These questions are not rhetorical. If they are used rhetorically or as a veiled attack, Oates is certainly right to strike back at them. It is the *how* of the violence, not the why, which critics have yet to treat with full sympathy and care, and until they do, discussion of Oates will always be hampered and incomplete. When Barbara Grizzuti Harrison, a few years ago, made a powerful case that something in Joan Didion's narrative voice seemed to cherish those everyday horrors which her essays and novels manifestly deplore, Harrison touched upon a vital tension in Didion's work and took our response to it to a new level of complexity and intensity. Few critics have given Oates the same kind of thought, have looked, for example, for any sort of resonance between the mayhem against bodies in her fiction and a violently-transformed idea of selfhood. Oates's resentment of the violence-question hardly means that the matter is to be dropped: it means that there is more and better thinking and questioning yet to be done.

What summary one can offer in the meantime, from the bibliographer's perspective, is simply this: that regardless of what long-term reputation Joyce Carol Oates may enjoy later, she is that rarest of contemporaries, the genuinely experimental writer. While the sanctioned imitation of Barth or Borges may deny itself any chance of genuine success, it may secure itself in a way against conspicuous failure, protected as it is by "schools" and sheltered by precedent. What Oates is doing has been codified by no school, by no critic, not even by herself. She is willing to ask and write about the hardest aesthetic and social questions of her time, and she will not countenance the easy answer, will not play to the expectations of an established tradition or of an established *avant-garde*, however much trouble that refusal may cost her fiction. Joyce Carol Oates is that rarest of novelists: the novelist who, because she takes actual risks, can actually fail. Would that one could say the same for more than a handful of artists of our time, a few careers now unfolding that stand a chance of making a real difference in our literature.

Bruce F. Michelson
Urbana, 1985

ACKNOWLEDGMENTS

A book is seldom the result of a single individual's efforts; this is never so evident as with a bibliography. It is fitting therefore that I should start with a word of thanks to all those who have contributed time and energy to give this project its final shape:

to Professor Bruce Michelson of the University of Illinois at Urbana-Champaign, former Senior Fulbright Lecturer to Belgium, for writing the preface and overseeing the annotations;

to Phyllis Vanlandingham, his talented assistant, for the long hours of work which resulted in many of the annotations; to David Farris and Mary Ellen Farrell of the English Library of the University of Illinois, who worked with them on the project; to the Graduate College of the University of Illinois for a grant which helped complete the critical chapters.

to Dr. Martin Wittek, Director of the Royal Library, for his understanding and administrative cooperation;

to the Commission for Educational Exchange between the United States, Belgium and Luxembourg, for a Special Grant which facilitated research in the initial stages;

to Mrs. Dorothy Deflandre-Moore, Former Executive Director of the Commission for Educational Exchange between the United States, Belgium and Luxembourg, for the guidance and unfailing support in this instance, for her clarity of judgment and generosity of spirit over the years;

to all those, too numerous to be named individually who have worked for me in various institutions; among them, special thanks must go to John Muirhead, Librarian at the John F. Kennedy Institute of the Freie Universität Berlin, to the staff of the American Library (U.S.I.S.) in Brussels, to Rosmarie Zimmermann, Head of the Nordamerika-Bibliothek of the Universität Zürich, to Mr. Grobe of the Niedersächsische Staats- und Universitätsbibliothek;

to the staff of the Library of Congress and in particular to J.H. Hass, John Kimball and S. Thorin who generously provided easy access to their superb and priceless collections;

to the reference librarians of the University of California, Berkeley, Stanford University, the University of Chicago and the New York Public Library;

to all those, librarians and editors of journals in the United States who kindly answered my letters and queries;

to my assistants at the Center for American Studies, Brussels, M. Lodeweyckx, Librarian, and C. Devillé, Secretary whose dedication and commitment were a constant encouragement to continue and complete the project;

to the Mizrack-Gannt family for providing me with a home away from home; their sense of hospitality gives cross-cultural friendship a new meaning for me;

to my own family for their patience, their understanding, their love;

to G. Kuris, my editor, for his professional understanding.

No bibliography can ever claim to be complete and even less definitive. I have attempted however to be reasonably comprehensive and, I trust, useful. I have enjoyed the help of many in my efforts to collect hundreds of items, sometimes difficult to identify and locate. All errors and omissions naturally remain my responsibility.

F.L.

I. PRIMARY SOURCES

THE WORKS OF JOYCE CAROL OATES

CHRONOLOGY

Year	Novels	Short Stories	Poems	Plays	Anthologies	Essays & Other Non-Fiction
1963		By the North Gate				
1964	With Shuddering Fall					
1966		Upon the Sweeping Flood and Other Stories				
1967	A Garden of Earthly Delights					
1968	Expensive People		Women in Love and Other Poems / Anonymous Sins and Other Poems			
1969	them					
1970		The Wheel of Love and Other Stories	Love and Its Derangements: Poems			
1971	Wonderland				Scenes from American Life: Contemporary Short Fiction	
1972		Marriages and Infidelities				The Edge of Impossibility: Tragic Forms in Literature
1973	Do with What You Will		Angel Fire / Dreaming America and Other Poems			
1974		The Hungry Ghosts: Seven Allusive Comedies / The Goddess and Other Women / Where Are You Going, Where Have You Been?: Stories of Young America	Love and Its Derangements and Other Poems	Miracle Play		New Heaven, New Earth: The Visionary Experience in Literature
1975	The Assassins: A Book of Hours	The Seduction and Other Stories / The Poisoned Kiss and Other Stories from the Portuguese	The Fabulous Beasts			
1976	Childwold	Crossing the Border / The Triumph of the Spider Monkey / Night-Side				
1977			Season of Peril			
1978	Son of the Morning	A Sentimental Education	Women Whose Lives Are Food, Men Whose Lives Are Money			
1979	Cybele / Unholy Loves	All the Good People I've Left Behind			The Best American Short Stories 1979 (with S. Ravenel)	
1980	Bellefleur		Celestial Timepiece	Three Plays		
1981	Angel of Light					Contraries
1982	A Bloodsmoor Romance		Invisible Woman		Night Walks: A Bedside Companion	
1983						The Profane Art: Essays and Reviews
1984	Mysteries of Winterthurn	Last Days	Luxury of Sin			
1985	Solstice					
1986	Marya: A Life					
forthc.	The Crosswick's Horror					

NOVELS

1. *Angel of Light.* New York: Dutton, 1981. 434p.
   London: Cape, 1981. [448]p.
   New York: Warner Books, 1982. 608p.

2. *The Assassins: A Book of Hours.* New York: Vanguard
   Press, 1975. 568p.
   New York: Fawcett Crest, 1983. 544p.

3. *Bellefleur.* Franklin Center, PA: Franklin Library, 1980.
   661p. (limited edition)
   New York: Dutton, 1980. 558p. (A Henry Robbins
   Book)
   London: Cape, 1981. 558p.

4. *A Bloodsmoor Romance.* New York: Dutton, 1982. 615p.
   New York: Warner Books, 1983. 672p.

5. *Childwold.* New York: Vanguard Press, 1976. 295p.
   London: Gollancz, 1977. 295p.
   New York: Fawcett Crest, 1983. 288p.

6. *The Crosswick's Horror.* New York: Dutton, forthcoming.

7. *Cybele.* Santa Barbara: Black Sparrow Press, 1979.
   204p.

8. *Do with Me What You Will.* New York: Vanguard Press,
   1973. 561p.
   New York: Fawcett Crest, 1983. 544p.
   London: Gollancz, 1974. 561p.
   London: Coronet, 1976. 541p.

9. *Expensive People.* New York: Vanguard Press, 1968.
   308p.
   London: Gollancz, 1969. 308p.
   New York: Fawcett Crest, 1970, 1974, 1982. 256p.
   London: Panther, 1972. 224p.

10. *A Garden of Earthly Delights.* New York: Vanguard
    Press, 1967. 440p.
    London: Gollancz, 1970. 440p.
    St. Albans: Panther, 1973. 398p.

11. *Marya: A Life.* New York: Dutton, forthcoming 1986.

12. *Mysteries of Winterthurn.* Franklin Center, PA:
    Franklin Library, 1984. 482p. (limited edition)
    New York: Dutton, 1984. 482p.

13. *Solstice.* New York: Dutton, 1985. 243p.
    South Yarmouth, MA: J. Curley, 1985. 388p.

14. *Son of the Morning.* New York: Vanguard Press, 1978.
    382p.
    London: Gollancz, 1979. 382p.

15. *them.* New York: Vanguard Press, 1969. 508p.
    Greenwich, CT: Fawcett Crest, 1970. 480p.
    London: Gollancz, 1971. 508p.
    London: Panther, 1972. 480p.
    Franklin Center, PA: Franklin Library, 1979.
    601p.

16. *Unholy Loves.* New York: Vanguard Press, 1979. 335p.
    London: Gollancz, 1980. 335p.
    New York: Fawcett Crest, 1984. 320p.

17. *With Shuddering Fall.* New York: Vanguard Press,
    1964. 316p.
    London: Cape, 1965. 316p.
    Greenwich, CT: Fawcett, 1971. 224p.

18. *Wonderland.* New York: Vanguard Press, 1971. 512p.
    London: Gollancz, 1972. 508p.
    Greenwich, CT: Fawcett, 1973. 508p.

SHORT STORIES AND TALES

19. "Accomplished Desires." *Esquire*, 69 (May 1968): 102-132.
    Repr. in *Prize Stories 1969: The O. Henry Awards*, William Abrahams, ed. Garden City, NY: Doubleday, 1969, pp. 43-61.
    Repr. in *The Wheel of Love and Other Stories* (# 402), pp. 127-149.
    Repr. in *The Fact of Fiction: Social Relevance in the Short Story*, Cyril M. Gulassa, comp. San Francisco: Canfield Press, 1972, pp. 298-315.
    Repr. in *The Process of Fiction*, Barbara McKenzie, ed. New York: Harcourt Brace Jovanovich, 1974, pp. 500-518.
    and in *Where Are You Going, Where Have You Been ?* (# 404), pp. 133-155.
    Repr. in *Women and Men, Men and Women*, William Smart, ed. New York: Harper & Row, 1975, pp. 196-226.
    Repr. in *Wild Saturday and Other Stories* (# 412), pp. 21-42.

20. "Adultery." *Critic* (Chicago), 26 (Apr.-May 1968): 40-47.

21. "All the Beautiful Women." *Saturday Evening Post*, 241 (June 29, 1968): 50-52.

22. "All the Good People I've Left Behind." *Redbook*, 149 (May 1977): 235-251.
    Repr. in *All the Good People I've Left Behind* (# 23), pp. 145-227.

23. *All the Good People I've Left Behind.* Santa Barbara: Black Sparrow Press, 1979. 227p.
    Contains: The Leap; High; Intoxication; The Tryst; Blood-Swollen Landscape; Eye-Witness; The Hallucination; Sentimental Journey; Walled City; All the Good People I've Left Behind.

24. "Alone." *Cosmopolitan*, 196 (May 1984): 330-331, 348.

25. "An American Adventure." *TriQuarterly*, 20 (Winter 1971): 312-324.
    Repr. in *Where Are You Going, Where Have You Been ?* (# 404), pp. 99-114.
    Repr. in *The Seduction and Other Stories* (# 326), pp. 13-24.

26. "Anatomical Studies." *Chatelaine*, 53 (Nov. 1980): 62, 148, 152, 156, 160.

27. "Ancient Airs, Voices." *Antioch Review* (forthcoming 1986).

28. "... & Answers." *Family Circle*, 82, i (Jan. 1973): 12-16, 116-118.
    Repr. in *The Goddess and Other Women* (# 156), pp. 153-166.

29. "And How Is Your Life." *Cosmopolitan*, 171 (Aug. 1971): 170-175.

30. "Angst." *University of Windsor Review*, 10, i (Fall-Winter 1974): 69-86.
    and in *The Hungry Ghosts* (# 179), pp. 179-200.

31. "The Antique Clock." *Malahat Review*, 56 (Oct. 1980): 118-125.

32. "Archways." *Cosmopolitan*, 153 (Mar. 1965): 76-81.
    Repr. in *Upon the Sweeping Flood and Other Stories* (# 385), pp. 166-185.

33. "Assailant." *Prairie Schooner*, 39, iv (Winter 1965-66): 330-336.
    Repr. in *The Wheel of Love and Other Stories* (# 402), pp. 300-307.

34. "Assault." *Review of Existential Psychology and Psychiatry*, 12, i (1973): 56-74.
    Repr. in *The Goddess and Other Women* (# 156), pp. 438-461.

35. "At the Seminary." *Kenyon Review*, 27, iii (Summer 1965): 483-502.
    Repr. in *Upon the Sweeping Flood and Other Stories* (# 385), pp. 103-124.

36. "Baby." *Ontario Review* (forthcoming).

37. "Back Country." *Shenandoah*, 34, i (1982-83): 3-14.

38. "Back There." *Epoch*, 22, i (Fall 1972): 87-103.
    Repr. in *Where Are You Going, Where Have You
    Been ?* (# 404), pp. 293-314.

39. "Ballad." *Southwest Review*, 70, ii (Spring 1985):
    216-229.

40. "Ballerina." *Georgia Review*, 34, iv (Winter 1980):
    735-750.

41. "The Bat." *Shenandoah*, 33, ii (1982): 19-33.

42. "Beautiful Girl." *Canto*, 2, iii (Fall 1978): 1-34.

43. "The Bequest." *New England Review*, 7, iii (Spring
    1985): 386-409.

44. "The Bingo Master" in *Dark Forces: New Stories of
    Suspense and Supernatural Horror*, Kirby
    McCauley, ed. New York: Viking Press, 1980, pp.
    106-128.

45. "Birds of Night." *Exile*, 7, iii-iv (1981): 10-35.

46. "The Birth of Tragedy." *Exile*, 1, iv (1974): 44-65.
    and in *The Hungry Ghosts* (# 179), pp. 103-130.

47. "The Birthday Celebration." *Virginia Quarterly Review*,
    56, i (Winter 1980): 51-62.

48. "Black Dahlia." *Ohio Review*, 34 (1985): 104-121.

49. "Black Eucharist." *Canto*, 1, iii (Fall 1977): 15-38.

50. *The Blessing.* Santa Barbara: Black Sparrow Press,
    June 1976. 16p. (limited edition) (Sparrow; 45)
    Repr. in *Night-Side* (# 260), pp. 331-347.

51. "Blindfold." *Southern Review* (Baton Rouge), n.s., 8,
    ii (Spring 1972): 438-452.
    Repr. in *The Goddess and Other Women* (# 156),
    pp. 35-50.

52. "A Bloodsmoor Romance." *Ms.*, 10 (June 1982): 60-61,
    98.

53. "Bloodstains." *Harper's*, 243 (Aug. 1971): 82-88.
    Repr. in *Night-Side* (# 260), pp. 168-185.

54. "Blood-Swollen Landscape." *Southern Review* (Baton
    Rouge), n.s., 11, i (Winter 1975): 212-225.
    Repr. in *Prize Stories 1976: The O. Henry
    Awards*, William Abrahams, ed. Garden City, NY:
    Doubleday, 1976, pp. 186-200.
    Repr. in *All the Good People I've Left Behind*
    (# 23), pp. 63-77.

55. "Bodies." *Harper's Bazaar*, 3099 (Feb. 1970): 122-125.
    and in *The Wheel of Love and Other Stories*
    (# 402), pp. 256-281.
    Repr. in *Strangeness: A Collection of Curious
    Tales*, Thomas M. Disch and Charles Naylor, eds.
    New York: Avon Books, 1978, pp. 124-144.

56. "The Boy." *Playgirl*, 12 (Dec. 1984): 74.

57. "Boy and Girl." *Prism International*, 8, iii (Spring
    1969): 4-17.
    Repr. in *The Wheel of Love and Other Stories*
    (# 402), pp. 282-299.
    Repr. in *Where Are You Going, Where Have You
    Been ?* (# 404), pp. 157-174.
    Repr. in *Wild Saturday and Other Stories* (# 412),
    pp. 62-78.

58. "Boys at a Picnic" in *By the North Gate* (# 61), pp.
    80-91.

59. "The Brain of Dr. Vicente." Fernandes; translated by
    J.C. Oates, in *The Poisoned Kiss and Other
    Stories* (# 292), pp. 26-28.

60. "By the North Gate" in *By the North Gate* (# 61), pp.
    236-253.

61. *By the North Gate*. New York: Vanguard Press, 1963.
    253p.
    Greenwich, CT: Fawcett, 1971. 208p.
    Contains: Swamps; The Census Taker; Ceremonies;
    Sweet Love Remembered; Boys at a Pic_i_ astoral
    Blood; An Encounter with the Blind; ___ Edge
    of the World; A Legacy; In the Old ___ The
    Fine White Mist of Winter; The ___per___ ___Spirit;
    By the North Gate.

62. "By the River." *December Magazine*, 10, i (1968):
     72-80.
     Repr. in *The Best American Short Stories*, Martha
     Foley and David Burnett, eds. Boston, MA:
     Houghton Mifflin, 1969, pp. 195-212.
     Repr. in *Marriages and Infidelities* (# 237), pp.
     127-147.
     Repr. in *Superfiction, or the American Story
     Transformed: An Anthology*, Joe David Bellamy,
     ed. New York: Vintage Books, 1975, pp. 91-112.

63. "Canal Road." *Southern Review* (Baton Rouge), n.s.,
     20, iii (Summer 1984): 610-631.

64. "Casualties." *Chatelaine*, 51 (July 1978): 40, 52, 54,
     56, 58, 60, 62.

65. "The Census Taker" in *By the North Gate* (# 61), pp.
     28-40.

66. "Ceremonies" in *By the North Gate* (# 61), pp. 41-65.
     Repr. in *Fourteen for Now: A Collection of
     Contemporary Stories*, John Simon, ed. New York:
     Harper & Row, 1969, pp. 196-226.

67. "The Changeling." *Missouri Review*, 3, ii (Winter 1980):
     43-61.

68. "Childhood." *Epoch*, 16, iii (Spring 1967): 204-222.
     Repr. under title "The Daughter" in *The Goddess
     and Other Women* (# 156), pp. 51-71 (revised
     version).

69. "The Children." *Transatlantic Review*, 32 (Summer
     1969): 48-63.
     Repr. in *Prize Stories 1971: The O. Henry
     Awards*, William Abrahams, ed. Garden City, NY:
     Doubleday, 1971, pp. 208-225.
     Repr. in *Marriages and Infidelities* (# 237), pp.
     216-236.

70. "Chloe." *Fiction International*, 15, i (1984): 132-148.

71. "   lavichord." *Confrontation*, 20 (Spring-Summer
              ): 29-39.

72. '   ling the Case of Bobby G.." *Atlantic*, 231
     (Feb. 1   84-88, 90-92.
     Repr. in *The Goddess and Other Women* (# 156),
     pp. 15-34.

73. "Conquistador." *Weekend Magazine*, 28, iv (June 17, 1978): 28–30.

74. "Convalescing." *Virginia Quarterly Review*, 45, iii (Summer 1969): 430–450.
    Repr. in *The Wheel of Love and Other Stories* (# 402), pp. 80–101.

75. "Corinne." *North American Review*, 260, iii (Fall 1975): 30–42.

76. "Crossing the Border." *New York Times Magazine* (Dec. 1, 1974): 127.
    Repr. in *Crossing the Border* (# 77), pp. 9–14.

77. *Crossing the Border. Fifteen Tales*. New York: Vanguard Press, 1976. 256p.
    London: Gollancz, 1978. 256p.
    New York: Fawcett Crest, 1983. 320p.
    Contains: Crossing the Border; Love. Friendship; Hello Fine Day Isn't It?; Through the Looking Glass; Natural Boundaries; Dreams; Customs; The Transformation of Vincent Scoville; The Golden Madonna; The Scream; The Liberation of Jake Hanley; An Incident in the Park; Falling in Love in Ashton, British Columbia; The Tempter; River Rising.

78. "The Cruel Master." Fernandes; translated by J.C. Oates, in *The Poisoned Kiss and Other Stories* (# 292), pp. 92–103.

79. "The Crystal Sea." *Saturday Night*, 97 (Jan. 1982): 40–51.

80. *Cupid and Psyche*. New York: Albondocani Press, 1970. 20p. (limited edition) (Albondocani Press Publication; 10)
    Repr. under title "The Dreaming Woman" in *The Seduction and Other Stories* (# 326), pp. 257–263.

81. "The Cure for Folly." *TriQuarterly*, 59 (Winter 1984): 29–52.

82. "Customs." *Fiddlehead*, 102 (Summer 1974): 5–14.
    Repr. in *Crossing the Border* (# 77), pp. 106–117.

83. *Daisy.* Santa Barbara: Black Sparrow Press, 1977. 34p.
    and in *Night-Side* (# 260), pp. 221-243.
    Repr. in *Major American Short Stories*, A. Walton
    Litz, ed. New York: Oxford University Press,
    1980, pp. 778-796.

84. "The Dark." *Southwest Review*, 55, iv (Autumn 1970):
    334-353.

85. "The Daughter" in *The Goddess and Other Women*
    (# 156), pp. 51-71.
    See "Childhood" (# 68).

86. "Dawn, Dusk." *Shenandoah*, 31, iv (1980): 79-86.

87. "The Dead" in *Marriages and Infidelities* (# 237), pp.
    453-488.
    Repr. in *Prize Stories 1973: The O. Henry
    Awards*, William Abrahams, ed. Garden City, NY:
    Doubleday, 1973, pp. 1-34.
    See "The Death of Dreams" (# 88).

88. "The Death of Dreams." *McCall's*, 98 (July 1971): 70,
    115-122.
    Repr. under title "The Dead" in *Marriages and
    Infidelities* (# 237), pp. 453-488.

89. "The Death of Mrs. Sheer" in *Upon the Sweeping Flood
    and Other Stories* (# 385), pp. 61-88.

90. "December." *Carolina Quarterly*, 35, ii (Winter 1983):
    21-30.

91. "Déjà Vu." *Missouri Review*, 2, i (Fall 1978): 53-69.

92. "Delia's Adventures." *Denver Quarterly*, 19, ii (Summer
    1984): 3-28.

93. "Democracy in America." *Shenandoah*, 24, iii (Spring
    1973): 21-38.
    Repr. in *The Hungry Ghosts* (# 179), pp. 10-30.

94. "Demons." *Southern Review* (Baton Rouge), n.s., 6, i
    (Winter 1970): 55-75.
    and in *The Wheel of Love and Other Stories*
    (# 402), pp. 232-255.
    Repr. in *Wild Saturday and Other Stories* (# 412),
    pp. 79-101.

95. "A Descriptive Catalogue." *Carolina Quarterly*, 25, iii
     (Fall 1973): 19–38.
     Repr. in *The Hungry Ghosts* (# 179), pp. 77–101.

96. "Détente." *Southern Review* (Baton Rouge), n.s., 17,
     iii (Summer 1981): 584–604.
     Repr. in *Pushcart Prize VII: Best of the Small
     Presses, 1982–83*, vol. 7, Bill Henderson, ed.
     Wainscott: Pushcart Press, 1982, pp. 270–294.
     Repr. in *Last Days* (# 208), pp. 113–136.

97. "Did You Ever Slip on Red Blood ?" *Harper's*, 244
     (Apr. 1972): 80–88.
     and in *Marriages and Infidelities* (# 237),   pp.
     338–360.

98. "Dies Irae." *New Letters*, 45, i (Fall 1978): 49–54.

99. "Distance." Fernandes; translated by J.C. Oates, in
     The Poisoned Kiss and Other Stories (# 292), pp.
     54–65.

100. "Do with Me What You Will." *Playboy*, 20 (June 1973):
     92–94, 190–193.
     and in *Antaeus*, 10 (Summer 1973): 66–83.

101. "The Doll." *Epoch*, 28, ii (Winter 1979): 202–218.
     Repr. in *The Arbor House Treasure of Horror
     and the Supernatural*, Bill Pronzini and Barry N.
     Malzberg, comps. New York: Arbor House, 1981,
     pp. 514–535.

102. "The Doomed Girl." *Bennington Review*, 8 (Sept.
     1980): 2–11.

103. "Double Solitaire." *Michigan Quarterly Review*
     (forthcoming).

104. "DOUBLE TRAGEDY STRIKES TENNESSEE HILL
     FAMILY." *Carolina Quarterly*, 24, i (Winter 1972):
     87–99.
     Repr. in *The Seduction and Other Stories*
     (# 326), pp. 210–223.

105. "The Dreaming Woman" in *The Seduction and Other
     Stories* (# 326), pp. 257–263.
     See "Cupid and Psyche" (# 80).

106. "Dreams." *Prairie Schooner*, 44, iv (Winter 1969-70): 331-351.
     Repr. in *Crossing the Border* (# 77), pp. 83-105.

107. "The Dungeon." *Iowa Review*, 6, i (Winter 1975): 1-11.
     Repr. in *Night-Side* (# 260), pp. 134-148.

108. "Dying." *Transatlantic Review*, 20 (Spring 1966): 64-84.
     and in *Upon the Sweeping Flood and Other Stories* (# 385), pp. 186-208.
     Repr. in *American Literary Anthology 1*, John Hawkes, et al., eds. New York: Noonday Press, 1968, pp. 67-85.

109. "The Dying Child." *Antioch Review*, 26, ii (Summer 1966): 247-263.
     Repr. in *The Goddess and Other Women* (# 156), pp. 283-302.

110. "Early Winter." Fiction Network Magazine (forthcoming).

111. "The Ebony Casket." *Exile*, 7, i-ii (1980): 21-32.

112. "Edge of the World" in *By the North Gate* (# 61), pp. 147-163.

113. "Elena." *Works in Progress*, 9 (Apr. 1973): 2-16.

114. "The Embrace." *Exile*, 3, iii-iv (1976): 5-19.

115. "The Enchanted Piano." Fernandes; translated by J.C. Oates. *Harper's Bazaar* (June 1971): 76.
     Repr. in *The Poisoned Kiss and Other Stories* (# 292), pp. 50-53.

116. "An Encounter with the Blind" in *By the North Gate* (# 61), pp. 114-127.

117. "Exile" in *Night-Side* (# 260), pp. 186-201.
     Repr. in *Tales*, 4 (Summer 1978): 3-16.

118. "The Expense of Spirit" in *By the North Gate* (# 61), pp. 217-235.

119. "Explorations." *Remington Review*, 1, ii (Oct. 1973):
      5-18.
      Repr. in *The Goddess and Other Women* (# 156),
      pp. 210-225.

120. "Expressway." *California Quarterly*, 13-14   (Spring-
      Summer 1978): 9-25.

121. "Extraordinary Popular Delusions." *Virginia Quarterly
      Review*, 48, ii (Spring 1972): 238-259.
      and in *Marriages and Infidelities* (# 237),   pp.
      148-170.

122. "Eye-Witness." *Michigan   Quarterly   Review*,   17,   i
      (Winter 1978): 26-34.
      Repr. in *All the Good People I've Left Behind*
      (# 23), pp. 79-87.

123. "Falling in Love in Ashton, British Columbia." *Epoch*,
      24, iii (Spring 1975): 279-289.
      Repr. in *Crossing the Border* (# 77), pp. 212-230.

124. "Famine Country." *Yale Review*, 66, iv (Summer 1977):
      534-550.
      and in *Night-Side* (# 260), pp. 149-167.

125. "A Far Countree." *Critic* (Chicago), 27 (Dec. 1968-
      Jan. 1969): 68-77.

126. "Fat." *Antaeus*, 2 (Spring 1971): 9-21.

127. "Fatal Woman." *Fiddlehead*, 114 (Summer 1977): 25-28.
      and in *Night-Side* (# 260), pp. 256-261.
      Repr. in *Playgirl*, 6 (June 1978): 95.
      Repr. in *The Arbor House Treasury of Mystery
      and Suspense*, Bill Pronzini, Barry N. Malzberg
      and Martin H. Greenberg, comps. New York:
      Arbor House, 1982, pp. 434-438.

128. "Fateful Mismatches." *Ontario Review*, 11 (Fall-Winter
      1979-80): 5-14.

129. "The Fine White Mist of Winter." *Literary Review*, 5,
      iii (Spring 1962): 349-363.
      Repr. in *By the North Gate* (# 61), pp. 198-216.
      and in *The Best American Short Stories*, Martha
      Foley and David Burnett, eds. Boston, MA:
      Houghton Mifflin, 1963, pp. 220-234.

and in *Prize Stories 1963: The O. Henry Awards*, Richard Poirier, ed. Garden City, NY: Doubleday, 1963, pp. 216-229.

130. "First Death." *Mademoiselle*, 84 (June 1978): 188-194.

131. "First Views of the Enemy." *Prairie Schooner*, 28, i (Spring 1964): 50-61.
Repr. in *The Best American Short Stories*, Martha Foley and David Burnett, eds. Boston, MA: Houghton Mifflin, 1965, pp. 259-270.
and in *Prize Stories 1965: The O. Henry Awards*, Richard Poirier and William Abrahams, eds. Garden City, NY: Doubleday, 1965, pp. 165-175.
Repr. in *Upon the Sweeping Flood and Other Stories* (# 385), pp. 89-102.
Repr. in *Other People's Lives: 34 Short Stories*, Leonard R.N. Ashley, comp. Boston, MA: Houghton Mifflin, 1970, pp. 409-418.
Repr. in *American Models: A Collection of Modern Stories*, James E. Miller, Robert Hayden and Robert O'Neal, eds. Glenview: Scott, Foresman, 1973, pp. 99-108.

132. "Five Pieces from Azulejos"; translated from the Portuguese by Joyce Carol Oates. *Transatlantic Review*, 45 (Spring 1973): 133-144.
Contains: The Seduction; In a Public Place; Journey; Impotence; Sunlight/Twilight.

133. "The Footbridge." *California Quarterly* (forthcoming).

134. "For I Will Consider My Cat Jeoffry." *Michigan Quarterly Review*, 23, iii (Summer 1984): 385-399.

135. "Four Seasons." *Virginia Quarterly Review*, 42, i (Winter 1966): 95-107.

136. "Four Summers." *Yale Review*, 56, iii (Spring 1967): 406-425.
Repr. in *The American Literary Anthology 2*, George Plimpton and Peter Ardery, eds. New York: Random House, 1969, pp. 342-361.
Repr. in *The Wheel of Love and Other Stories* (# 402), pp. 209-231.
Repr. in *Where Are You Going, Where Have You Been ?* (# 404), pp. 175-196.
Repr. in *Fiction 100: An Anthology of Short Stories*, James H. Pickering, ed. New York: Macmillan, 1978, pp. 728-738.

137. "Free." *Quarterly Review of Literature*, 17, iii-iv
      (1971): 415-440.
      Repr. in *The Goddess and Other Women* (# 156),
      pp. 125-152.

138. "Friday Evening." *Penthouse* (Mar. 1980): 110-113,
      176-177.

139. "Frissons." *Blast*, 3 (Aug. 1984): 237-256.

140. "The Funeral." *Miami Herald Tropic Magazine Section*
      (June 19, 1983): 16.

141. *Funland*. Concord, NH: William Ewert, 1983. (limited
      edition)
      Repr. in *Last Days* (# 208), pp. 40-53.

142. "Further Confessions." *Chicago Review*, 28, iv (Spring
      1977): 61-77.
      and in *Night-Side* (# 260), pp. 309-330.
      Repr. in *The Slaying of the Dragon: Modern
      Tales of the Playful Imagination*, Franz
      Rottensteiner, ed. New York: Harcourt Brace
      Jovanovich, 1984, pp. 209-234.

143. "A Garden of Earthly Delights." *Shenandoah*, 17, ii
      (Winter 1966): 21-43.

144. "Gargoyle." *StoryQuarterly*, 5-6 (June 1977): 93-101.

145. "Gay." *Playboy*, 23 (Dec. 1976): 104, 106, 120.
      Repr. in *The Best American Short Stories 1977
      and the Yearbook of the American Short Story*,
      Martha Foley, ed. Boston, MA: Houghton Mifflin,
      1977, pp. 235-255.

146. "Getting and Spending" in *The Seduction and Other
      Stories* (# 326), pp. 44-67.

147. "Ghost Town." *Literary Review*, 25, iv (Summer 1982):
      571-610.

148. "The Giant Woman." *Kansas Quarterly*, 8, i (Winter
      1976): 45-55.
      Repr. in *Night-Side* (# 260), pp. 202-220.

149. "Gifts." *Kenyon Review*, 28, iv (Fall 1966): 499-520.
     Repr. in *The Seduction and Other Stories*
     (# 326), pp. 25-43.

150. *The Girl*. Cambridge, MA: Pomegranate Press, 1974.
     34p. (limited edition)
     and in *The Goddess and Other Women* (# 156),
     pp. 3-14.

151. "A Girl at the Edge of the Ocean." *Falcon*, 4 (Spring
     1972): 51-67.
     Repr. in *The Goddess and Other Women* (# 156),
     pp. 324-343.
     and in *Where Are You Going, Where Have You
     Been ?* (# 404), pp. 271-291.
     Repr. in *Wild Saturday and Other Stories* (# 412),
     pp. 102-121.

152. "The Girl with the Beautiful Face." *University Review*,
     33, iii (Spring 1967): 180-188.

153. "A Girl Worth Twenty Million" in *Cosmopolitan's Winds
     of Love: Romantic and Erotic Tales*. New York:
     Cosmopolitan Books, 1975, pp. 68-82.

154. "A Girl Worth Two Million." *Cosmopolitan*, 166 (Feb.
     1969): 120-127.

155. "The Goddess." *Antaeus*, 13-14 (Spring-Summer 1974):
     200-217.
     and in *The Goddess and Other Women* (# 156),
     pp. 402-424.

156. *The Goddess and Other Women*. New York: Vanguard
     Press, 1974. 468p.
     London: Gollancz, 1975. 468p.
     Contains: The Girl; Concerning the Case of
     Bobby G.; Blindfold; The Daughter; In the
     Warehouse; Ruth; The Maniac; ... & Answers; I
     Must Have You; Magna Mater; Explorations; Small
     Avalanches; The Voyage to Rosewood; Waiting;
     The Dying Child; Narcotic; A Girl at the Edge of
     the Ocean; Unpublished Fragments; A Premature
     Autobiography; Psychiatric Services; The
     Goddess; Honeybit; Assault; The Wheel.

157. "Going-Away Party." *Antaeus*, 36 (Winter 1980): 113-130.
     Repr. in *Story: Fiction Past Present*, Boyd Litzinger and Joyce Carol Oates, eds. Lexington, MA: D.C. Heath, 1984.

158. "Golden Gloves." *Washington Post Magazine* (Aug. 4, 1985): 13-15, 29.

159. "The Golden Madonna." *Playboy*, 21 (Mar. 1974): 118.
     Repr. in *Crossing the Border* (#77), pp. 148-168.

160. "The Granite Springs Elegies." *California Quarterly*, 22 (Summer 1983): 7-18.

161. "Growing Seasons & Killing Frosts." *Agni Review*, 17 (Fall 1982): 57-66.

162. "The Hallucination." *Chicago Review*, 26, iv (Spring 1975): 19-30.
     Repr. in *Pushcart Prize [I]: Best of the Small Presses*, Bill Henderson, ed. Yonkers: Pushcart Book Press, 1976, pp. 404-416.
     Repr. in *All the Good People I've Left Behind* (#23), pp. 89-101.

163. "Happy." *Vanity Fair*, 47 (Dec. 1984): 124.

164. "Happy Onion." *Antioch Review*, 31, iv (Winter 1971-72): 459-475.
     Repr. in *Marriages and Infidelities* (#237), pp. 237-259.
     Repr. in *Where Are You Going, Where Have You Been ?* (#404), pp. 33-56.

165. "Harriet Stillman." *Saturday Night*, 93 (Nov. 1978): 32-44, 87-94.

166. "Harrow Street at Linden." *Massachusetts Review*, 24, iv (Winter 1983): 793-817.

167. "The Haunted House." *Kansas Quarterly*, 12, i (Winter 1980): 31-43.

168. "The Heavy Sorrow of the Body." *Northwest Review*, 11, ii (1968): 4-26.
     Repr. in *The Wheel of Love and Other Stories* (#402), pp. 308-333.

169. "Hell" in *The Seduction and Other Stories* (# 326), pp. 250-256.

170. "Hello Fine Day Isn't It ?" *Malahat Review*, 38 (Apr. 1976): 53-60.
and in *Crossing the Border* (# 77), pp. 39-47.

171. "Help..." *Southern Review* (Baton Rouge), n.s., 10, iii (Summer 1974): 698-721.
Repr. under title "The Seduction" in *The Seduction and Other Stories* (# 326), pp. 107-128.

172. "High." *Southern Review* (Baton Rouge), n.s., 14, i (Winter 1978): 125-136.
Repr. in *All the Good People I've Left Behind* (# 23), pp. 19-31.

173. "Honeybit." *Confrontation*, 9 (Fall 1974): 25-33.
and in *The Goddess and Other Women* (# 156), pp. 425-437.

174. "Honeymoon." *Greensboro Review*, 21 (Winter 1976-77): 57-81.

175. "How I Contemplated the World from the Detroit House of Correction and Began My Life over Again." *TriQuarterly*, 15 (Spring 1969): 5-21.
Repr. in *The Wheel of Love and Other Stories* (# 402), pp. 170-189.
and in *The Best American Short Stories 1970 and the Yearbook of the American Short Story*, Martha Foley and David Burnett, eds. Boston, MA: Houghton Mifflin, 1970, pp. 207-222.
and in *Prize Stories 1970: The O. Henry Awards*, William Abrahams, ed. Garden City, NY: Doubleday, 1970, pp. 275-291.
Repr. in *Anti-Story: An Anthology of Experimental Fiction*, Philip Stevick, ed. New York: Free Press, 1971, pp. 23-39.
Repr. in *Cutting Edges: Young American Fiction for the '70s*, Jack Hicks, ed. New York: Holt, Rinehart & Winston, 1973, pp. 275-291.
Repr. in *Where Are You Going, Where Have You Been ?* (# 404), pp. 115-132.
and in *The Process of Fiction*, Barbara McKenzie, ed. New York: Harcourt Brace Jovanovich, 1974, pp. 475-489.
and in *What Is the Short Story ?*, Eugene Current-Garcia and Walton R. Patrick, eds. Glenview: Scott, Foresman, 1974, pp. 476-488.

Repr. in *The Challenge of Conflict*, Paul C. Holmes and Anita J. Lehman. New York: Harper & Row, 1976, pp. 159-171.
Repr. in *The Best of TriQuarterly*, Jonathan Brent, ed. New York: Washington Square Press, 1982, pp. 12-27.
Repr. in *Wild Saturday and Other Stories* (# 412), pp. 166-184.

176. "How My Father Was Murdered." *Atlantic*, 228 (Sept. 1971): 72-76.

177. "How We Fall in Love." *New Orleans Review*, 1, iv (Summer 1969): 326-330.

178. "Hull and the Motions of Grace." *Northwest Review*, 21, i (1983): 86-116.

179. *The Hungry Ghosts: Seven Allusive Comedies*. Los Angeles: Black Sparrow Press, 1974. 200p.
Contains: Democracy in America; Pilgrims' Progress; Up from Slavery; A Descriptive Catalogue; The Birth of Tragedy; Rewards of Fame; Angst.

180. "Husband and Wife." Fernandes; translated by J.C. Oates. *Carolina Quarterly*, 24, iii (Fall 1972): 31-35.
Repr. in *The Poisoned Kiss and Other Stories* (# 292), pp. 111-118.

181. "I Must Have You." *Ohio Review*, 14, iii (Spring 1973): 54-64.
Repr. in *The Goddess and Other Women* (# 156), pp. 167-181.

182. "I Was in Love." *Shenandoah*, 21, iii (Spring 1970): 39-56.
and in *The Wheel of Love and Other Stories* (# 402), pp. 388-408.

183. "Ich Bin Ein Berliner." *Esquire*, 98 (Dec. 1982): 142-148.
Repr. in *Great Esquire Fiction: The Finest Stories from the First Fifty Years*, L. Rust Hills, ed. New York: Viking Press, 1983, pp. 557-571. (Penguin Books)
Repr. in *Last Days* (# 208), pp. 97-112.

184. "Images" in *By the North Gate* (# 61), pp. 128-146.

185. "Immortal Longings." *Exile*, 3, iii-iv (1976): 193-199.

186. "The Impostors." *Review of Existential Psychology and Psychiatry*, 13, ii (1974): 169-183.
    Repr. in *The Seduction and Other Stories* (# 326), pp. 170-188.

187. "Impotence." Fernandes; translated by J.C. Oates. *Transatlantic Review*, 45 (Spring 1973): 139-140.
    Repr. in *The Poisoned Kiss and Other Stories* (# 292), pp. 136-137.
    See "Five Pieces from Azulejos" (# 132).

188. "Improvisation." *New Letters*, 49, ii (Winter 1983): 77-83.

189. "In the Autumn of the Year." *Bennington Review*, 1 (Apr. 1978): 10-18.
    and in *A Sentimental Education* (# 328), pp. 91-112.
    Repr. in *Prize Stories 1979: The O. Henry Awards*, William Abrahams, ed. Garden City, NY: Doubleday, 1979, pp. 150-172.

190. "In the Old World." *Mademoiselle*, 49 (Aug. 1959): 258, 314-323.
    Repr. in *By the North Gate* (# 61), pp. 180-197.

191. "In Parenthesis." *Chelsea*, 44 (Oct. 1985): 123-137.

192. "In a Public Place." Fernandes; translated by J.C. Oates. *Transatlantic Review*, 45 (Spring 1973): 135-137.
    Repr. in *The Poisoned Kiss and Other Stories* (# 292), pp. 66-69.
    See "Five Pieces from Azulejos" (# 132).

193. "In the Region of Ice." *Atlantic*, 218 (Aug. 1966): 78-85.
    Repr. in *Prize Stories 1967: The O. Henry Awards*, William Abrahams, ed. Garden City, NY: Doubleday, 1967, pp. 1-17.
    Repr. in *The Wheel of Love and Other Stories* (# 402), pp. 13-33.
    and in *Fifty Years of the American Short Story. From the O. Henry Awards 1919-1970*, William Abrahams, ed. Garden City, NY: Doubleday, 1970, pp. 500-515.

Repr. in *Points of Departure: A Collection of Short Fiction*, Herbert Goldstone, Irving Cummings and Thomas Churchill, eds. Englewood Cliffs: Prentice-Hall, 1971, pp. 188-205.
Repr. in *Live and Learn: Stories about Students and Their Teachers*, Stephanie Spinner, ed. New York: Macmillan, 1973, pp. 176-200.
Repr. in *Where Are You Going, Where Have You Been ?* (# 404), pp. 57-77.
Repr. in *Modern Stories in English*, William H. New and H. Rosengarten, eds. New York: Crowell, 1975, pp. 300-315.
Repr. in *Women and Fiction: Short Stories by and about Women*, Susan Cahill, ed. New York: New American Library, 1978, pp. 316-332.
Repr. in *I he Treasury of American Short Stories*, Nancy Sullivan, comp. Garden City, NY: Doubleday, 1981, pp. 691-705.
Repr. in *Wild Saturday and Other Stories* (# 412), pp. 146-165.

194. "In Traction." *Fiction Network Magazine* (forthcoming).

195. "In the Warehouse." *Transatlantic Review*, 26 (Summer 1967): 96-102.
Repr. in *The Goddess and Other Women* (# 156), pp. 72-80.

196. "An Incident in the Park" in *Crossing the Border* (# 77), pp. 202-211.

197. "The Insomniac." *Exile*, 5, i-ii (1977): 104-116.

198. "An Interior Monologue." *Esquire*, 71 (Feb. 1969): 84-85, 92-93.
Repr. in *The Wheel of Love and Other Stories* (# 402), pp. 409-423.

199. "Intoxication." *Boston University Journal*, 24, iii (Feb. 1977): 35-44.
Repr. in *All the Good People I've Left Behind* (# 23), pp. 33-47.

200. "Johanna." *Chatelaine*, 51 (Feb. 1978): 40, 52, 54, 56, 58, 60-62.

201. "Journey." Fernandes; translated by J.C. Oates. *Transatlantic Review*, 45 (Spring 1973): 137-139. Repr. in *The Poisoned Kiss and Other Stories* (# 292), pp. 182-185. See "Five Pieces from Azulejos" (# 132).

202. "Joy Let Us Praise Thee." *Southwest Review*, 51, iv (Autumn 1966): 377-389.

203. "The Joyful Wedding." *Cosmopolitan*, 189 (Aug. 1980): 271-272.

204. "Knowing." *Ontario Review*, 4 (Spring-Summer 1976): 25-42.

205. "The Lady with the Pet Dog." *Partisan Review*, 39, ii (1972): 222-238. and in *Marriages and Infidelities* (# 237), pp. 390-411. Repr. in *Bitches and Sad Ladies: An Anthology of Short Fiction by and about Women*, Pat Rotter, ed. New York: Harper Magazine Press, 1974, pp. 14-32.

206. *The Lamb of Abyssalia.* Cambridge, MA: Pomegranate Press, 1979. 33p. Repr. in *Night Walks* (# 848), pp. 207-217. Repr. in *Last Days* (# 208), pp. 223-232.

207. "Last Days." *Michigan Quarterly Review*, 22, iii (Summer 1983): 360-376. Repr. in *Last Days* (# 208), pp. 19-39.

208. *Last Days.* New York: Dutton, 1984. 241p. Contains: The Witness; Last Days; Funland; The Man Whom Women Adored; Night. Sleep. Death. The Stars; Ich Bin Ein Berliner; Détente; My Warszawa, 1980; Old Budapest; Lamb of Abyssalia; Our Wall.

209. "The Leap." *Confrontation*, 16 (Spring-Summer 1978): 3-11. Repr. in *All the Good People I've Left Behind* (# 23), pp. 9-18.

210. "A Lecture upon the Shadow." *Southern Humanities Review*, 2, i (Winter 1968): 53-69.

211. "A Legacy." *Arizona Quarterly*, 17, ii (Summer 1961):
      159–172.
      Repr. in *By the North Gate* (# 61), pp. 164–179.

212. "The Lesson." *Chatelaine*, 52 (Sept. 1979): 46, 60, 62,
      64, 66, 68, 70.

213. "The Letter." Fernandes; translated by J.C. Oates.
      Literary Review, 17, i (Fall 1973): 86–92.
      Repr. in *The Poisoned Kiss and Other Stories*
      (# 292), pp. 150–158.

214. "Letters to Fernandes from a Young American Poet."
      Translated by J.C. Oates. *Chelsea*, 30–31 (June
      1972): 51–58,
      Repr. in *The Poisoned Kiss and Other Stories*
      (# 292), pp. 138–149.

215. "The Liberation of Jake Hanley." *Queen's Quarterly*,
      82, i (Spring 1975): 44–58.
      Repr. in *Crossing the Border* (# 77), pp. 181–
      201.

216. "Little Wife." *Kenyon Review* (forthcoming Spring 1986).

217. "'Loss.'" Fernandes; translated by J.C. Oates.
      Southwest Review, 56, iv (Autumn 1971):
      310–316.
      Repr. in *The Poisoned Kiss and Other Stories*
      (# 292), pp. 29–38.

218. "Lost." *Exile*, 6, i–ii (1979): 22–38.

219. "The Lost Suitor." *Avenue*, 8 (Feb. 1984): 94, 96,
      98–105.

220. "Love. Friendship." *Chatelaine*, 48 (Jan. 1975):
      30–31, 61–68.
      Repr. in *Crossing the Border* (# 77), pp. 15–38.

221. "Love and Death." *Atlantic*, 225 (June 1970): 57–66.
      Repr. in *Black and White: Stories of American
      Life*, Donald B. Gibson and Carol Anselment, eds.
      New York: Washington Square Press, 1971, pp.
      141–163.
      Repr. in *Marriages and Infidelities* (# 237), pp.
      55–82.

and in *Collection: Literature for the 70s*, Nancy
S. Messner, Gerald Messner and Dennis Roby,
comps. Lexington, MA: D.C. Heath, 1972, pp.
298-315.
Repr. in *Archetypal Themes in the Modern Story*,
Jack Matthews, ed. New York: St. Martin's
Press, 1973, pp. 34-50.

222. "Love, Careless Love." *Northwest Review*, 14, i (1974):
6-66.

223. "A Love Story." *Cosmopolitan*, 162 (July 1967):
116-122.

224. "The Lover." *Exile*, 2, ii (1974): 5-20.
Repr. in *Night-Side* (# 260), pp. 65-85.

225. "The Lovers." *Canto*, 3, iv (Feb. 1981): 80-107.

226. "The Loves of Franklin Ambrose." *Playboy*, 19 (Jan.
1972): 146-148, 152, 276-277.
and in *Aspects of Love*. Chicago: Playboy Press,
1972, pp. 50-64.
Repr. under title "Up from Slavery" in *The
Hungry Ghosts* (# 179), pp. 61-76.
Repr. in *29 Short Stories: An Introductory
Anthology*, Michael Timko, ed. New York: Knopf,
1975, pp. 296-306.

227. "Loving
Losing
Loving... a Man." *Southern Review* (Baton Rouge),
n.s., 7, iv (Autumn 1971): 1103-1119.
Repr. in *Marriages and Infidelities* (# 237), pp.
319-337.

228. "The Madwoman." *Review of Existential Psychology and
Psychiatry*, 12, iii (1973): 229-234.
Repr. in *The Seduction and Other Stories*
(# 326), pp. 202-209.

229. "Magic." *Antioch Review*, 40, iv (Fall 1982): 413-427.

230. "Magna Mater" in *The Goddess and Other Women*
(# 156), pp. 182-209.

231. "Maimed." Fernandes; translated by J.C. Oates, in
The Poisoned Kiss and Other Stories (# 292), pp.
74-77.

232.   "'The Man That Turned into a Statue'" in *Upon the
       Sweeping Flood and Other Stories* (# 385), pp.
       151-165.

233.   "The Man Whom Women Adored." *North American
       Review*, 266, i (Mar. 1981): 10-18.
       Repr. in *Prize Stories 1982: The O. Henry
       Awards*, William Abrahams, ed. Garden City, NY:
       Doubleday, 1982, pp. 229-253.
       Repr. in *Last Days* (# 208), pp. 54-76.

234.   "The Maniac." *Viva*, 1 (Oct. 1973): 80-85.
       Repr. in *The Goddess and Other Women* (# 156),
       pp. 106-124.

235.   "Manslaughter." *Malahat Review*, 08 (June 1984):
       68-79.

236.   "Mara." *TriQuarterly*, 36 (Spring 1976): 156-184.

237.   *Marriages and Infidelities; Short Stories*. New York:
       Vanguard Press, 1972. 497p.
       London: Gollancz, 1974. 497p.
       Contains: The Sacred Marriage; Puzzle; Love and
       Death; 29 Inventions; Problems of Adjustment in
       Survivors of Natural/Unnatural Disasters; By the
       River; Extraordinary Popular Delusions; Stalking;
       Scenes of Passion and Despair; Plot; The
       Children; Happy Onion; Normal Love; Stray
       Children; Wednesday's Child; Loving, Losing,
       Loving a Man; Did You Ever Slip on Red Blood ?;
       The Metamorphosis; Where I Lived, and What I
       Lived For; The Lady with the Pet Dog; The
       Spiral; The Turn of the Screw; The Dead;
       Nightmusic.

238.   "Marya and Sylvester." *Western Humanities Review*,
       35, iv (Winter 1981): 305-319.

239.   "Master Race." *Partisan Review*, 51, iv (1984):
       566-590.

240.   "Matter & Energy." *Partisan Review*, 36, iii (1969):
       418-447.
       Repr. in *The Wheel of Love and Other Stories*
       (# 402), pp. 334-361.

241. "Meredith Dawe." *TriQuarterly*, 26 (Winter 1973): 282-298.

242. "The Metamorphosis" in *Marriages and Infidelities* (# 237), pp. 361-378.
     Repr. in *Experience and Expression: Reading and Responding to Short Fiction*, John L. Kimmey, ed. Glenview: Scott, Foresman, 1976, pp. 453-463.
     See "Others' Dreams" (# 275).

243. "A Middle-Class Education" in *A Sentimental Education* (# 328), pp. 75-90.
     Repr.: New York: Albondocani Press, 1980. [28]p.

244. "The Mime." *Penthouse* (Jan. 1978): 76-83.

245. "Minor Characters." *Massachusetts Review*, 22, iii (Summer 1981): 245-272.

246. "The Mirror." *South Carolina Review*, 14, ii (Spring 1982): 51-64.

247. "The Molesters." *Quarterly Review of Literature*, 15, iii-iv (1968): 393-409.

248. "The Murder" in *Night-Side* (# 260), pp. 244-255.

249. "The Murderer." Fernandes; translated by J.C. Oates. *Greensboro Review*, 16 (Spring 1974): 74-77.
     Repr. in *The Poisoned Kiss and Other Stories* (# 292), pp. 132-135.

250. "Murderess." *Western Humanities Review*, 33, i (Winter 1979): 19-34.

251. "Mutilated Woman." *Michigan Quarterly Review*, 19, ii (Spring 1980): 230-250.
     Repr. in *Prize Stories 1981: The O. Henry Awards*, William Abrahams, ed. Garden City, NY: Doubleday, 1981, pp. 191-211.

252. "My Warszawa." *Kenyon Review*, n.s., 3, iv (Fall 1981): 1-47.
     Repr. in *Prize Stories 1983: The O. Henry Awards*, William Abrahams, ed. Garden City, NY: Doubleday, 1983, pp. 26-79.

Repr. under title "My Warszawa, 1980" in *Last Days* (# 208), pp. 137-187.

253. "My Warszawa, 1980." See "My Warszawa" (# 252).

254. "Nairobi." *Paris Review*, 25 (Spring 1983): 216-223.
Repr. in *The Best American Short Stories 1984*, John Updike and Shannon Ravenel, eds. Boston, MA: Houghton Mifflin, 1984, pp. 177-183.

255. "Narcotic." *Mademoiselle*, 75 (Oct. 1972): 190-191.
Repr. in *The Goddess and Other Women* (# 156), pp. 303-323.
Repr. in *Last Night's Stranger: One Night Stands and Other Staples of Modern Life*, Pat Rotter, ed. New York: A & W Publishers, 1981, pp. 254-274.

256. "Natural Boundaries." *Family Circle*, 85, ii (Aug. 1974): 69, 147-155.
Repr. in *Crossing the Border* (# 77), pp. 67-82.

257. "New Year's Eve." *Chatelaine*, 52 (Jan. 1979): 36-43.

258. "Night. Sleep. Death. The Stars." *Queen's Quarterly*, 90, iii (Autumn 1983): 720-734.
Repr. in *Last Days* (# 208), pp. 77-94.

259. "Night-Side." *Queen's Quarterly*, 84, iii (Autumn 1977): 399-419.
and in *Night-Side* (# 260), pp. 1-29.
Repr. in *Specter! A Chrestomathy of "Spookery"!*, Bill Pronzini, ed. New York: Arbor House, 1982, pp. 259-287.

260. *Night-Side: Eighteen Tales.* New York: Vanguard Press, 1977. 370p.
London: Gollancz, 1979. 370p.
New York: Fawcett Crest, 1984. 320p.
Contains: Night-Side; The Widows; Lover; The Snow-Storm; The Translation; The Dungeon; Famine Country; Bloodstains; Exile; The Giant Woman; Daisy; The Murder; Fatal Woman; The Sacrifice; The Thaw; Further Confessions; The Blessing; A Theory of Knowledge.

261. "Night Song." *Greensboro Review*, 25 (Winter 1978-79): 34-59.

262. "Nightmusic." *Mundus Artium*, 5, i-ii (July 1972): 6-12.
     and in *Marriages and Infidelities* (# 237), pp. 489-497.

263. "Nightshade." *StoryQuarterly*, 11 (1980): 86-94.

264. "The Nordic Soul." *Washington Post Magazine* (Aug. 5, 1984): 8-9, 17-18, 20, 23, 28-30.

265. "Normal Love." *Atlantic*, 227 (Jan. 1971): 80-85.
     Repr. in *Marriages and Infidelities* (# 237), pp. 260-277.
     Repr. in *Intimate Relationships: Marriage, Family and Lifestyles through Literature*, Rose M. Somerville, ed. Englewood Cliffs: Prentice-Hall, 1975, pp. 49-58.

266. "Norman and the Killer." *Southwest Review*, 50, ii (Spring 1965): 121-140.
     Repr. in *Upon the Sweeping Flood and Other Stories* (# 385), pp. 125-150.
     Repr. in *Argosy Magazine* (Apr. 1967).
     Repr. in *A Treasury of Modern Mysteries*, vol. 1, Agatha Christie, et al. Garden City, NY: Doubleday, 1973, pp. 143-160.
     Repr. in *The Web She Weaves: An Anthology of Mystery & Suspense Stories by Women*, Marcia Muller and Bill Pronzini [eds]. New York: Morrow, 1983, pp. 143-160.

267. "North Wind" in *Banquet*, Joan Norris, ed. Lincoln, MA: Penmaen Press, 1978, pp. 9-34.

268. "Notes on Contributors." *TriQuarterly*, 20 (Winter 1971): 426-428.
     Repr. in *The Seduction and Other Stories* (# 326), pp. 165-169.

269. "November Morning." *Columbia Magazine* (Fall 1978): 19-24.

270. "The Obsession." *Ladies' Home Journal*, 88 (Oct. 1971): 96-97, 151-152, 154-158.

271. "Old Budapest." *Kenyon Review*, n.s., 5, iv (Fall 1983): 8-36.
     Repr. in *Last Days* (# 208), pp. 188-222.

272. "An Old-Fashioned Love Story." *Exile*, 8, iii-iv (1981): 125-131.

273. "On the Gulf." *South Carolina Review*, 7, i (Nov. 1974): 85-101.
     Repr. in *The Seduction and Other Stories* (# 326), pp. 88-106.

274. "The Orphan." *Agni Review* (forthcoming).

275. "Others' Dreams." *New American Review*, 13 (Nov. 1971): 198-214.
     Repr. under title "The Metamorphosis" in *Marriages and Infidelities* (# 237), pp. 361-378.

276. "Our Lady of the Easy Death of Alferce." Fernandes; translated by J.C. Oates. *Prism International*, 11, i (Summer 1971): 137-142.
     Repr. in *The Poisoned Kiss and Other Stories* (# 292), pp. 17-25.

277. "Our Wall." *Partisan Review*, 49, i (1982): 45-53.
     Repr. in *Last Days* (# 208), pp. 233-241.

278. "Out of Place." *Virginia Quarterly Review*, 44, iii (Summer 1968): 428- 440.
     Repr. in *The Seduction and Other Stories* (# 326), pp. 154-164.

279. "The Outing." *Mademoiselle*, 86 (Mar. 1980): 212-217.

280. "Pain." *New Letters*, 51, iii (Spring 1985): 3-30.

281. "Paradise: A Post-Love Story." *Shenandoah*, 27, iv (Summer 1976): 17-41.

282. "Parricide." Fernandes; translated by J.C. Oates. *Yale Review*, 63, iii (Spring 1974): 405-412.
     Repr. in *The Poisoned Kiss and Other Stories* (# 292), pp. 39-49.

283. "Passions and Meditations." *Partisan Review*, 40, iii (1973): 370-380.
     Repr. in *The Seduction and Other Stories* (# 326), pp. 129-139.

284. "Pastoral Blood" in *By the North Gate* (# 61), pp. 92-113.
     Repr. in *Where Are You Going, Where Have You Been ?* (# 404), pp. 315-335.

285. "The Pedlar." *New England Review*, 5, i-ii (Autumn-Winter 1982): 146-152.

286. "Pilgrim's Progress" in *The Hungry Ghosts* (# 179), pp. 31-59.
     See "Saul Bird Says: Relate ! Communicate ! Liberate !" (# 316).

287. *Plagiarized Material*. Fernandes. Translated by Joyce Carol Oates. Los Angeles: Black Sparrow Press, Apr. 1974. [15]p. (Sparrow; 19)
     Repr. in *The Poisoned Kiss and Other Stories* (# 292), pp. 159-181.

288. "Plot." *Paris Review*, 13 (Summer 1971): 81-100.
     Repr. in *Marriages and Infidelities* (# 237), pp. 194-215.
     Repr. in *Scenes from American Life* (J.C. Oates, ed.) (# 849), pp. 217-232.

289. "Plover Hill." *Prairie Schooner*, 56, iv (Winter 1982-83): 3-25.

290. "Poetics 105." *Descant*, 22, i (Fall 1977): 2-9.

291. "The Poisoned Kiss." Fernandes; translated by J.C. Oates. *Greensboro Review*, 16 (Spring 1974): 73-74.
     Repr. in *The Poisoned Kiss and Other Stories* (# 292), pp. 119-120.

292. *The Poisoned Kiss and Other Stories from the Portuguese*. Fernandes/Joyce Carol Oates. New York: Vanguard Press, 1975. 189p.
     London: Gollancz, 1976. 189p.
     Contains: Our Lady of the Easy Death of Alferce; The Brain of Dr. Vicente; Loss; Parricide; The Enchanted Piano; Distance; In a Public Place; The Seduction; Maimed; Two Young Men; The Secret Mirror; The Cruel Master; Sunlight/Twilight; Husband and Wife; The Poisoned Kiss; The Son of God and His Sorrow; The Murderer; Impotence; Letters to Fernandes from a Young American Poet; The Letter; Plagiarized Material; Journey.

293. "Poor Lizzie." *Exile*, 8, iii-iv (1981): 109-121.

294. "The Precipice" in *A Sentimental Education* (# 328), pp. 35-60.
     Repr. in *Mississippi Review*, 8, i-ii (Winter-Spring 1979): 140-168.

295. "A Premature Autobiography" in *The Goddess and Other Women* (# 156), pp. 364-383.

296. "Presque Isle." *Agni Review*, 13 (Fall 1980): 41-58.
     Repr. in *The Best American Short Stories 1981*, Hortense Calisher and Shannon Ravenel, eds. Boston, MA: Houghton Mifflin, 1981, pp. 255-270.

297. "Private Life." *Yale Review*, 59, i (Autumn 1969): 79-96.
     Repr. in *Coming Together: Modern Stories by Black and White Americans*, Adam A. Casmier and Sally Souder, eds. Belmont, CA: Dickenson Publishing, 1972, pp. 311-325.

298. "Problems of Adjustment in Survivors of Natural/ Unnatural Disasters." *Boston Review of the Arts*, 2 (June 1972): 17-25.
     and in *Marriages and Infidelities* (# 237), pp. 101-126.

299. "Prose and Poetry." *Carleton Miscellany*, 9 (Spring 1968): 36-54.

300. "Psychiatric Services" in *The Goddess and Other Women* (# 156), pp. 384-401.
     Repr. in *On the Job: Fiction about Work by Contemporary American Writers*, William O'Rourke, ed. New York: Vintage Books, 1977, pp. 324-339.

301. "The Psychoanalytical Love Affair." *Cosmopolitan*, 47 (Sept. 1964): 93-99.

302. "Puppies." *Carolina Quarterly* (forthcoming).

303. "Puzzle." *Redbook*, 136 (Nov. 1970): 72-73.
     Repr. in *Marriages and Infidelities* (# 237), pp. 37-54.

304. "Queen of the Night" in *A Sentimental Education* (# 328), pp. 1-33.
     Repr.: Northridge: Lord John Press, 1979. 44p. (limited edition)
     Repr. in *The Arbor House Celebrity Book of Horror Stories*, Charles Waugh and Martin H. Greenberg, eds. New York: Arbor House, 1982, pp. 264-294.

305. "Rabies and Race: An Hypothesis." *Partisan Review*, 50, ii (1983): 202-212.

306. "Raven's Wing." *Esquire*, 102 (Aug. 1984): 94-96, 98.
     To be reprinted in *The Best American Short Stories 1985*, Gail Godwin, ed. Forthcoming 1986.

307. "The Reliquary." *Queen's Quarterly*, 86, iii (Autumn 1979): 409-419.

308. "Reunion." *New England Review*, 1, iv (Summer 1979): 405-425.

309. "Rewards of Fame" in *The Hungry Ghosts* (# 179), pp. 131-177.

310. "River Rising." *Chatelaine*, 49 (May 1976): 52, 80, 82, 84, 86, 88, 90.
     and in *Crossing the Border* (# 77), pp. 242-256.

311. "The Room of Contamination." *Western Humanities Review*, 34, iii (Summer 1980): 205-221.

312. "The Rose Wall." *Twilight Zone* (Apr. 1981): 46-51.

313. "Ruth" in *The Goddess and Other Women* (# 156), pp. 81-105.
     Repr. in *Short Story International*, 9 (Aug. 1985): 137-158.

314. "The Sacred Marriage." *Southern Review* (Baton Rouge), n.s., 8, iii (Summer 1972): 603-634.
     and in *Marriages and Infidelities* (# 237), pp. 3-36.

315. "The Sacrifice." *Fiction International*, 4-5 (1975): 12-26.
     Repr. in *Night-Side* (# 260), pp. 262-288.

316. "Saul Bird Says: Relate! Communicate! Liberate!"
     Playboy, 17 (Oct. 1970): 92, 94, 96, 247-248,
     250, 252-254, 256.
     Repr. in *Prize Stories 1972: The O. Henry
     Awards*, William Abrahams, ed. Garden City, NY:
     Doubleday, 1972, pp. 16-43.
     Repr. under title "Pilgrim's Progress" in *The
     Hungry Ghosts* (# 179), pp. 31-59.

317. "Scenes of Passion & Despair." *Shenandoah*, 22, iv
     (Summer 1971): 3-14.
     Repr. in *Marriages and Infidelities* (# 237), pp.
     180-193.

318. "Scherzo." *Ohio Review*, 20, i (Winter 1979): 20-49.

319. "Schwilk." *California Quarterly*, 16-17 (Summer-Fall
     1980): 11-28.

320. "The Scream." *Michigan Quarterly Review*, 14, ii
     (Spring 1975): 270-280.
     Repr. in *Crossing the Border* (# 77), pp. 169-
     180.

321. "The Seasons." *Ploughshares*, 9, iv (1983): 176-196.
     Repr. in *Prize Stories 1985: The O. Henry
     Awards*, William Abrahams, ed. Garden City, NY:
     Doubleday, 1985, pp. 254-270.

322. "The Secret Mirror." Fernandes; translated by J.C.
     Oates. *December Magazine*, 13, i-ii (1971):
     138-140.
     Repr. in *The Poisoned Kiss and Other Stories*
     (# 292), pp. 87-91.

323. "Secret Observations on the Goat Girl." *Pequod*
     (University of Maine), 18 (Mar. 1985): 101-105.

324. "The Seduction" in *The Seduction and Other Stories*
     (# 326), pp. 107-128.
     See "Help" (# 171).

325. "The Seduction." Fernandes; translated by J.C.
     Oates. *Transatlantic Review*, 45 (Spring 1973):
     133-135.
     Repr. in *The Poisoned Kiss and Other Stories*
     (# 292), pp. 70-73.
     See "Five Pieces from Azulejos" (# 132).

326. *The Seduction and Other Stories.* Los Angeles: Black
     Sparrow Press, 1975. 263p.
     New York: Fawcett Crest, 1980. 320p.
     Contains: An American Adventure; Gifts; Getting
     and Spending; Splendid Architecture; On the
     Gulf; The Seduction; Passions and Meditations;
     6:27 p.m.; Out of Place; Notes on Contributors;
     The Impostors; Year of Wonders; The Madwoman;
     Double Tragedy Strikes Tennessee Hill Family;
     The Stone House; Hell; The Dreaming Woman.

327. "A Sentimental Education" in *A Sentimental Education*
     (# 328), pp. 113-196.

328. *A Sentimental Education; Stories.* Los Angeles:
     Sylvester & Orphanos, 1978. 102p. (limited
     edition)
     New York: Dutton, 1980. 196p.
     Contains: Queen of the Night; The Precipice; The
     Tryst; A Middle-Class Education; In the Autumn
     of the Year; A Sentimental Education.

329. "Sentimental Journey." *South Carolina Review*, 9, ii
     (Apr. 1977): 3-19.
     Repr. in *All the Good People I've Left Behind*
     (# 23), pp. 103-122.

330. "Shame." *Atlantic*, 221 (June 1968): 80-88.
     Repr. in *The Wheel of Love and Other Stories*
     (# 402), pp. 102-126.

331. "The Silent Child." *Epoch*, 15, iii (Spring 1966):
     195-214.

332. "Silkie." *Malahat Review*, 23 (July 1972): 106-114.
     Repr. in *The Best American Short Stories 1973
     and the Yearbook of the American Short Story*,
     Martha Foley, ed. Boston, MA: Houghton Mifflin,
     1973, pp. 228-237.
     Repr. in *Where Are You Going, Where Have You
     Been ?* (# 404), pp. 223-234.

333. "Silver Storm." *Agni Review*, 20 (Spring 1984): 49-63.

334. "Sin." *Fiction International*, 12 (Winter 1980): 44-57.
     and in *Moral Fiction: An Anthology*, Joe David
     Bellamy, ed. Canton, NY: Fiction International,
     1980, pp. 44-57.

335. "Sisters." *South Carolina Review*, 12, ii (Spring 1980):
      2-15.

336. "6:27 p.m." *Redbook*, 138 (Dec. 1971): 82-83, 190-194.
      Repr. in *The Seduction and Other Stories*
      (# 326), pp. 140-153.
      Repr. in *Solo: Women on Woman Alone*, Linda and
      Leo Hamalian, eds. New York: Delacorte Press,
      1977, pp. 48-62.

337. "Small Avalanches." *Cosmopolitan*, 173 (Nov. 1972):
      230-233.
      Repr. in *The Goddess and Other Women* (# 156),
      pp. 226-239.

338. "The Snow-Storm." *Mudemoiselle*, 79 (Sept. 1974):
      140-141.
      Repr. in *Night-Side* (# 260), pp. 86-109.

339. "Softball." *Shenandoah*, 29, iv (Summer 1978): 57-75.

340. "The Son of God and His Sorrow." Fernandes;
      translated by J.C. Oates. *Massachusetts Review*,
      12, iv (Autumn 1971): 681-688.
      Repr. in *The Poisoned Kiss and Other Stories*
      (# 292), pp. 121-131.

341. "Sonata." *Northwest Review*, 18, i (1979): 4-22.

342. "Sonata Quasi una Fantasia..." *Fiction*, 7,iii - 8,i
      (1985): 92-98.

343. "*The Spider*, Love." *TriQuarterly*, 47 (Winter 1980):
      90-105.

344. "The Spiral." *Shenandoah*, 20, ii (Winter 1969): 3-21.
      Repr. in *Marriages and Infidelities* (# 237), pp.
      412-432.

345. "Splendid Architecture." *Antioch Review*, 28, iii (Fall
      1968): 305-324.
      Repr. in *The Seduction and Other Stories*
      (# 326), pp. 68-87.

346. "Stalking." *North American Review*, 257, ii (Summer
      1972): 41-43.
      and in *Marriages and Infidelities* (# 237), pp.
      171-179.

Repr. in *Where Are You Going, Where Have You Been ?* (# 404), pp. 235-244.
Repr. in *The Short Story: An Introduction*, Wilfred Stone, Nancy Huddleston Packer and Robert Hoopes, eds. New York: McGraw-Hill, 1976, pp. 480-485.

347. *The Step-Father.* Northridge: Lord John Press, 1978. 29p. (limited edition)

348. "Stigmata." *Colorado Quarterly*, 11, iv (Spring 1963): 332-349.
Repr. in *Prize Stories 1964: The O. Henry Awards*, Richard Poirier, ed. Garden City, NY: Doubleday, 1964, pp. 30-48.
Repr. in *Upon the Sweeping Flood and Other Stories* (# 385), pp. 13-35.
Repr. in *Quest for Meaning: Modern Short Stories*, Glenn O. Carey, ed. New York: McKay, 1975, pp. 227-244.

349. "The Stone House." *Quarterly Review of Literature*, 13, iii-iv (1965): 381-411.
Repr. in *The Seduction and Other Stories* (# 326), pp. 224-249.

350. "The Storm." *Cosmopolitan*, 191 (Sept. 1981): 296-298, 300, 302.

351. "Story of an Ordinary Girl." *Texas Quarterly*, 11, ii (Summer 1968): 217-230.
Repr. in *The Seduction and Other Stories* (# 326), pp. 224-249.

352. "Stray Children." *Salmagundi*, 15 (Winter 1971): 20-39.
Repr. in *Marriages and Infidelities* (# 237), pp. 278-301.
Repr. in *Where Are You Going, Where Have You Been ?* (# 404), pp. 197-221.
Repr. in *Wild Saturday and Other Stories* (# 412), pp. 122-145.

353. "Sunday Blues." *Fiction*, 5, i (Dec. 1976-Apr. 1977): 17-20.

354. "Sunday Dinner." *TriQuarterly*, 10 (Fall 1967): 63-101.
Repr. in *Under 30: Fiction, Poetry and Criticism of the New American Writers*, Charles Newman and William A. Henkin, Jr., eds. Bloomington, IN: Indiana University Press, 1969, pp. 63-101.

355. "The Sunken Woman." *Playboy*, 28 (Dec. 1981):
        196-197, 199, 223, 340, 344-346, 348, 350-351, 356.

356. "Sunlight/Twilight." Fernandes; translated by J.C.
        Oates. *Transatlantic Review*, 45 (Spring 1973):
        140-144.
        Repr. in *The Poisoned Kiss and Other Stories*
        (# 292), pp. 104-110.
        See "Five Pieces from Azulejos" (# 132).

357. "Superstitious." *Bennington Review* (forthcoming).

358. "The Survival of Childhood." *Southwest Review*, 49, ii
        (Spring 1964): 106-123.
        Repr. in *Upon the Sweeping Flood and Other
        Stories* (# 385), pp. 36-60.

359. "Swamps" in *By the North Gate* (# 61), pp. 11-27.

360. "The Sweet Enemy." *Southern Review* (Baton Rouge),
        n.s., 3, iii (Summer 1967): 653-720.

361. "Sweet Love Remembered." *Epoch*, 10, iii (Spring
        1960): 131-141.
        Repr. in *By the North Gate* (# 61), pp. 66-79.

362. "The Tattoo." *Mademoiselle*, 83 (July 1977): 144,
        146-153.
        Repr. in *Prize Stories 1978: The O. Henry
        Awards*, William Abrahams, ed. Garden City, NY:
        Doubleday, 1979, pp. 129-147.

363. "The Tempter." *Fiction*, 3, ii-iii (1975): 45-48.
        Repr. in *Crossing the Border* (# 77), pp. 231-241.

364. "Testimony." *Southern Review* (Baton Rouge) (forth-
        coming Summer 1986).

365. "The Thaw." *Viva*, 4 (Feb. 1977): 70-73, 106-108.
        and in *Night-Side* (# 260), pp. 289-308.

366. "Theft." *Northwest Review*, 19, iii (1981): 40-86.
        Repr. in *The Best American Short Stories 1982*,
        John Gardner and Shannon Ravenel, eds. Boston,
        MA: Houghton Mifflin, 1982, pp. 311-358.

367. "A Theory of Knowledge" in *Night-Side* (# 260), pp.
        348-370.

368. "The Thief." *North American Review*, 251, v (Sept. 1966): 10-17.

369. "Three Women" in *The Stone Wall Book of Short Fictions*, Robert Coover and Kent Dixon, eds. Iowa City: Stone Wall Press, 1973, pp. 36-38.

370. "Through the Looking Glass." *Malahat Review*, 15 (July 1970): 78-93.
    Repr. in *The Best Little Magazine Fiction, 1971*, Curt Johnson and Alvin Greenberg, eds. New York: New York University Press, 1971, pp. 252-269.
    Repr. in *Crossing the Border* (# 77), pp. 48-66.

371. "To My Lover, Who Has Abandoned Me..." *Cosmopolitan*, 170 (Jan. 1971): 134-141.

372. "The Transformation of Vincent Scoville." *Canadian Fiction Magazine*, 15 (Autumn 1974): 17-43.
    Repr. in *Crossing the Border* (# 77), pp. 118-147.

373. "The Translation." *TriQuarterly*, 40 (Fall 1977): 105-125.
    and in *Night-Side* (# 260), pp. 110-133.
    Repr. in *The Best American Short Stories 1978: Selected from US and Canadian Magazines* by Ted Solotaroff with Shannon Ravenel. Boston, MA: Houghton Mifflin, 1978, pp. 26-45.

374. *The Triumph of the Spider Monkey.* Santa Barbara: Black Sparrow Press, 1976. 89p.
    New York: Fawcett Crest, 1976. 158p.

375. "The Tryst." *Atlantic*, 238 (Aug. 1976): 40-46.
    Repr. in *A Sentimental Education* (# 328), pp. 61-74.
    Repr. in *All the Good People I've Left Behind* (# 23), pp. 49-61.
    Repr. in *Cosmopolitan*, 191 (Aug. 1981): 246-247, 298, 300, 302.

376. "The Turn of the Screw." *Iowa Review*, 2, ii (Spring 1971): 36-48.
    Repr. in *Marriages and Infidelities* (# 237), pp. 433-452.

377. "29 Inventions." *Antioch Review*, 30, iii-iv (Fall-Winter 1970-71): 380-391.
      Repr. in *Marriages and Infidelities* (# 237), pp. 83-100.

378. "Two Poets." *Northwest Review*, 8, i (1967): 7-26.

379. "Two Young Men." Fernandes; translated by J.C. Oates. *Aspen Leaves*, 1, ii (June 1974): 95-101.
      Repr. in *The Poisoned Kiss and Other Stories* (# 292), pp. 78-86.

380. "Unmailed, Unwritten Letters." *Hudson Review*, 22, i (Spring 1969): 19-39.
      Repr. in *The Wheel of Love and Other Stories* (# 402), pp. 55-79.
      and in *The Best Little Magazine Fiction, 1970*, Curt L. Johnson, ed. New York: New York University Press, 1970, pp. 200-222.
      and in *Prize Stories 1970: The O. Henry Awards*, William Abrahams, ed. Garden City, NY: Doubleday, 1970, pp. 253-274.

381. "Unpublished Fragments" in *The Goddess and Other Women* (# 156), pp. 344-363.
      Repr. in *Fiction International*, 1 (Fall 1983): 18-29.

382. "An Unsolved Crime." *Colorado Quarterly*, 27, ii (Summer 1978): 5-22.

383. "Up from Slavery" in *The Hungry Ghosts* (# 179), pp. 61-76.
      See "The Loves of Franklin Ambrose" (# 226).

384. "Upon the Sweeping Flood." *Southwest Review*, 48, ii (Spring 1963): 130-142.
      Repr. in *The Best American Short Stories 1964*, Martha Foley and David Burnett, eds. Boston, MA: Houghton Mifflin, 1964, pp. 241-256.
      Repr. in *Fifty Best American Short Stories, 1915-1965*, Martha Foley, ed. Boston, MA: Houghton Mifflin, 1965, pp. 799-814.
      Repr. in *Upon the Sweeping Flood and Other Stories* (# 385), pp. 230-250.
      Repr. in *The Young American Writers*, Richard Kostelanetz, ed. New York: Funk & Wagnalls, 1967, pp. 276-293.

Repr. in *Killing Time: A Guide to Life in the Happy Valley*, Robert Disch and Barry N. Schwartz, eds. Englewood Cliffs: Prentice-Hall, 1972, pp. 204-217.
Repr. in *Southwest Review*, 59, iv (Autumn 1974): 363-378.
and in *The Choices of Fiction*, Donald E. Morse, ed. Cambridge, MA: Winthrop Publishers, 1974, pp. 243-256.
Repr. in *Major American Short Stories*, A. Walton Litz, ed. New York: Oxford University Press, 1975, pp. 720-734.

385. *Upon the Sweeping Flood and Other Stories.* New York: Vanguard Press, 1966. 250p.
Greenwich, CT: Fawcett, 1971. 224p.
London: Gollancz, 1973. 250p.
London: Coronet, 1976. 224p.
Contains: Stigmata; The Survival of Childhood; The Death of Mrs. Sheer; First Views of the Enemy; At the Seminary; Norman and the Killer; "The Man That Turned into a Statue"; Archways; Dying; What Death with Love Should Have to Do; Upon the Sweeping Flood.

386. "The Victim." *Iowa Review*, 13, ii (Spring 1983): 15-31.

387. "The Voyage to Rosewood." *Shenandoah*, 18, iv (Summer 1967): 3-22.
Repr. in *The Goddess and Other Women* (# 156), pp. 240-260.

388. "The Voyeur." *Southwest Review*, 63, i (Winter 1978): 56-64.

389. "Waiting." *Epoch*, 17, iii (Spring 1968): 250-269.
Repr. in *The Goddess and Other Women* (# 156), pp. 261-282.

390. "Walled City." *Queen's Quarterly*, 83, iv (Winter 1976): 578-594.
Repr. in *All the Good People I've Left Behind* (# 23), pp. 123-144.

391. "Washington Square." *Antioch Review*, 36, iii (Summer 1978): 293-314.

392. "The Way Back in from Out There." *Southwest Review*, 52, iii (Summer 1967): 209-223.

393. "The Way We Live." *Agni Review*, 10-11 (Spring 1979): 106-127.

394. "The Wedding Party." *Aspen Leaves*, 83, iv (Winter 1976): 578-594.

395. "Wednesday." *Esquire*, 74 (Aug. 1970): 80, 123.
    Repr. under title "Wednesday's Child" in *Marriages and Infidelities* (# 237), pp. 302-318.

396. "Wednesday's Child" in *Marriages and Infidelities* (# 237), pp. 302-318.
    See "Wednesday" (# 395).

397. "What Death with Love Should Have to Do." *Literary Review*, 9, i (Autumn 1965): 19-36.
    Repr. in *Upon the Sweeping Flood and Other Stories* (# 385), pp. 209-229.

398. "What Herbert Breuer and I Did to Each Other." *McCall's*, 97 (Apr. 1970): 102-103, 143-146, 148, 154.

399. "What Is the Connection between Men and Women ?" *Mademoiselle*, 70 (Feb. 1970): 244-245, 278-281.
    and in *The Wheel of Love and Other Stories* (# 402), pp. 424-440.

400. "The Wheel." *Epoch*, 22, iii (Spring 1973): 249-254.
    Repr. in *The Goddess and Other Women* (# 156), pp. 462-468.

401. "The Wheel of Love." *Esquire*, 68 (Oct. 1967): 134-137, 158, 160, 162.
    Repr. in *The Wheel of Love and Other Stories* (# 402), pp. 190-208.
    Repr. in *Love Stories*, Martin Levin, comp. New York: Popular Library, 1979, pp. 160-172.

402. *The Wheel of Love and Other Stories*. New York: Vanguard Press, 1970. 440p.
    London: Gollancz, 1971. 440p.
    Greenwich, CT: Fawcett, 1972. 383p.
    Contains: In the Region of Ice; Where Are You Going, Where Have You Been ?; Unmailed,

Unwritten Letters; Convalescing; Shame;
Accomplished Desires; Wild Saturday; How I
Contemplated the World from the Detroit House of
Correction and Began My Life over Again; The
Wheel of Love; Four Summers; Demons; Bodies;
Boy and Girl; The Assailant; The Heavy Sorrow
of the Body; Matter and Energy; You; I Was in
Love; An Interior Monologue; What Is the
Connection between Men and Women ?

403. "Where Are You Going, Where Have You Been ?"
Epoch, 16, i (Fall 1966): 59-76.
Repr. in *The Best American Short Stories 1967*,
Martha Foley and David Burnett, eds. Boston,
MA: Houghton Mifflin, 1967, pp. 193-209.
Repr. in *Prize Stories 1968: The O. Henry
Awards*, William Abrahams, ed. Garden City, NY:
Doubleday, 1968, pp. 296-313.
Repr. in *The Wheel of Love and Other Stories*
(# 402), pp. 34-54.
and in *Fifty Years of the American Short Story:
From the O. Henry Awards, 1919-1970*, William
Abrahams, ed. Garden City, NY: Doubleday,
1970, pp. 516-531.
and in *Student's Choice: An Anthology of Short
Stories*, Richard Kraus and William Wiegand, eds.
Columbus, OH: Charles Merrill, 1970, pp. 75-89.
Repr. in *Where Are You Going, Where Have You
Been ?* (# 404), pp. 11-31.
Repr. in *200 Years of Great American Short
Stories*, Martha Foley, ed. Boston, MA: Houghton
Mifflin, 1975, pp. 914-929.
Repr. in *American Short Stories*, Eugene
Current-Garcia and Walton R. Patrick, eds.
Glenview: Scott, Foresman, 1976, pp. 657-672.
Repr. in *In the Looking Glass*, Nancy Dean and
Myra Stark, eds. New York: Putnam, 1977, pp.
213-231.
Repr. in *Wild Saturday and Other Stories* (# 412),
pp. 1-20.
Repr. in *The Norton Anthology of Literature by
Women: The Tradition in English*, Sandra M.
Gilbert and Susan Gubar [eds]. New York;
London: Norton, 1985, pp. 2276-2291.

404. *Where Are You Going, Where Have You Been ?: Stories of Young America.* Greenwich, CT: Fawcett, 1974. 352p.
Contains: Where Are You Going, Where Have You Been ?; Happy Onion; In the Region of Ice; Wild Saturday; An American Adventure; How I Contemplated the World from the Detroit House of Correction and Began My Life over Again; Accomplished Desires; Boy and Girl; Four Summers; Stray Children; Silkie; Stalking; You; A Girl at the Edge of the Ocean; Back There; Pastoral Blood; Year of Wonders.

405. "Where the Continent Ends." *Northwest Review*, 13, i (1973): 24-88.

406. "Where I Lived, and What I Lived For." *Virginia Quarterly Review*, 46, iv (Autumn 1970): 613-623.
Repr. in *Marriages and Infidelities* (# 237), pp. 379-389.

407. "White Shadow." *Kenyon Review*, n.s., 1, iv (Fall 1979): 141-151.

408. "Why Did You Cry for Me ?" *Cosmopolitan*, 57 (July 1964): 93-97.

409. "The Widows." *Hudson Review*, 28, i (Spring 1975): 35-62.
Repr. in *Night-Side* (# 260), pp. 30-64.

410. *Wild Nights.* Athens, OH: Croissant, 1985. 56p. (limited edition)

411. "Wild Saturday." *Mademoiselle*, 71 (Sept. 1970): 136-137.
and in *The Wheel of Love and Other Stories* (# 402), pp. 150-169.
Repr. in *Where Are You Going, Where Have You Been ?* (# 404), pp. 79-98.
Repr. in *Wild Saturday and Other Stories* (# 412), pp. 43-61.

412. *Wild Saturday and Other Stories.* London: Dent, 1984. 184p.
Contains: Where Are You Going, Where Have You Been ?; Accomplished Desires; Wild Saturday; Boy and Girl; Demons; A Girl at the Edge of the Ocean; Stray Children; In the Region of Ice; How I Contemplated the World from the Detroit House of Correction and Began My Life over Again.

413. "The Witness." *Antaeus*, 49–50 (Spring–Summer 1983): 123–137.
      Repr. in *Last Days* (# 208), pp. 3–18.

414. "The Woman Who Disappeared." *University Review*, 34, iv (Summer 1968): 243–257.

415. "Years of Wonders" in *Where Are You Going, Where Have You Been ?* (# 404), pp. 337–352.
      Repr. in *The Seduction and Other Stories* (# 326), pp. 189–201.

416. "You." *Cosmopolitan*, 168 (Feb. 1970): 134–141.
      and in *The Wheel of Love and Other Stories* (# 402), pp. 362–387.
      Repr. in *Where Are You Going, Where Have You Been ?* (# 404), pp. 245–270.

POEMS

417. *Abandoned Airfield, 1977.* Northridge: Lord John Press, 1977. (broadside)
Repr. in *Ontario Review,* 8 (Spring-Summer 1978): 74-75.
and in *Women Whose Lives Are Food, Men Whose Lives Are Money* (# 831), p. 32.
Repr. in *Invisible Woman* (# 600), pp. 79-80.

418. "Acceleration Near the Point of Impact." *Esquire,* 78 (Nov. 1972): 89.
Repr. in *Angel Fire* (# 439), p. 42.
Repr. in *Love and Its Derangements and Other Poems* (# 623), p. 170.

419. "Addiction." *University of Windsor Review,* 11, ii (Spring-Summer 1976): 76.
Repr. in *Women Whose Lives Are Food, Men Whose Lives Are Money* (# 831), p. 22.

420. "Adult Life: Mourning." *Literary Review,* 15, ii (Winter 1971-72): 184.

421. "After Love a Formal Feeling Comes." *Prism International,* 10, ii (Autumn 1970): 83.
and in *Love and Its Derangements* (# 624), p. 39.
Repr. in *Love and Its Derangements and Other Poems* (# 623), p. 107.

422. "After the Storm ..." *Poem,* 20 (Mar. 1974): 34-35.
Repr. in *The Fabulous Beasts* (# 523), p. 68.

423. "After Sunset." *Canadian Literature,* 70 (Autumn 1976): 58-59.
Repr. in *Women Whose Lives Are Food, Men Whose Lives Are Money* (# 831), p. 29.

424. "After Terror ..." *Canadian Forum*, 54 (Jan. 1975): 29.
      and in *The Fabulous Beasts* (# 523), p. 5.
      Repr. in *Invisible Woman* (# 600), p. 87.

425. "After Twelve Years of Travelling [sic]." *Mademoiselle*,
      76 (Mar. 1973): 56.
      and under title "'After Twelve Years of Travelling
      [sic] Constantly ...'" in *Dreaming America &
      Other Poems* (# 504), [n.p.]
      Repr. under title "After Twelve Years of
      Traveling Constantly ..." in *The Fabulous Beasts*
      (# 523), p. 24.

426. "'After Twelve Years of Travelling [sic] Constantly ...'"
      See "After Twelve Years of Travelling [sic]"
      (# 425).

427. "An Age of Miracles" in *The Fabulous Beasts* (# 523),
      pp. 22-23.

428. "Alarms." *Southwest Review*, 52, iv (Autumn 1967):
      343.
      Repr. in *Anonymous Sins and Other Poems*
      (# 441), pp. 50-51.
      Repr. in *Love and Its Derangements and Other
      Poems* (# 623), p. 50.

429. "'All Things Are Full of Gods.'" *Seneca Review*, 5, ii
      (Dec. 1974): 6.
      Repr. in *The Fabulous Beasts* (# 523), p. 85.

430. "Alone, a Threnody." *Antioch Review*, 42, i (Winter
      1984): 88.

431. "American City" in *Anonymous Sins and Other Poems*
      (# 441), pp. 18-19.
      Repr. in *Love and Its Derangements and Other
      Poems* (# 623), p. 25.
      Repr. in *Introducing Poems*, Linda W. Wagner and
      C. David Mead, eds. New York: Harper & Row,
      1976, pp. 167-168.

432. "American Expressway" in *Love and Its Derangements*
      (# 624), pp. 41-43.
      Repr. in *Connexion* [1, iv (Apr. 1971)]: [n.p.]
      Repr. in *Love and Its Derangements and Other
      Poems* (# 623), p. 108.

433. "American Independence" in *Women Whose Lives Are Food, Men Whose Lives Are Money* (# 831), pp. 56-57.

434. "American Morocco: A Child's Song." *Southwest Review*, 54, i (Summer 1969): 271-273.
and in *Anonymous Sins and Other Poems* (# 441), pp. 24-27.
Repr. in *Love and Its Derangements and Other Poems* (# 623), pp. 30-33.
See "Three Dances of Death" (# 785).

435. "An American Tradition" in *The Fabulous Beasts* (# 523), p. 28.

436. "Ancient Snapshots." *Poetry*, 142 (Aug. 1983): 257.

437. "And So I Grew up to Be Nineteen and to Murder." *Southern Review* (Baton Rouge), n.s., 4, iv (Autumn 1968): 1032-1034.
Repr. in *Anonymous Sins and Other Poems* (# 441), pp. 57-59.
Repr. in *Love and Its Derangements and Other Poems* (# 623), p. 54.

438. "Angel Fire" in *Angel Fire* (# 439), pp. 30-31.
Repr. in *Love and Its Derangements and Other Poems* (# 623), p. 161.

439. *Angel Fire: Poems*. Baton Rouge: Louisiana State University Press, 1973. 62p.
Repr. in *Love and Its Derangements and Other Poems* (# 623), pp. 135-188.
Contains: Part I. Lovers' Bodies: Lovers' Bodies; The Small Still Voice behind the Great Romances; Contrary Motions; At This Moment; Where the Wind Went Crazy; Dancer; At Our Fingers' Tips There Are Small Faces; A Woman's Song; Structures; Hate; Insomnia; Bloodstains; Unpronouncing of Names; Several Embraces; Making an End; Where the Shadow Is Darkest. Part II. Domestic Miracles: Domestic Miracles; Our Common Past; A Young Wife; A City Graveyard; A Secular Morning; Leaving the Mountains; Mile-High Monday; Angel Fire. Part III. Revelations: Firing a Field; A Midwestern Song; Children Not Kept at Home; What We Fear from Dreams & Waking; Acceleration Near the Point of

Impact; Family; How I Became Fiction; Things
Happen to Us; The Nightmare; Entering the
Desert; Mouth; The Secret Sweetness of
Nightmares; Becoming Garbage; Prophecies;
Southern Swamp; Elegy of the Letter "I"; City of
Locks; Revelations in Small Sunbaked Squares;
Iris into Eye.

440. "Anonymous Sins" in *Anonymous Sins and Other Poems*
      (# 441), pp. 73-74.
      Repr. in *Love and Its Derangements and Other
      Poems* (# 623), p. 65.

441. *Anonymous Sins and Other Poems*. Baton Rouge:
      Louisiana State University Press, 1969. 79p.
      Repr. in *Love and Its Derangements and Other
      Poems* (# 623), pp. 12-69.
      Contains: The Dark; Lines for Those to Whom
      Tragedy Is Denied; Five Confessions; American
      City; Three Dances of Death; Tinkly Song; At an
      Old Downtown Square; Unborn Child; Gravity; A
      Drawing of Darkness; The Ride; A Girl at the
      Center of Her Life; Of the Violence of Self-Death;
      Marriage; On Being Borne Reluctantly to New
      York State, by Train; Foetal Song; Alarms;
      Sleepwalking; Centuries of Lovers; To Whose
      Country Have I Come ?; And So I Grew up to Be
      Nineteen and to Murder; A Woman in Her Secret
      Life; Women in Love; A Rising and Sinking and
      Rising in My Mind; An Internal Landscape; Cupid
      and Psyche; In the Night; Transparencies; Like
      This ... So This; Anonymous Sins; Dead Actors;
      A Crowded River, Sunday; Vanity.

442. "Another." *Hudson Review*, 34, i (Spring 1981): 62.
      Repr. in *Invisible Woman* (# 600), p. 28.

443. "Appetite. Terror." *Texas Quarterly*, 21, i (Spring
      1978): 6-7.
      Repr. under title "Appetite and Terror on the
      Wide White Sands of Western Florida" in *Invisible
      Woman* (# 600), pp. 35-36.

444. "Appetite and Terror" in *Celestial Timepiece* (# 471),
      [n.p.]

445. "Appetite and Terror on the Wide White Sands of
      Western Florida." See "Appetite. Terror" (# 443).

446. "Approaching the Speed of Light" in *The Fabulous Beasts* (# 523), p. 67.

447. "At an Old Downtown Square." *Sage*, 12, i (Spring 1968): 15-16.
     Repr. in *Anonymous Sins and Other Poems* (# 441), p. 32.
     Repr. in *Love and Its Derangements and Other Poems* (# 623), p. 37.

448. "At Our Fingers' Tips There Are Small Deadly Faces" in *Red Clay Reader* 7, Charleen Whisnant, ed. Charlotte, NC: Southern Review, 1970, p. 66.
     Repr. under title "At Our Fingers' Tips There Are Small Faces" in *Angel Fire* (# 439), p. 9.
     Repr. under title "At Our Fingers' Tips There Are Small Faces" in *Love and Its Derangements and Other Poems* (# 623), p. 141.

449. "At Our Fingers' Tips There Are Small Faces." See "At Our Fingers' Tips There Are Small Deadly Faces" (# 448).

450. "At Peace, at Rest." *Modern Poetry Studies*, 7, ii (Autumn 1976): 82-83.
     Repr. in *Women Whose Lives Are Food, Men Whose Lives Are Money* (# 831), p. 28.

451. "At the Seashore." *Prism International*, 14, iii (Winter 1975): 54.
     Repr. in *Women Whose Lives Are Food, Men Whose Lives Are Money* (# 831), p. 28.

452. "At This Moment." *Quarry* (Kingston, ON), 20, i (Winter 1971): 36.
     Repr. in *Angel Fire* (# 439), p. 6.
     Repr. in *Love and Its Derangements and Other Poems* (# 623), p. 138.

453. "Autistic Child, No Longer Child" in *Invisible Woman* (# 600), p. 44.

454. "The Autistic Child Twenty Years after, Scraping His Shoes." *Mainline*, 1 (Feb. 1968): [n.p.]

455. "Baby." *Harper's*, 264 (Mar. 1982): 70.
     and in *Invisible Woman* (# 600), p. 11.

456.   "Back Country." *Georgia Review*, 33, iv (Winter 1979):
       876-877.
       Repr. in *Invisible Woman* (# 600), pp. 46-47.

457.   "Beauty Is an Accusation." *Colorado State Review*, 3,
       ii (Spring 1968): 10.

458.   "Becoming Garbage" in *Angel Fire* (# 439), p. 51.
       Repr. in *Love and Its Derangements and Other
       Poems* (# 623), p. 178.

459.   "Being Faithful." *Malahat Review*, 31 (July 1974):
       85-86.
       Repr. in *The Fabulous Beasts* (# 523), pp. 63-64.

460.   "Detrayal" in *Invisible Woman* (# 600), p. 32.

461.   "Blizzard." *Southwest Review*, 59, i (Winter 1974):
       53-54.
       Repr. in *The Fabulous Beasts* (# 523), p. 43.

462.   "Bloodstains" in *Red Clay Reader 7*, Charleen
       Whisnant, ed. Charlotte, NC: Southern Review,
       1970, p. 66.
       Repr. in *Angel Fire* (# 439), p. 14.
       and in *Three Women* (# 369), p. 36.
       Repr. in *Love and Its Derangements and Other
       Poems* (# 623), p. 146.

463.   "Boredom." *Virginia Quarterly Review*, 57, iv (Autumn
       1981): 636-637.
       Repr. in *Invisible Woman* (# 600), pp. 62-63.

464.   "Breaking and Entering." *Malahat Review*, 31 (July
       1974): 87-88.
       Repr. in *The Fabulous Beasts* (# 523), p. 25.

465.   "Breaking Apart." *Southern Review* (Baton Rouge),
       n.s., 6, iii (Summer 1970): 723-724.
       and in *Love and Its Derangements* (# 624), p. 32.
       Repr. in *Love and Its Derangements and Other
       Poems* (# 623), p. 101.

466.   "Broken Connections." *Hudson Review*, 26, iii (Autumn
       1973): 500-501.
       Repr. in *The Fabulous Beasts* (# 523), pp. 3-4.

467. "The Broken Man." *Modern Poetry Studies*, 7, ii (Autumn 1976): 85-86.
     Repr. in *Women Whose Lives Are Food, Men Whose Lives Are Money* (# 831), p. 40.

468. "The Buried Self." *Canadian Literature*, 75 (Winter 1977): 73.
     and in *Season of Peril* (# 736), p. 21.

469. "'But I Love ...'" *Canadian Forum*, 54 (Jan. 1975): 29.
     and in *The Fabulous Beasts* (# 523), p. 42.

470. "Celestial Timepiece" in *Celestial Timepiece* (# 471), [n.p.]
     Repr. in *Invisible Woman* (# 600), pp. 50-51.

471. *Celestial Timepiece*. Dallas: Pressworks, 1980. [25]p. (limited edition)
     Contains: Snow-Drunk; The River; Last Things; Those Weathers; Elegy; Appetite and Terror; Homage to Virginia Woolf; The Forbidden; The Great Cobweb; In the Country of Pain; The Great Egg; Celestial Timepiece.

472. "Centuries of Lovers" in *Anonymous Sins and Other Poems* (# 441), p. 54.
     Repr. in *Love and Its Derangements and Other Poems* (# 623), p. 52.

473. "The Child-Bride." *Kenyon Review*, n.s., 2, iv (Fall 1980): 33-34.
     Repr. in *Invisible Woman* (# 600), pp. 69-70.

474. "The Child-Martyr." *Fiction Midwest*, 1, ii (1973): [n.p.]
     Repr. in *The Fabulous Beasts* (# 523), pp. 51-53.

475. "Children Not Kept at Home" in *Angel Fire* (# 439), p. 39.
     Repr. in *Love and Its Derangements and Other Poems* (# 623), p. 167.

476. "Christmas chez Nous: In Response to a Query." *North American Review*, 269, i (Mar. 1984): 43.

477. "A City Graveyard." *Prairie Schooner*, 45, iii (Fall
      1971): 230-231.
      Repr. in *Angel Fire* (# 439), p. 26.
      Repr. in *Love and Its Derangements and Other
      Poems* (# 623), p. 157.

478. "City of Locks" in *Angel Fire* (# 439), pp. 57-58.
      Repr. in *Love and Its Derangements and Other
      Poems* (# 623), p. 185.

479. "Closure." *Chicago Tribune Magazine* (Mar. 10, 1974):
      34.
      Repr. in *The Fabulous Beasts* (# 523), p. 62.

480. "Coast Guard Rescue Maneuvers." *Queen's Quarterly*,
      81, i (Spring 1974): 85.
      Repr. in *The Fabulous Beasts* (# 523), p. 29.

481. "The Cocoon" in *The Triumph of the Spider Monkey*
      (# 374), pp. 19-20.

482. "Contrary Motions." *Prism International*, 10, ii
      (Autumn 1970): 82.
      Repr. in *Angel Fire* (# 439), p. 5.
      Repr. in *Love and Its Derangements and Other
      Poems* (# 623), p. 137.

483. "Coronary Thrombosis." *Michigan Quarterly Review*,
      14, iv (Fall 1975): 426.
      Repr. in *Women Whose Lives Are Food, Men Whose
      Lives Are Money* (# 831), p. 44.

484. "The Courtship of the Spider Monkey" in *The Triumph
      of the Spider Monkey* (# 374), p. 16.

485. "The Creation." *Hudson Review*, 28, iv (Winter
      1975-76): 530.
      Repr. in *Women Whose Lives Are Food, Men Whose
      Lives Are Money* (# 831), p. 71.

486. "A Crowded River, Sunday." *Literary Review*, 12, iii
      (Spring 1969): 397-398.
      and in *Anonymous Sins and Other Poems* (# 441),
      pp. 77-78.
      Repr. in *Love and Its Derangements and Other
      Poems* (# 623), p. 67.

487. "Cupid and Psyche" in *Women in Love and Other Poems* (# 829), p. 9.
     Repr. in *Prairie Schooner*, 44, iii (Fall 1969): 302.
     and in *Anonymous Sins and Other Poems* (# 441), pp. 66-67.
     Repr. in *Love and Its Derangements and Other Poems* (# 623), p. 60.

488. "The Current" (prose poem). *Michigan Quarterly Review*, 21, iv (Fall 1982): 577-578.

489. "Dancer." *Literary Review*, 15, ii (Winter 1971-72): 182.
     Repr. in *Angel Fire* (# 439), p. 8.
     Repr. in *Love and Its Derangements and Other Poems* (# 623), p. 140.

490. "Dancer, Harshly Photographed." *Hudson Review*, 37, iii (Autumn 1984): 393-394.

491. "The Dark" in *Anonymous Sins and Other Poems* (# 441), pp. 3-4.
     Repr. in *Love and Its Derangements and Other Poems* (# 623), p. 12.

492. "Dazed" in *Women in Love and Other Poems* (# 829), p. 11.

493. "Dead Actors." *Literary Review*, 12, iii (Spring 1969): 394-395.
     and in *Anonymous Sins and Other Poems* (# 441), pp. 75-76.
     Repr. in *Love and Its Derangements and Other Poems* (# 623), p. 66.

494. "The Demons." *Kansas Quarterly*, 6, iii (Summer 1974): 13.
     Repr. in *Women Whose Lives Are Food, Men Whose Lives Are Money* (# 831), p. 27.

495. "Detroit by Daylight." *Prairie Schooner*, 42, ii (Summer 1968): 126.

496. "Disfigured Woman." *Michigan Quarterly Review*, 16, iii (Summer 1977): 262.

497. "Disintegration" in *Love and Its Derangements* (# 624),
      p. 44.
      Repr. in *Love and Its Derangements and Other
      Poems* (# 623), p. 110.

498. "Diving." *Mainline*, 7 (July 1970): 21.
      and in *Love and Its Derangements* (# 624), p. 50.
      Repr. in *Love and Its Derangements and Other
      Poems* (# 623), p. 116.

499. "Doctor's Wife" in *Anonymous Sins and Other Poems*
      (# 441), pp. 16-17.
      Repr. in *Love and Its Derangements and Other
      Poems* (# 623), pp. 23-25.
      See "Five Confessions" (# 535).

500. "Domestic Miracles" in *Angel Fire* (# 439), p. 23.
      Repr. in *Invisible Woman* (# 600), p. 94.
      Repr. in *Love and Its Derangements and Other
      Poems* (# 623), p. 155.

501. "Don't You Know the Private Life Is Over ?" in *Love
      and Its Derangements* (# 624), pp. 45-46.
      Repr. in *Love and Its Derangements and Other
      Poems* (# 623), p. 111.

502. "A Drawing of Darkness." *Southern Review* (Baton
      Rouge), n.s., 4, iv (Autumn 1968): 1031.
      Repr. in *Anonymous Sins and Other Poems*
      (# 441), p. 37.
      Repr. in *Love and Its Derangements and Other
      Poems* (# 623), p. 40.

503. "Dreaming America." *Hudson Review*, 26, iii (Autumn
      1973): 501-502.
      and in *Dreaming America & Other Poems* (# 504),
      [n.p.]
      Repr. in *The Fabulous Beasts* (# 523), pp. 83-84.
      Repr. in *American Poets in 1976*, William Heyen,
      ed. Indianapolis: Bobbs-Merrill, 1976, pp.
      209-210.
      Repr. in *Invisible Woman* (# 600), pp. 81-82.

504. *Dreaming America & Other Poems.* [New York]: Aloe
      Editions, 1973. [6]l. (limited edition)
      Contains: Flight; Dreaming America; Mourning
      and Melancholia: In Memory of Sylvia Plath;
      Lorelei; Promiscuity; "After Twelve Years of
      Travelling [sic] Constantly ..."

505. "Drownings." *Denver Quarterly*, 4, ii (Summer 1969): 91.
     Repr. in *Love and Its Derangements* (# 624), p. 38.
     Repr. in *Love and Its Derangements and Other Poems* (# 623), p. 106.

506. "Duet." *Southern Humanities Review*, 4, ii (Spring 1970): 112.
     and in *Love and Its Derangements* (# 624), p. 14.
     Repr. in *Love and Its Derangements and Other Poems* (# 623), p. 86.

507. "Dying." *Connexion*, 1, ii (Apr. 1969): [n.p.]

508. "Earth-Rituals." *Hudson Review*, 28, iv (Winter 1975-76): 529.
     Repr. in *Season of Peril* (# 736), p. 19.
     Repr. in *Women Whose Lives Are Food, Men Whose Lives Are Money* (# 831), p. 78.

509. "Easter Anise Bread" in *John Keats's Porridge, Favorite Recipes of American Poets*, Victoria McCabe, [ed.]. Iowa City: University of Iowa Press, 1975, p. 74.

510. "Eating" in *Three Women* (# 369), pp. 36-37.

511. "Ebony Casket." *Harper's*, 260 (Apr. 1980): 118-120.

512. "Eclipse." *Fiddlehead*, 84 (Mar.-Apr. 1970): 18.

513. "Ecstasy of Boredom at the Berlin Wall." *Ontario Review*, 16 (Spring-Summer 1982): 84-85.
     and in *Invisible Woman* (# 600), pp. 64-65.

514. "Ecstasy of Flight." *Ontario Review*, 16 (Spring-Summer 1982): 80-81.
     and in *Invisible Woman* (# 600), p. 59.

515. "Ecstasy of Motion." *Ontario Review*, 16 (Spring-Summer 1982): 82-83.
     and in *Invisible Woman* (# 600), pp. 60-61.

516. "Elegy" in *Celestial Timepiece* (# 471), [n.p.]

517. "Elegy of the Letter 'I'" in *Angel Fire* (# 439), pp. 55-56.
      Repr. in *Love and Its Derangements and Other Poems* (# 623), p. 182.

518. "Enigma." *American Poetry Review*, 5 (Sept.-Oct. 1976): 33.
      Repr. in *Women Whose Lives Are Food, Men Whose Lives Are Money* (# 831), p. 41.

519. "Entering the Desert." *New Letters*, 38, i (Autumn 1971): 33-34.
      Repr. in *Angel Fire* (# 439), pp. 47-48.
      Repr. in *Love and Its Derangements and Other Poems* (# 623), p. 175.

520. "The Eternal Children." *Western Humanities Review*, 29, iii (Summer 1975): 260-261.
      Repr. in *Women Whose Lives Are Food, Men Whose Lives Are Money* (# 831), p. 11.

521. "*F-.*" *Iowa Review*, 9, iii (Summer 1978): 94.
      Repr. in *Invisible Woman* (# 600), pp. 52-53.

522. "Fabulous Beast." *Little Magazine*, 8, iii-iv (Fall-Winter 1974-75): 27.
      Repr. in *The Fabulous Beasts* (# 523), p. 79.

523. *The Fabulous Beasts: Poems.* Ill. by A.G. Smith, Jr.
      Baton Rouge: Louisiana State University Press, 1975. 86p.
      Contains: I. Broken Connections: Broken Connections; After Terror ...; The Impasse; Wonders of the Invisible World; A Posthumous Sketch. II. Forbidden Testimonies: Forbidden Testimony; An Age of Miracles; "After Twelve Years of Traveling Constantly ..."; Breaking and Entering; The Fear of Going Blind; Two Insomniacs; An American Tradition; Coast Guard Rescue Maneuvers; Lovers; A Heroine without a Story; Lies Lovingly Told; To a Victim; A Friend Moving Out of Our Lives; The Survivor; In the Street; Spaces; Lorelei; "But I Love ..."; Blizzard; Sinners in the Hand of a Righteous God; Flight; Seizure. III. The Child-Martyr: The Child-Martyr; Occult; In Case of Accidental Death; Promiscuity; What Has Not Been Lost in the Deserts of North America ?; Midday; Closure;

Being Faithful; Fireflies; Mourning and Melancholia: In Memory of Sylvia Plath; Approaching the Speed of Light; After the Storm; While We Slept ...; The Forgiveness of Sins; London Winter; 20.26 Knots; In Air; Music; A Vision. IV. The Fabulous Beasts: Fabulous Beast; Wooded Forms; In Realms of Day; Dreaming America; "All Things Are Full of Gods"; Waiting.

524. "Family." *Boston Review of the Arts*, 2 (Aug. 1972): 15.
Repr. in *Angel Fire* (# 439), p. 43.
Repr. in *Love and Its Derangements and Other Poems* (# 623), p. 171.

525. "The Fear of Going Blind." *Esquire*, 76 (Dec. 1971): 280.
Repr. in *The Fabulous Beasts* (# 523), p. 26.

526. "Feast-Day." *New Letters*, 45, ii (Winter 1978): 31-33.

527. "Fertilizing the Continent." *Capilano Review*, 6 (Fall 1974): 74.
Repr.: Northridge: Santa Susana Press, 1976. [n.p.]
Repr. in *Women Whose Lives Are Food, Men Whose Lives Are Money* (# 831), p. 79.
Repr. in *Invisible Woman* (# 600), p. 86.

528. "Fever" in *Angel Fire* (# 439), pp. 17-18.
Repr. in *Love and Its Derangements and Other Poems* (# 623), p. 150.
See "Several Embraces" (# 742).

529. "Fever Dream on the Eve of Illness" in *Season of Peril* (# 736), p. 22.
Repr. in *Dreamworks*, 1, ii (1980): 123.

530. "Fever Song." *Texas Quarterly*, 21, i (Spring 1978): 8-9.
and in *Women Whose Lives Are Food, Men Whose Lives Are Money* (# 831), p. 21.

531. "Fireflies." *Southern Review* (Baton Rouge), n.s., 11, ii (Spring 1975): 377.
and in *The Fabulous Beasts* (# 523), p. 65.

532. "Firing a Field." *Massachusetts Review*, 13, iii
      (Summer 1972): 469–470.
      Repr. in *Angel Fire* (# 439), pp. 35–36.
      Repr. in *Love and Its Derangements and Other
      Poems* (# 623), p. 165.
      Repr. in *Invisible Woman* (# 600), pp. 90–91.

533. "First Dark." *Paris Review*, 23 (Summer 1981): 130.
      Repr. in *Invisible Woman* (# 600), p. 43.

534. "First Death, 1950." *Georgia Review*, 31, iii (Autumn
      1977): 598–599.
      Repr. in *Invisible Woman* (# 600), pp. 48–49.

535. "Five Confessions" in *Anonymous Sins and Other Poems*
      (# 441), pp. 8–17.
      Repr. in *Love and Its Derangements and Other
      Poems* (# 623), pp. 16–25.
      Contains: A Nap without Sleep; A Married
      Woman's Song; Pain; New Wife; Doctor's Wife.

536. "Flight." *Hudson Review*, 26, iii (Autumn 1973):
      502–503.
      and in *Dreaming America & Other Poems* (# 504),
      [n.p.]
      Repr. in *The Fabulous Beasts* (# 523), pp. 45–46.
      Repr. in *American Poets in 1976*, William Heyen,
      ed. Indianapolis: Bobbs-Merrill, 1976, pp.
      205–206.

537. "Foetal Song." *Chelsea*, 22–23 (June 1968): 60–61.
      Repr. in *Anonymous Sins and Other Poems*
      (# 441), pp. 48–49.
      Repr. in *Love and Its Derangements and Other
      Poems* (# 623), p. 48.
      Repr. in *I Hear My Sisters Saying: Poems by
      Twentieth-Century Women*, Carol Konek and
      Dorothy Walters, eds. New York: Crowell, 1976,
      pp. 96–98.

538. "The Food-Chain Blues" in *The Triumph of the Spider
      Monkey* (# 374), p. 20.

539. "Footprints." *Nation*, 224 (Apr. 16, 1977): 475.
      and in *Season of Peril* (# 736), p. 20.
      Repr. in *Invisible Woman* (# 600), p. 40.

540. "The Forbidden" in *Celestial Timepiece* (# 471), [n.p.]
     Repr. in *Invisible Woman* (# 600), p. 23.

541. "Forbidden Testimony." *Southern Review* (Baton Rouge), n.s., 11, ii (Spring 1975): 379.
     and in *The Fabulous Beasts* (# 523), p. 21.

542. "Ford." *Michigan Quarterly Review*, 20, i (Winter 1981): 617-618.

543. "Forgetful America." *Hudson Review*, 34, i (Spring 1981): 60-61.

544. "The Forgiveness of Sins." *Queen's Quarterly*, 18, i (Spring 1974): 84.
     Repr. in *The Fabulous Beasts* (# 523), p. 71.

545. "Former Movie Queen, Dying of Cancer, Watches an Old Movie of Hers at a Film Festival in San Francisco." *Southern Review* (Baton Rouge), n.s., 13, iv (Autumn 1977): 757-759.
     Repr. in *Women Whose Lives Are Food, Men Whose Lives Are Money* (# 831), pp. 8-10.

546. "Free Fall." *Poem*, 20 (Mar. 1974): 39.

547. "A Friend Moving Out of Our Lives." *Quarry* (Kingston, ON), 20, i (Winter 1971): 36-37.
     Repr. in *Best Poems of 1971. Borestone Mountain Poetry Awards, 1972.* Palo Alto: Pacific Books Pubs, 1972, pp. 76-77.
     Repr. in *The Fabulous Beasts* (# 523), pp. 36-37.

548. "Friendly Conversation." *Southern Humanities Review*, 6, i (Winter 1972): 70.

549. "From the Dark Side of the Earth." *Niagara Magazine*, 1 (Summer 1974): 32. (Poets of Western New York and Ontario)
     Repr. in *Women Whose Lives Are Food, Men Whose Lives Are Money* (# 831), p. 12.

550. "The Funnel." *Modern Poetry Studies*, 3, vi (1972): 260.

551. "Gala Power Black-Out of New York City, July '77" (prose poem). *New Republic* (Sept. 17, 1977): 36.
     Repr. in *Women Whose Lives Are Food, Men Whose Lives Are Money* (# 831), p. 58.

552. "Giant Sunday Rats." *Texas Quarterly*, 21, i (Spring
      1978): 8.

553. "A   Girl   at   the   Center   of   Her   Life." *Southern
      Humanities Review*, 3, i (Winter 1968): 58-59.
      Repr. in *Anonymous Sins and Other Poems*
      (# 441), pp. 40-41.
      Repr. in *Contemporary Poetry in America*, Miller
      Williams, ed. New York: Random House, 1973,
      p. 163.
      Repr. in *Love and Its Derangements and Other
      Poems* (# 623), p. 42.

554. "Giving Oneself a Form Again." *Beloit Poetry Journal*,
      19, iii (Spring 1969): 23.
      Repr. in *Love and Its Derangements* (# 624),
      p. 20.
      Repr. in *Love and Its Derangements and Other
      Poems* (# 623), p. 90.

555. "The Good Life Here on Earth." *McCall's*, 97 (Jan.
      1970): 31.
      and in *Love and Its Derangements* (# 624), p. 18.
      Repr. in *Love and Its Derangements and Other
      Poems* (# 623), p. 89.

556. "Good Morning" in *Invisible Woman* (# 600), p. 33.

557. "The   Grave   Dwellers." *Prism   International*,   9,   ii
      (Autumn 1969): 57.
      Repr. in *Love and Its Derangements* (# 624),
      p. 11.
      Repr. in *Love and Its Derangements and Other
      Poems* (# 623), p. 83.

558. "Gravity" in *Anonymous Sins and Other Poems* (# 441),
      pp. 35-36.
      Repr. in *Love and Its Derangements and Other
      Poems* (# 623), p. 39.

559. "The Great Cobweb" in *Celestial Timepiece* (# 471),
      [n.p.]

560. "The Great Egg" in *Celestial Timepiece* (# 471),
      [n.p.]
      Repr. in *Invisible Woman* (# 600), pp. 66-68.

561. "Growing Together" in *Love and Its Derangements* (# 624), p. 19.
     Repr. in *Michigan Quarterly Review*, 10, iv (Fall 1971): 254.
     Repr. in *Love and Its Derangements and Other Poems* (# 623), p. 89.
     Repr. in *I Hear My Sisters Saying: Poems by Twentieth-Century Women*, Carol Konek and Dorothy Walters, eds. New York: Crowell, 1976, pp. 50-51.

562. "Guilt." *Concerning Poetry*, 8, ii (Fall 1975): 60.
     Repr. in *Women Whose Lives Are Food, Men Whose Lives Are Money* (# 831), pp. 30-31.

563. "Happy Birthday." *Boston University Journal*, 23, i (Winter 1975): 25.
     Repr. in *Women Whose Lives Are Food, Men Whose Lives Are Money* (# 831), p. 53.

564. "A Happy Song: Not for Adults." *Colorado State Review*, 3, i (Winter 1968): 44-46.
     Repr. in *Anonymous Sins and Other Poems* (# 441), pp. 27-30.
     Repr. in *Love and Its Derangements and Other Poems* (# 623), pp. 33-36.
     See "Three Dances of Death" (# 785).

565. "Hate." *Modern Poetry Studies*, 1, v (1970): 232.
     Repr. in *Angel Fire* (# 439), p. 12.
     Repr. in *Love and Its Derangements and Other Poems* (# 623), p. 144.

566. "Hauled from River, Sunday 8 a.m.." *Southern Review* (Baton Rouge), n.s., 13, iv (Autumn 1977): 756.
     Repr. in *Women Whose Lives Are Food, Men Whose Lives Are Money* (# 831), p. 7.

567. "He Traveled by Jet First Class to Tangier." *Prairie Schooner*, 49, iii (Fall 1975): 212-214.
     Repr. in *Women Whose Lives Are Food, Men Whose Lives Are Money* (# 831), pp. 66-67.

568. "A Heroine without a Story" in *The Fabulous Beasts* (# 523), pp. 31-32.

569. "High-Wire Artist." *Southern Review* (Baton Rouge),
      n.s., 18, ii (Spring 1982): 382-383.
      and in *Invisible Woman* (# 600), pp. 71-72.

570. "Holy Saturday." *Missouri Review*, 1, i (Spring 1978):
      17.
      and in *Women Whose Lives Are Food, Men Whose
      Lives Are Money* (# 831), p. 24.

571. "Homage to Virginia Woolf" in *Celestial Timepiece*
      (# 471), [n.p.]
      Repr. in *Invisible Woman* (# 600), p. 73.

572. "Honeymoon" in *Invisible Woman* (# 600), p. 24.

573. "How Gontle." *Mainline*, 7 (July 1970): 14.
      and in *Love and Its Derangements* (# 624), p. 60.
      Repr. in *Love and Its Derangements and Other
      Poems* (# 623), p. 124.
      Repr. in *Invisible Woman* (# 600), p. 95.

574. "How I Became Fiction." *Poetry Northwest*, 12, iii
      (Autumn 1971): 24.
      Repr. in *Angel Fire* (# 439), p. 44.
      Repr. in *Love and Its Derangements and Other
      Poems* (# 623), p. 172.

575. "How I Became Fictional." *University of Windsor
      Review*, 3, ii (Spring 1968): 28-29.

576. "How Liquid Rises Magically in a Tube." *Malahat
      Review*, 31 (July 1974): 84-85.

577. "How Sweet to Be a Wound ..." in *Women in Love and
      Other Poems* (# 829), p. 13.

578. "How We Are Flowers." *Prism International*, 9, ii
      (Autumn 1969): 58.
      Repr. in *Love and Its Derangements* (# 624),
      p. 7.
      Repr. in *Love and Its Derangements and Other
      Poems* (# 623), p. 80.

579. "'I don't like for people to scream at me 'cause all I do
      is holler back.'" *Epos*, 20 (Summer 1969): 8-9.
      Repr. in *Love and Its Derangements* (# 624), pp.
      55-56.
      Repr. in *Love and Its Derangements and Other
      Poems* (# 623), p. 120.

580. "I Saw a Woman." *Shenandoah*, 35, i (1983-84): 32-33.

581. "Ice Age." *Poetry Northwest*, 17, iv (Winter 1976-77): 15.
    Repr. in *Season of Peril* (# 736), p. 15.
    Repr. in *Women Whose Lives Are Food, Men Whose Lives Are Money* (# 831), p. 43.
    Repr. in *Invisible Woman* (# 600), p. 97.

582. "If You Must Go and I Must Stay." *Southern Review* (Baton Rouge), n.s., 11, ii (Spring 1975): 378.
    Repr. in *Women Whose Lives Are Food, Men Whose Lives Are Money* (# 831), p. 35.

583. "Ill-Used." *Modern Poetry Studies*, 1, v (1970): 233.

584. "Imaginery Ballet." *December Magazine*, 10, i (1968): 132.

585. "The Impasse." *Prairie Schooner*, 47, iv (Winter 1973-74): 314.
    Repr. in *The Fabulous Beasts* (# 523), p. 6.
    Repr. in *American Poets in 1976*, William Heyen, ed. Indianapolis: Bobbs-Merrill, 1976, pp. 203-204.

586. "In Air." *Quarry* (Santa Cruz), 3 (1973): 68-69.
    Repr. in *The Fabulous Beasts* (# 523), p. 74.

587. *In Case of Accidental Death.* Cambridge, MA: Pomegranate Press, 1972. (broadside; limited edition)
    Repr. in *The Fabulous Beasts* (# 523), p. 57.

588. "In the Country of Pain" in *Celestial Timepiece* (# 471), [n.p.]

589. "In Hot May." *Pebble*, 5 (Winter 1970-71): [n.p.]
    and in *Love and Its Derangements* (# 624), p. 27.
    Repr. in *Love and Its Derangements and Other Poems* (# 623), p. 96.

590. "In Medias Res." *Michigan Quarterly Review*, 14, iv (Fall 1975): 425.
    Repr. in *Women Whose Lives Are Food, Men Whose Lives Are Money* (# 831), p. 77.

591. "In Memory of an Ex-Friend, a Murderer." *Literary Review*, 11, iii (Spring 1968): 391-393.

592. "In the Night." *Poetry Northwest*, 8, iii (Autumn 1967): 20.
       Repr. in *Anonymous Sins and Other Poems* (# 441), p. 68.
       Repr. in *Love and Its Derangements and Other Poems* (# 623), p. 61.

593. "(In Parenthesis)." *TriQuarterly*, 56 (Winter 1983): 161-162.

594. "In Realms of Day" (prose poem). *Poem*, 20 (Mar. 1974): 33.
       Repr. in *The Fabulous Beasts* (# 523), p. 82.

595. "In the Street." *Prairie Schooner*, 47, iv (Winter 1973-74): 315.
       Repr. in *The Fabulous Beasts* (# 523), p. 39.

596. "An Infant's Song" in *Women Whose Lives Are Food, Men Whose Lives Are Money* (# 831), p. 76.

597. "Insomnia." *Malahat Review*, 20 (Oct. 1971): 46.
       Repr. in *Angel Fire* (# 439), p. 13.
       Repr. in *Love and Its Derangements and Other Poems* (# 623), p. 145.

598. "An Internal Landscape" in *Women in Love and Other Poems* (# 829), p. 10.
       Repr. in *Atlantic*, 223 (Apr. 1969): 63.
       and in *Anonymous Sins and Other Poems* (# 441), p. 65.
       Repr. in *Love and Its Derangements and Other Poems* (# 623), p. 59.

599. "Invisible Woman" in *Invisible Woman* (# 600), p. 3.

600. *Invisible Woman: New and Selected Poems, 1970-1982.* Princeton, NJ: Ontario Review Press, 1982. 99p. (Ontario Review Press Poetry Series)
       Contains: I. Sun-Truths: Invisible Woman; The Stone Orchard; Nightless Nights; The Wasp; Last Things; Season of Peril; Baby; A Miniature Passion; Sun-Truths; The Mourning; The Mourning II; The Loss; Poem Jubilant in Place of Mourning. II. The Forbidden: The Forbidden;

Honeymoon; There Are Northern Lakes ...;
Tachycardiac Seizure; The Proofs of God;
Another; Leavetaking, at Dusk; Night Driving,
New Year's Eve; Betrayal; Good Morning; Query,
Not to Be Answered; Appetite and Terror on the
Wide White Sands of Western Florida; Psalm;
Snowfall; Snow-Drunk in Ontario; Footprints.
III. First Dark: First Dark; Autistic Child, No
Longer Child; Jesus, Heal Me; Back Country;
First Death, 1950; Celestial Timepiece; F-; The
Present Tense. IV. A Report to an Academy:
Ecstasy of Flight; Ecstasy of Motion; Boredom;
Ecstasy of Boredom at the Berlin Wall; The Great
Egg; The Child-Bride; High-Wire Artist; Homage
to Virginia Woolf; A Report to an Academy.
V. Selected Poems 1970-1978: Abandoned Airfield,
1977; Dreaming America; Last Harvest; Visionary
Adventures of a Wild Dog Pack; Fertilizing the
Continent; After Terror ...; "Promiscuity"; The
Suicide; Firing a Field; Shelley at Viareggio;
Domestic Miracles; How Gentle; Skyscape; Ice
Age.

601. "Iris into Eye." *Poetry Northwest*, 11, iii (Autumn 1970): 26-27.
Repr. under title "Wonderland" (signed T.W. Monk) in *Wonderland* (# 18), pp. 13-14.
Repr. in *Angel Fire* (# 439), pp. 61-62.
Repr. in *Love and Its Derangements and Other Poems* (# 623), p. 188.

602. "Is Infidelity a Kind of Suicide ?" *Southern Review* (Baton Rouge), n.s., 4, iv (Autumn 1968): 1035-1036.

603. "Jesus, Heal Me." *New Republic*, 182 (Jan. 26, 1980): 26.
Repr. in *Invisible Woman* (# 600), p. 45.

604. "Jigsaw Puzzle." *Salmagundi*, 13 (Summer 1970): 61.
and in *Love and Its Derangements* (# 624), p. 40.
Repr. in *Love and Its Derangements and Other Poems* (# 623), p. 107.

605. "A Landscape of Back Yards." *Colorado State Review*, 4, i (Winter 1969): 12.
Repr. in *Love and Its Derangements* (# 624), pp. 57-58.

Repr. in *Love and Its Derangements and Other
Poems* (# 623), pp. 121-122.
See "Landscapes" (# 608).

606. "A Landscape of Forms" in *Love and Its Derangements*
(# 624), pp. 58-59.
Repr. in *Southwest Review*, 56, iii (Summer
1971): 232.
Repr. in *Love and Its Derangements and Other
Poems* (# 623), pp. 122-123.
See "Landscapes" (# 608).
See "Two Landscapes" (# 797).

607. "A Landscape of Love." *Southern Humanities Review*,
3, i (Winter 1969): 59.
Repr. in *Love and Its Derangements* (# 624),
p. 59.
Repr. in *Southwest Review*, 56, iii (Summer
1971): 233.
Repr. in *Love and Its Derangements and Other
Poems* (# 623), pp. 123-124.
See "Landscapes" (# 608).
See "Two Landscapes" (# 797).

608. "Landscapes" in *Love and Its Derangements* (# 624),
pp. 57-59.
Repr. in *Love and Its Derangements and Other
Poems* (# 623), pp. 121-124.
Contains: A Landscape of Back Yards; A
Landscape of Forms; A Landscape of Love.

609. "Last Harvest" in *Season of Peril* (# 736), p. 14.
Repr. in *Women Whose Lives Are Food, Men Whose
Lives Are Money* (# 831), p. 23.
Repr. in *Invisible Woman* (# 600), p. 83.

610. "Last Things." *Virginia Quarterly Review*, 55, iv
(Autumn 1979): 713.
Repr. in *Celestial Timepiece* (# 471), [n.p.]
Repr. in *Invisible Woman* (# 600), p. 9.

611. "Leavetaking." *Hudson Review*, 32, ii (Summer 1979):
190.
Repr. under title "Leavetaking, at Dusk" in
Invisible Woman (# 600), p. 29.
Repr. in *Portfolio One/1983. Ten Illustrated
Poetry Broadsides*. Roslyn Harbor: Stone House
Press, 1983.

612. "Leavetaking, at Dusk." See "Leavetaking" (# 611).

613. "Leaving the Mountains" in *Angel Fire* (# 439), p. 28.
     Repr. in *Love and Its Derangements and Other Poems* (# 623), p. 159.

614. "Lies Lovingly Told." *Poetry Northwest*, 15, iii (Autumn 1974): 26.
     Repr. in *The Fabulous Beasts* (# 523), p. 33.

615. "Light." *Quarry* (Kingston, ON), 19, ii (Winter 1970): 11.

616. "Like This ... So This." *Poetry Northwest*, 10, iii (Autumn 1969): 63.
     and in *Anonymous Sins and Other Poems* (# 441), p. 72.
     Repr. in *Love and Its Derangements and Other Poems* (# 623), p. 64.

617. "Lines for Those to Whom Tragedy Is Denied." *Ohio University Review*, 10 (1968): 25-27.
     Repr. in *Anonymous Sins and Other Poems* (# 441), pp. 5-7.
     Repr. in *Contemporary Poetry in America*, Miller Williams, ed. New York: Random House, 1973, pp. 162-163.
     Repr. in *Love and Its Derangements and Other Poems* (# 623), p. 13.
     Repr. in *I Hear My Sisters Saying: Poems by Twentieth-Century Women*, Carol Konek and Dorothy Walters, eds. New York: Crowell, 1976, pp. 246-249.

618. "London Winter." *Strivers' Row*, 1 (Fall 1974): 66.
     Repr. in *The Fabulous Beasts* (# 523), p. 72.

619. "Lorelei." *Prism International*, 13, i (Summer 1973): 121.
     and in *Dreaming America & Other Poems* (# 504), [n.p.]
     Repr. in *The Fabulous Beasts* (# 523), p. 41.

620. "The Loss." *Virginia Quarterly Review*, 57, iv (Autumn 1981): 637-638.
     Repr. in *Invisible Woman* (# 600), p. 17.

621. "Love." *Southern Humanities Review*, 3, i (Winter 1968): 59.

622. "Love and Its Derangements." *Pebble*, 5 (Winter 1970–71): [n.p.]
and in *Love and Its Derangements* (# 624), pp. 30–31.
Repr. in *Love and Its Derangements and Other Poems* (# 623), p. 99.

623. *Love and Its Derangements and Other Poems.* Greenwich, CT: Fawcett [1974]. 189p.
Contains: Anonymous Sins and Other Poems; Love and Its Derangements; Angel Fire.

624. *Love and Its Derangements: Poems.* Baton Rouge: Louisiana State University Press, 1970. 60p.
Repr. in *Love and Its Derangements and Other Poems* (# 623), pp. 77–124.
Contains: Parachuting; Sleeping Together; "Only the Exhaustive Can Be Truly Interesting"; How We Are Flowers; The Sirens; Turning into Another Person; The Grave Dwellers; "Woman Is the Death of the Soul"; Loving; Duet; Traveling with You; Two of Us Staring into Another Dimension; The Good Life Here on Earth; Growing Together; Giving Oneself a Form Again; Wounds; A Lover; Morning on Our Beach; You/Your; Public Love; In Hot May; The Struggle to Wake from Sleep; My Fate Met Me; Love and Its Derangements; Breaking Apart; Mysterious Motions Subside; Love Picnic; Passing an Afternoon; What I Fear ...; Drownings; After Love a Formal Feeling Comes; Jigsaw Puzzle; American Expressway; Disintegration; Don't You Know the Private Life Is Over?; Madness; Portrait; Mirage; Diving; Love and Time; The Secret of the Water Off Point Pelee; Ordinary Summer Days; "I don't like for people to scream at me 'cause all I do is holler back"; Landscapes: Back Yards, Forms, Love; How Gentle.

625. "Love and Time." *Quarry* (Kingston, ON), 19, ii (Winter 1970): 12.
and in *Love and Its Derangements* (# 624), p. 51.
Repr. in *Love and Its Derangements and Other Poems* (# 623), p. 117.

626. "Love Anecdote." *Poetry*, 142 (Aug. 1983): 258.

627. "Love Picnic." *Chelsea*, 28 (Aug. 1970): 93.
and in *Love and Its Derangements* (# 624), pp. 34-35.
Repr. in *Love and Its Derangements and Other Poems* (# 623), p. 102.

628. "Love Poem." *Hudson Review*, 26, iii (Autumn 1973): 503.
Repr. in *Women Whose Lives Are Food, Men Whose Lives Are Money* (# 831), p. 73.

629. "A Lover." *Literary Review*, 12, iii (Spring 1969): 396.
Repr. in *Love and Its Derangements* (# 624), p. 22.
Repr. in *Love and Its Derangements and Other Poems* (# 623), p. 92.

630. "Lovers." *Poem*, 20 (Mar. 1974): 36-37 (in slightly different form).
Repr. in *The Fabulous Beasts* (# 523), p. 30.

631. "The Lovers." *California Quarterly*, 11-12 (Winter-Spring 1977): 44.
Repr. in *Women Whose Lives Are Food, Men Whose Lives Are Money* (# 831), p. 19.

632. "Lovers Asleep." *Canadian Forum*, 54 (Jan. 1975): 28.
Repr. in *Women Whose Lives Are Food, Men Whose Lives Are Money* (# 831), p. 17.

633. "Lovers' Bodies." *Carolina Quarterly*, 22, ii (Spring 1970): 28.
Repr. in *Angel Fire* (# 439), p. 3.
Repr. in *Love and Its Derangements and Other Poems* (# 623), p. 135.

634. "Loving." *Tamarack Review*, 55 (Third Quarter 1970): 68-69.
and in *Love and Its Derangements* (# 624), p. 13.
Repr. in *Love and Its Derangements and Other Poems* (# 623), p. 85.

635. "Luxury of Being Despised." *Bennington Review*, 13 (June 1982): 28.
Repr. in *First Person Singular* (# 1077), p. 194.
Repr. in *Luxury of Sin* (# 637), [n.p.]

636. "Luxury of Sin." *Georgia Review*, 35, iv (Winter
      1981): 805.
      Repr. in *Luxury of Sin* (# 637), [n.p.]

637. *Luxury of Sin*. Northridge: Lord John Press, 1984.
      [n.p.]
      Contains: Luxury of Sin; Luxury of Being
      Despised; The Madwoman's Repentance; Night;
      Self-Portrait As a Still Life; The Sacred Fount.

638. "Madness." *Saturday Review*, 53 (Feb. 7, 1970): 45.
      and in *Love and Its Derangements* (# 624), p. 47.
      Repr. in *Love and Its Derangements and Other
      Poems* (# 623), p. 113.

639   "The Madness of Crowds." *Black Moss*, 2, 1 (1970):
      [n.p.]
      and in *Printed Matter, an Anthology of Black
      Moss*, Robert Hawkins, ed. Windsor, ON: Sun
      Parlor Advertising, 1970, pp. 28–29.
      Repr. in *Malahat Review*, 20 (Oct. 1971): 47.
      and in *Wonderland* (# 18), p. 275.

640. "The Madwoman's Repentance." *Southern Review*
      (Baton Rouge), n.s., 19, ii (Spring 1983): 356–
      357.
      Repr. in *Luxury of Sin* (# 637), [n.p.]

641. "The Magic Show." *Malahat Review*, 57 (Jan. 1981):
      124.

642. "Making an End" in *Angel Fire* (# 439), p. 19.
      Repr. in *Love and Its Derangements and Other
      Poems* (# 623), p. 152.

643. "Man and Wife." *Modern Poetry Studies*, 7, ii (Autumn
      1976): 84–85.

644. "Many Are Called." *Hudson Review*, 28, iv (Winter
      1975–76): 530.
      Repr. in *American Poets in 1976*, William Heyen,
      ed. Indianapolis: Bobbs-Merrill, 1976, p. 211.
      Repr. in *Women Whose Lives Are Food, Men Whose
      Lives Are Money* (# 831), p. 80.

645. "Marriage." *December Magazine*, 10, i (1968): 132.
      Repr. in *Anonymous Sins and Other Poems*
      (# 441), p. 44.
      Repr. in *Love and Its Derangements and Other
      Poems* (# 623), p. 45.

646. "A Married Woman's Song." *University of Windsor Review*, 4, i (Fall 1968): 74-76.
Repr. in *Anonymous Sins and Other Poems* (# 441), pp. 10-13.
Repr. in *Love and Its Derangements and Other Poems* (# 623), pp. 18-20.
See "Five Confessions" (# 535).

647. "Metamorphoses." *Little Magazine*, 9, iii (Summer 1975): 53.
Repr. in *Women Whose Lives Are Food, Men Whose Lives Are Money* (# 831), p. 26.

648. "The Metamorphosis." *Literary Review*, 15, ii (Winter 1971-72): 183.

649. "Midday." *Chicago Tribune Magazine* (Mar. 10, 1974): 34.
Repr. in *The Fabulous Beasts* (# 523), p. 61.

650. "A Midwestern Song" in *Angel Fire* (# 439), pp. 37-38.
Repr. in *Love and Its Derangements and Other Poems* (# 623), p. 166.

651. "Mile-High Monday." *Salmagundi*, 19 (Spring 1972): 66.
Repr. in *Angel Fire* (# 439), p. 29.
Repr. in *Love and Its Derangements and Other Poems* (# 623), p. 160.

652. "A Miniature Passion" in *Invisible Woman* (# 600), p. 12.

653. "Miniatures: East Europe." *Denver Quarterly*, 18, iii (Autumn 1983): 5-12.

654. "The Miraculous Birth." *New York Times Magazine* (Dec. 23, 1984): 13.

655. "Mirage" in *Love and Its Derangements* (# 624), p. 49.
Repr. in *Love and Its Derangements and Other Poems* (# 623), p. 115.

656. "Morning on Our Beach." *Southern Review* (Baton Rouge), n.s., 6, iii (Summer 1970): 722-723.
and in *Love and Its Derangements* (# 624), p. 23.
Repr. in *Love and Its Derangements and Other Poems* (# 623), p. 93.

657. "A Mother to Her Child." *Beloit Poetry Journal*, 18, ii
      (Winter 1967-68): 18-22.
      Repr. in *Anonymous Sins and Other Poems*
      (# 441), pp. 20-24.
      Repr. in *Love and Its Derangements and Other
      Poems* (# 623), pp. 26-30.
      See "Three Dances of Death" (# 785).

658. "The Mountain Lion." *Southern Review* (Baton Rouge),
      n.s., 20, iii (Summer 1984): 600-602.

659. "The Mourning" in *Invisible Woman* (# 600), p. 15.

660. "The Mourning II" in *Invisible Woman* (# 600), p. 16.

661. "Mourning and Melancholia: In Memory of Sylvia Plath"
      in *Dreaming America & Other Poems* (# 504),
      [n.p.]
      Repr. in *Strivers' Row*, 1 (Fall 1974): 65.
      Repr. in *The Fabulous Beasts* (# 523), p. 66.

662. "Mouth." *Mediterranean Review*, 2, i (Autumn 1971):
      63.
      Repr. in *Angel Fire* (# 439), p. 49.
      Repr. in *Love and Its Derangements and Other
      Poems* (# 623), p. 176.

663. "Moving Out." *Hudson Review*, 32, ii (Summer 1979):
      189-190.
      Repr. in *Anthology of Magazine Verse and
      Yearbook of American Poetry 1981*, Alan F. Pater,
      ed. Beverly Hills: Monitor Book, 1981, pp.
      330-331.

664. "Music." *Poem*, 20 (Mar. 1974): 40.
      Repr. in *The Fabulous Beasts* (# 523), p. 75.

665. "The Music of Erosion, Strange Music" in *Women in
      Love and Other Poems* (# 829), p. 12.

666. "Mute Mad Child." *Southern Review* (Baton Rouge),
      n.s., 19, ii (Spring 1983): 357-358.

667. "My Fate Met Me." *Carolina Quarterly*, 22, ii (Spring
      1970): 30.
      and in *Love and Its Derangements* (# 624), p. 29.
      Repr. in *Love and Its Derangements and Other
      Poems* (# 623), p. 98.

668. "Mysterious Motions Subside." *Southern Review* (Baton Rouge), n.s., 6, iii (Summer 1970): 725-726.
and in *Love and Its Derangements* (# 624), p. 33.
Repr. in *Love and Its Derangements and Other Poems* (# 623), p. 102.

669. "Mythology." *Paris Review*, 21 (Spring 1979): 244.

670. "A Nap without Sleep." *Poetry Northwest*, 8, iii (Autumn 1967): 18-20.
Repr. in *Anonymous Sins and Other Poems* (# 441), pp. 8-10.
Repr. in *Love and Its Derangements and Other Poems* (# 623), pp. 16-18.
See "Five Confessions" (# 535).

671. "The Natural Human Fear of Being Soiled." *Literary Review*, 15, ii (Winter 1971-72): 181.

672. "New-Jersey White-Tailed Deer." *Michigan Quarterly Review*, 23, ii (Spring 1984): 253-255.

673. "New Wife" in *Anonymous Sins and Other Poems* (# 441), pp. 14-15.
Repr. in *Love and Its Derangements and Other Poems* (# 623), pp. 22-23.
See "Five Confessions" (# 535).

674. "Night." *Poetry*, 142 (Aug. 1983): 255-256.
Repr. in *Luxury of Sin* (# 637), [n.p.]

675. "Night Driving, New Year's Eve." *Hudson Review*, 30, iv (Winter 1977-78): 544-545.
Repr. in *Invisible Woman* (# 600), pp. 30-31.

676. "A Night Scene." *Sage*, 12, i (Spring 1968): 14.

677. "Night Thoughts." *California Quarterly*, 18-19 (Summer-Fall 1981): 78-79.

678. *Nightless Nights*. Concord, NH: William B. Ewert, 1981. (limited edition)
Repr. in *Southern Review* (Baton Rouge), n.s., 18, ii (Spring 1982): 381-382.
and in *Invisible Woman* (# 600), pp. 5-6.

679. "The Nightmare." *Prairie Schooner*, 45, iii (Fall 1971):
      229.
      Repr. in *Angel Fire* (# 439), p. 46.
      Repr. in *Love and Its Derangements and Other
      Poems* (# 623), p. 174.

680. "The Noisy Sorrowful Ones." *Canadian Literature*, 70
      (Autumn 1976): 60.
      Repr. in *Women Whose Lives Are Food, Men Whose
      Lives Are Money* (# 831), p. 59.

681. "North" in *Angel Fire* (# 439), p. 18.
      Repr. in *Love and Its Derangements and Other
      Poems* (# 623), p. 151.
      See "Several Embraces" (# 742).

682. "Not-Being." *Georgia Review*, 28, iv (Winter 1974):
      678-679.
      Repr. in *Women Whose Lives Are Food, Men Whose
      Lives Are Money* (# 831), p. 72.

683. "A November of the Soul." *Quarry* (Santa Cruz), 3
      (1973): 66-67.

684. "Numberless Girls." *Beloit Poetry Journal*, 18, ii
      (Winter 1967-68): 22-23.

685. "Occult." *Canadian Forum*, 54 (Jan. 1975): 29.
      and in *The Fabulous Beasts* (# 523), pp. 55-56.

686. "Of the Violence of Self-Death" in *Anonymous Sins and
      Other Poems* (# 441), pp. 42-43.
      Repr. in *Love and Its Derangements and Other
      Poems* (# 623), p. 44.

687. "Office Hours." *Prism International*, 13, i (Summer
      1973): 122-123.

688. "Offspring" in *Season of Peril* (# 736), p. 17.

689. "On Being Borne Reluctantly to New York State, by
      Train." *Mainline*, 1 (Feb. 1968): [n.p.]
      Repr. in *Wisconsin Review*, 3, ii (Spring 1968):
      11.
      Repr. in *Anonymous Sins and Other Poems*
      (# 441), pp. 45-47.
      Repr. in *Love and Its Derangements and Other
      Poems* (# 623), p. 46.

690. "'Only the Exhaustive Can Be Truly Interesting.'"
Prism International, 9, ii (Autumn 1969): 56.
Repr. in *Love and Its Derangements* (# 624), p. 6.
Repr. in *Love and Its Derangements and Other Poems* (# 623), p. 79.

691. "The Oracle." *Poem*, 20 (Mar. 1974): 31.

692. "Ordinary Miracles; Poem. View from the Campus."
Saturday Review, 52 (Dec. 20, 1969): 8.

693. "Ordinary Summer Days" in *Love and Its Derangements* (# 624), p. 54.
Repr. in *Love and Its Derangements and Other Poems* (# 623), p. 119.

694. "Our Common Past" in *Red Clay Reader 7*, Charleen Whisnant, ed. Charlotte, NC: Southern Review, 1970, p. 67.
Repr. in *Angel Fire* (# 439), p. 24.
Repr. in *Love and Its Derangements and Other Poems* (# 623), p. 155.

695. "Our Dead." *Mademoiselle*, 72 (Apr. 1971): 166.
Repr. in *Angel Fire* (# 439), p. 16.
Repr. in *Love and Its Derangements and Other Poems* (# 623), pp. 148-149.
See "Several Embraces" (# 742).

696. "Pain" (prose poem) in *Anonymous Sins and Other Poems* (# 441), pp. 13-14.
Repr. in *Love and Its Derangements and Other Poems* (# 623), pp. 21-22.
Repr. in *Southern Review* (Baton Rouge), n.s., 20, iii (Summer 1984): 602-604.
See "Five Confessions" (# 535).

697. "Painting the Balloon Face." *Paris Review*, 21 (Spring 1979): 245-246.

698. "Parachuting" in *Love and Its Derangements* (# 624), p. 3.
Repr. in *Love and Its Derangements and Other Poems* (# 623), p. 77.

699. "Parallel Lives." *Literary Review*, 15, ii (Winter 1971-72): 185.

700.   "Passing   an   Afternoon."   *Carleton   Miscellany*,   11
        (Winter 1970): 90-91.
        and in *Love and Its Derangements* (# 624), p. 36.
        Repr. in *Love and Its Derangements and Other
        Poems* (# 623), p. 104.

701.   "Pastoral." *Ohio University Review*, 10 (1968): 24.

702.   "The   Playground."   *Hudson   Review*,   28,   iv   (Winter
        1975-76): 531.

703.   "Playlet"   (prose   poem).   *TriQuarterly*,   56   (Winter
        1983): 163-164.

704.   "Poem   for   Louise"   in   *The   Triumph   of   the   Spider
        Monkey* (# 846), p. 75.

705.   "Poem   Jubilant   in   Place   of   Mourning"   in   *Invisible
        Woman* (# 600), pp. 18-19.

706.   "Portrait"   in   *Love   and   Its   Derangements*   (# 624),
        p. 48.
        Repr. in *Mainline*, 9 (Aug. 1971): [n.p.]
        Repr.   in   *Love   and   Its   Derangements   and   Other
        Poems* (# 623), p. 114.

707.   "Portrait: Woman with a Girl's Face." *Southern Review*
        (Baton   Rouge),   n.s.,   16,   ii   (Spring   1980):
        402-403.

708.   *A   Posthumous   Sketch* (prose   poem).   [Los   Angeles]:
        Black   Sparrow   Press,   July   1973.   [15]p.
        (Sparrow; 10)
        Repr. in *The Fabulous Beasts* (# 523), pp. 8-18.

709.   "Power." *Sage*, 12, i (Spring 1968): 16.

710.   "Prelude." *Southern Review* (Baton Rouge), n.s., 16,
        ii (Spring 1980): 401-402.

711.   "The Present Tense." *Atlantic*, 244 (Nov. 1979): 81.
        Repr.   in   *Anthology   of   Magazine   Verse   and
        Yearbook of American Poetry 1981*, Alan F. Pater,
        ed. Beverly Hills: Monitor Book, 1981, p. 330.
        Repr. in *Invisible Woman* (# 600), pp. 54-55.

712.   "Pretty Death." *Ohio Review*, 18, i (Winter 1977): 12.
        Repr. in *Women Whose Lives Are Food, Men Whose
        Lives Are Money* (# 831), p. 37.

713. "Preventing the Death of the Brain." *Nation*, 219 (Nov. 16, 1974): 510.
Repr. in *Women Whose Lives Are Food, Men Whose Lives Are Money* (# 831), p. 45.

714. "Primitive People Do Not Know Remorse." *Chelsea*, 22-23 (June 1968): 60-62.

715. "'Promiscuity'." *Prism International*, 13, i (Summer 1973): 119-120.
and in *Dreaming America & Other Poems* (# 504), [n.p.]
Repr. in *The Fabulous Beasts* (# 523), pp. 58-59.
Repr. in *American Poets in 1976*, William Heyen, ed. Indianapolis: Bobbs-Merrill, 1976, pp. 208-209.
Repr. in *Invisible Woman* (# 600), p. 88.

716. "The Proofs of God." *Hudson Review*, 34, i (Spring 1981): 61-62.
Repr. in *Invisible Woman* (# 600), p. 27.

717. "Prophecies." *Salmagundi*, 21 (Winter 1973): 85-86.
and in *Angel Fire* (# 439), pp. 52-53.
Repr. in *Love and Its Derangements and Other Poems* (# 623), p. 179.

718. "Psalm." *Texas Quarterly*, 21, i (Spring 1978): 6.
Repr. in *Invisible Woman* (# 600), p. 37.

719. "Public Love." *Malahat Review*, 16 (Oct. 1970): 16-17.
and in *Love and Its Derangements* (# 624), pp. 25-26.
Repr. in *Love and Its Derangements and Other Poems* (# 623), p. 95.

720. *Public Outcry*. Pittsburgh: Slow Loris Press, 1976. (broadside; limited edition)
Repr. in *Women Whose Lives Are Food, Men Whose Lives Are Money* (# 831), p. 55.

721. "Query." *Missouri Review*, 1, i (Spring 1978): 16.
Repr. under title "Query, Not to Be Answered" in *Invisible Woman* (# 600), p. 34.

722. "Query, Not to Be Answered." See "Query" (# 721).

723. "A Report to an Academy." *Paris Review*, 21 (Spring 1979): 246-247.
      Repr. in *Invisible Woman* (# 600), pp. 74-75.

724. "The Resurrection of the Dead." *Southern Review* (Baton Rouge), n.s., 13, iv (Autumn 1977): 754-755.
      Repr. in *Women Whose Lives Are Food, Men Whose Lives Are Money* (# 831), pp. 48-49.

725. "The Return" (prose poem). *Michigan Quarterly Review*, 21, iv (Fall 1982): 576-577.

726. "Revelations." *Modern Poetry Studies*, 7, ii (Autumn 1976); 81-82.
      Repr. in *Women Whose Lives Are Food, Men Whose Lives Are Money* (# 831), p. 60.

727. "Revelations in Small Sunbaked Squares." *Salmagundi*, 21 (Winter 1973): 86-87.
      and in *Angel Fire* (# 439), pp. 59-60.
      Repr. in *Love and Its Derangements and Other Poems* (# 623), p. 186.

728. "The Ride." *Beloit Poetry Journal*, 18, ii (Winter 1967-68): 23-24.
      Repr. in *Anonymous Sins and Other Poems* (# 441), pp. 38-39.
      Repr. in *Love and Its Derangements and Other Poems* (# 623), p. 41.

729. "A Rising and Sinking and Rising in My Mind." *Southern Review* (Baton Rouge), n.s., 4, iv (Autumn 1968): 1030.
      and in *Women in Love and Other Poems* (# 829), p. 8.
      Repr. in *Anonymous Sins and Other Poems* (# 441), p. 64.
      Repr. in *Love and Its Derangements and Other Poems* (# 623), p. 59.

730. "Rising to Trees" in *Season of Peril* (# 736), p. 24.
      Repr. in *Centennial Review*, 22, iv (Autumn 1978): 415.

731. "The River." *New Letters*, 45, ii (Winter 1978): 31.
      Repr. in *Celestial Timepiece* (# 471), [n.p.]
      Repr. in *New Letters*, 49, iii-iv (Spring-Summer 1983): 256.

732. *Rumpled Bed.* Derry: Rook Society, 1976. (Rook broadside; 8)
     Repr. in *Helios*, n.s., 5, i (1977): 62.
     Repr. in *Women Whose Lives Are Food, Men Whose Lives Are Money* (# 831), p. 46.

733. "The Sacred Fount" in *Luxury of Sin* (# 637), [n.p.]

734. "Sane and Sanitary Love." *Mainline*, 6 (1970): [n.p.]

735. "Season of Peril" in *Season of Peril* (# 736), p. 16.
     Repr. in *Invisible Woman* (# 600), p. 10.

736. *Season of Peril.* Santa Barbara: Black Sparrow Press, 1977. 24p.
     Contains: A Song on Coming Back from Nothing; Last Harvest; Ice Age; Season of Peril; Offspring; Skyscape; Earth-Rituals; Footprints; The Buried Self; Fever Dream on the Eve of Illness; Small Miracles; Rising to Trees.

737. "The Secret of the Water Off Point Pelee." *Tamarack Review*, 55 (Third Quarter 1970): 69–70.
     and in *Love and Its Derangements* (# 624), pp. 52–53.
     Repr. in *Love and Its Derangements and Other Poems* (# 623), p. 118.

738. "The Secret Sweetness of Nightmares." *University Review*, 37, iv (Summer 1971): 275.
     Repr. in *Angel Fire* (# 439), p. 50.
     Repr. in *Love and Its Derangements and Other Poems* (# 623), p. 177.

739. "A Secural Morning." *Little Magazine*, 5, iii–iv (Fall–Winter 1971–72): 22.
     Repr. in *Angel Fire* (# 439), p. 27.
     Repr. in *Love and Its Derangements and Other Poems* (# 623), p. 158.

740. "Seizure." *Ohio Review*, 15, i (Fall 1973): 61–62.
     Repr. in *Best Poems of 1973. Borestone Mountain Poetry Awards, 1974.* Palo Alto: Pacific Books, 1974, pp. 74–75.
     Repr. in *The Fabulous Beasts* (# 523), pp. 47–48.

741. "Self-Portrait As a Still Life." *Southern Review* (Baton
      Rouge), n.s., 19, ii (Spring 1983): 358-359.
      Repr. in *Luxury of Sin* (# 637), [n.p.]

742. "Several Embraces" in *Angel Fire* (# 439), pp. 16-18.
      Repr. in *Love and Its Derangements and Other
      Poems* (# 623), pp. 148-152.
      Contains: Our Dead; Two Bodies; Fever; North.

743. "Shelley at Viareggio" in *Invisible Woman* (# 600), pp.
      92-93.

744. "Sinners in the Hand of a Righteous God." *Beloit
      Poetry Journal*, 24, iv (Summer 1974): 16.
      Repr. in *The Fabulous Beasts* (# 523), p. 44.

745. "The Sirens." *Western Humanities Review*, 23, iii
      (Summer 1969): 205.
      Repr. in *Love and Its Derangements* (# 624),   pp.
      8-9.
      Repr. in *Love and Its Derangements and Other
      Poems* (# 623), p. 81.

746. "Skyscape." *New Republic*, 176 (Feb. 5, 1977): 27.
      and in *Season of Peril* (# 736), p. 18.
      Repr. in *Women Whose Lives Are Food, Men Whose
      Lives Are Money* (# 831), p. 25.
      Repr. in *Invisible Woman* (# 600), p. 96.

747. "The Sleep That Is Love." *Ohio University Review*, 10
      (1968): 23.

748. "Sleeping Together." *Transatlantic Review*, 37-38
      (Autumn-Winter 1970-71): 77.
      and in *Love and Its Derangements* (# 624), pp.
      4-5.
      Repr. in *Love and Its Derangements and Other
      Poems* (# 623), p. 78.

749. "Sleepwalking" in *Anonymous Sins and Other Poems*
      (# 441), pp. 52-53.
      Repr. in *Love and Its Derangements and Other
      Poems* (# 623), p. 51.

750. "Slow, Dragging Song of the Neurosurgeon."
      University Review, 36, iii (Spring 1970): 237-238.

751. "Small Miracles" in *Season of Peril* (# 736), p. 23.
     Repr. in *Paris Review*, 23 (Spring 1981): 249.

752. "The Small Still Voice behind the Great Romances."
     Modern Poetry Studies, 1, v (1970): 231-232.
     Repr. in *Angel Fire* (# 439), p. 4.
     Repr. in *Love and Its Derangements and Other
     Poems* (# 623), p. 136.

753. "Snow-Drunk" in *Celestial Timepiece* (# 471), [n.p.]

754. "Snow-Drunk in Ontario" in *Invisible Woman* (# 600),
     p. 39.

755. *Snowfall*. Northridge: Lord John Press, 1978. (broad-
     side; limited edition)
     Repr. in *Invisible Woman* (# 600), p. 38.

756. "Snowstorm in April." *American Poetry Review*, 5
     (Sept.-Oct. 1976): 33.

757. "So Cold, So Icy ..." (prose poem). *Michigan
     Quarterly Review*, 21, iv (Fall 1982): 578.

758. "A Song on Coming Back from Nothing" in *Season of
     Peril* (# 736), pp. 11-13.

759. "The Soul Glutton." *Poem*, 20 (Mar. 1974): 32.

760. "Southern Swamp." *Prairie Schooner*, 45, iii (Fall
     1971): 230.
     Repr. in *Angel Fire* (# 439), p. 54.
     Repr. in *Love and Its Derangements and Other
     Poems* (# 623), p. 181.

761. "Spaces." *Prism International*, 13, i (Summer 1973):
     116-117.
     Repr. in *The Fabulous Beasts* (# 523), p. 40.

762. "The Spectre." *New Letters*, 40, iv (Summer 1974): 27.
     Repr. in *Women Whose Lives Are Food, Men Whose
     Lives Are Money* (# 831), p. 18.

763. "Staring." *Mainline*, 3 (Nov. 1968): 27.

764. *The Stone Orchard*. Northridge: Lord John Press,
     1980. (broadside; limited edition)
     Repr. in *Malahat Review*, 60 (Jan. 1981): 125.
     Repr. in *Invisible Woman* (# 600), p. 4.

765. "Stranded." *Southern Humanities Review*, 6, i (Winter
      1972): 71.

766. "Structures." *Modern Poetry Studies*, 1, v (1970): 234.
      Repr. in *Angel Fire* (# 439), p. 11.
      Repr. in *Love and Its Derangements and Other
      Poems* (# 623), p. 143.

767. "The Struggle." *Modern Poetry Studies*, 7, ii (Autumn
      1976): 83-84.

768. "The Struggle to Wake from Sleep." *TriQuarterly*, 16
      (Fall 1969): 45.
      Repr. in *Love and Its Derangements* (# 624), p. 28
      Repr. in *Love and Its Derangements and Other
      Poems* (# 623), p. 97.

769. "Struggling with Invisible Shapes" in *Windsor Salt; An
      Anthology of Windsor Poetry*, C.H. Gervais, ed.
      Windsor, ON: Bandit Black Moss Press, 1979,
      p. 27.

770. "The Suicide." *American Poetry Review*, 5 (Sept.-Oct.
      1976): 33.
      Repr. in *Women Whose Lives Are Food, Men Whose
      Lives Are Money* (# 831), p. 39.
      Repr. in *Invisible Woman* (# 600), p. 89.

771. "Sun-Truths" in *Invisible Woman* (# 600), pp. 13-14.

772. "The Survivor." *Canadian Forum*, 54 (Jan. 1975): 28.
      and in *The Fabulous Beasts* (# 523), p. 38.

773. "A Survivor's Tale." *California Quarterly*, 11-12
      (Winter-Spring 1977): 45.

774. "Sweetest Gloomsday." *Texas Quarterly*, 21, i (Spring
      1978): 7.

775. "Tachycardiac Seizure" in *Invisible Woman* (# 600),
      p. 26.

776. "That." *Nation*, 225 (July 2, 1977): 23.
      Repr. in *Women Whose Lives Are Food, Men Whose
      Lives Are Money* (# 831), p. 75.

777. "Them" in *Women in Love and Other Poems* (# 829),
      p. 14.

778. "There Are Northern Lakes..." *Mademoiselle*, 84 (Mar.
      1978): 86.
      Repr. in *Invisible Woman* (# 600), p. 25.

779. "There Are Those Who Die." *Prairie Schooner*, 49, iii
      (Fall 1975): 212.
      Repr. in *Women Whose Lives Are Food, Men Whose
      Lives Are Money* (# 831), p. 36.

780. "Thimble-Sized Soul." *Paris Review*, 23 (Summer 1981):
      129.

781. "Things Happen to Us." *Southwest Review*, 58, ii
      (Spring 1973): 124.
      and in *Angel Fire* (# 439), p. 45.
      Repr. in *Love and Its Derangements and Other
      Poems* (# 623), p. 173.

782. "Things Run Down." *Nation*, 231 (Sept. 27, 1980): 292.

783. "This Can't Be Happening." *Quarry* (Kingston, ON),
      19, ii (Winter 1970): 11-12.

784. "Those Weathers" in *Celestial Timepiece* (# 471), [n.p.]

785. "Three Dances of Death" in *Anonymous Sins and Other
      Poems* (# 441), pp. 20-30.
      Repr. in *Love and Its Derangements and Other
      Poems* (# 623), pp. 26-36.
      Contains: A Mother to Her Child; American
      Morocco: A Child's Song; A Happy Song: Not for
      Adults.

786. "The Time Traveler." *Hudson Review*, 37, iii (Autumn
      1984): 394-395.

787. "Tinkly Song." *South Dakota Review*, 6, ii (Summer
      1968): 46.
      Repr. in *Anonymous Sins and Other Poems*
      (# 441), p. 31.
      Repr. in *Love and Its Derangements and Other
      Poems* (# 623), p. 36.

788. "To a Victim" in *The Fabulous Beasts* (# 523), p. 34.

789. "To Whose Country Have I Come ?" in *Women in Love
      and Other Poems* (# 829), p. 7.
      Repr. in *Anonymous Sins and Other Poems*
      (# 441), pp. 55-56.

Repr. in *Love and Its Derangements and Other Poems* (# 623), p. 53.

790. "The Train" in *The Triumph of the Spider Monkey* (# 374), p. 19.

791. "Transparencies." *Western Humanities Review*, 23, iii (Summer 1969): 207.
and in *Anonymous Sins and Other Poems* (# 441), pp. 69-71.
Repr. in *Love and Its Derangements and Other Poems* (# 623), p. 62.

792. "Traveling with You." *Southern Humanities Review*, 4, ll (Spring 1970): 112-113.
and in *Love and Its Derangements* (# 624), pp. 15-16.
Repr. in *Love and Its Derangements and Other Poems* (# 623), p. 86.

793. "Turning into Another Person." *Black Moss*, 1, iii (Winter 1970): 6.
and in *Love and Its Derangements* (# 624), p. 10.
Repr. in *Love and Its Derangements and Other Poems* (# 623), p. 82.

794. "20.26 Knots." *Strivers' Row*, 1 (Fall 1974): 66-67.
Repr. in *The Fabulous Beasts* (# 523), p. 73.

795. "Two Bodies" in *Angel Fire* (# 439), p. 17.
Repr. in *Love and Its Derangements and Other Poems* (# 623), p. 149.
See "Several Embraces" (# 742).

796. "Two Insomniacs." *Prism International*, 13, i (Summer 1973): 118.
Repr. in *The Fabulous Beasts* (# 523), p. 27.

797. "Two Landscapes." *Southwest Review*, 56, iii (Summer 1971): 232-233.
Contains: A Landscape of Forms; A Landscape of Love.

798. "Two Masquers." *Virginia Quarterly Review*, 60, iii (Summer 1984): 428.

799. "Two of Us Staring into Another Dimension." *Southern Humanities Review*, 4, ii (Spring 1970): 113.
and in *Love and Its Derangements* (# 624), p. 17.
Repr. in *Love and Its Derangements and Other Poems* (# 623), p. 88.

800. "Unborn Child." *Small Pond*, 13 (Spring 1968): 16.
Repr. in *Anonymous Sins and Other Poems* (# 441), pp. 33-34.
Repr. in *Love and Its Derangements and Other Poems* (# 623), p. 38.

801. "Unborn Souls." *Poem*, 20 (Mar. 1974): 38.

802. "Unpronouncing of Names." *Modern Poetry Studies*, 1, v (1970): 233.
Repr. in *Angel Fire* (# 439), p. 15.
Repr. in *Love and Its Derangements and Other Poems* (# 623), p. 147.

803. "'Untitled Poem' with Commentary." *McCall's*, 97 (Jan. 1970): 31.

804. "Upon Being Asked 'What Is It Your Practice to Do on Christmas' by a Mass-Market Magazine with a Circulation of 75 Billion Readers." *Centennial Review*, 22, iv (Autumn 1978): 415.

805. "The Vampire." *Southern Review* (Baton Rouge), n.s., 20, iii (Summer 1984): 604.

806. "Vanity." *Prairie Schooner*, 42, iv (Winter 1968-69): 299.
Repr. in *Anonymous Sins and Other Poems* (# 441), p. 79.
Repr. in *Love and Its Derangements and Other Poems* (# 623), p. 69.

807. "'Vietnam'. 1968." *South Dakota Review*, 6, ii (Summer 1968): 10-11.

808. "Violations." *Fiddlehead*, 84 (Mar.-Apr. 1970): 17.

809. "A Vision." *Queen's Quarterly*, 81, i (Spring 1974): 84.
Repr. in *The Fabulous Beasts* (# 523), p. 76.

810. "Visionary Adventures of a Wild Dog Pack" in *Women Whose Lives Are Food, Men Whose Lives Are Money* (# 831), p. 5.
Repr. in *Invisible Woman* (# 600), pp. 84-85.

811. "Waiting." *Prairie Schooner*, 47, iv (Winter 1973-74):
      315.
      Repr. in *The Fabulous Beasts* (# 523), p. 86.

812. "Walking in Safety." *Malahat Review*, 20 (Oct. 1971):
      47.

813. "The Wasp." *Atlantic*, 248 (Nov. 1981): 28.
      Repr. in *Invisible Woman* (# 600), p. 7.

814. "Wealthy Lady." *Epoch*, 24, i (Fall 1974): 71-73.
      Repr. in *Women Whose Lives Are Food, Men Whose
      Lives Are Money* (# 831), pp. 63-65.

815. "What Has Been Your Life ?" *Michigan Quarterly
      Review*, 16, iii (Summer 1977): 261.

816. "What Has Not Been Lost in the Deserts of North
      America?" *Prairie Schooner*, 47, iv (Winter
      1973-74): 316.
      Repr. in *The Fabulous Beasts* (# 523), p. 60.

817. "What I Fear ..." *Denver Quarterly*, 4, ii (Summer
      1969): 90.
      Repr. in *Love and Its Derangements* (# 624), p. 37.
      Repr. in *Love and Its Derangements and Other
      Poems* (# 623), p. 105.

818. "What We Fear from Dreams & Waking" in *Angel Fire*
      (# 439), pp. 40-41.
      Repr. in *Love and Its Derangements and Other
      Poems* (# 623), p. 168.

819. "Where the Shadow Is Darkest." *Southern Review*
      (Baton Rouge), n.s., 6, iii (Summer 1970):
      724-725.
      Repr. in *Angel Fire* (# 439), p. 20.
      Repr. in *Love and Its Derangements and Other
      Poems* (# 623), p. 152.

820. "Where the Wind Went Crazy" in *Angel Fire* (# 439),
      p. 7.
      Repr. in *Love and Its Derangements and Other
      Poems* (# 623), p. 139.

821. "While We Slept ..." *Canadian Forum*, 54 (Jan. 1975):
      29.
      and in *The Fabulous Beasts* (# 523), p. 69.

822. "Winter Landscape: Children Teasing Death." *New Letters*, 45, ii (Winter 1978): 33-34.

823. "A Woman Comes to Rest." *Mainline*, 6 (1970): [n.p.]

824. "A Woman in Her Secret Life." *Epos*, 20 (Winter 1968-69): 4.
    and in *Women in Love and Other Poems* (# 829), p. 5.
    Repr. in *Anonymous Sins and Other Poems* (# 441), pp. 60-61.
    Repr. in *Love and Its Derangements and Other Poems* (# 623), p. 57.

825. *Woman Is the Death of the Soul*. Toronto: Coach House Press, 1970. (broadside) (Orange Bear Reader; 2)
    and *Epoch*, 19, iii (Spring 1970): 226.
    and in *Love and Its Derangements* (# 624), p. 12.
    Repr. in *Love and Its Derangements and Other Poems* (# 623), p. 84.

826. "A Woman Walking in a Man's Sight." *Southern Humanities Review*, 6, i (Winter 1972): 69.

827. "A Woman's Song" in *Angel Fire* (# 439), p. 10.
    Repr. in *Love and Its Derangements and Other Poems* (# 623), p. 141.

828. "Women in Love" in *Women in Love and Other Poems* (# 829), p. 6.
    Repr. in *Anonymous Sins and Other Poems* (# 441), pp. 62-63.
    Repr. in *Love and Its Derangements and Other Poems* (# 623), p. 58.

829. *Women in Love and Other Poems*. New York: Albondocani Press, 1968. 14p. (Albondocani Press Publication; 3)
    Contains: A Woman in Her Secret Life; Women in Love; To Whose Country Have I Come ?; A Rising and Sinking and Rising in My Mind; Cupid and Psyche; An Internal Landscape; Dazed; The Music of Erosion, Strange Music; How Sweet to Be a Wound ...; Them.

830. "Women Whose Lives Are Food, Men Whose Lives Are Money." *Boston University Journal*, 23, i (Winter 1975): 26-27.
    Repr. in *Women Whose Lives Are Food, Men Whose Lives Are Money* (# 831), pp. 3-4.

831. *Women Whose Lives Are Food, Men Whose Lives Are
      Money: Poems.* Ill. by Elizabeth Hansell. Baton
      Rouge; London: Louisiana State University Press,
      1978. 80p.
      Contains: Part I. Women Whose Lives Are Food,
      Men Whose Lives Are Money: Women Whose Lives
      Are Food, Men Whose Lives Are Money; Visionary
      Adventures of a Wild Dog Pack; Hauled from
      River, Sunday 8 a.m.; Former Movie Queen,
      Dying of Cancer, Watches an Old Movie of Hers at
      a Film Festival in San Francisco; The Eternal
      Children; From the Dark Side of the Earth.
      Part II. Metamorphoses: Lovers Asleep; The
      Spectre; The Lovers; Fever Song; Addiction;
      Last Harvest; Holy Saturday; Skyscape;
      Metamorphoses; The Demons; At the Seashore;
      After Sunset; Guilt; Abandoned Airfield, 1977.
      Part III. The Resurrection of the Dead: If You
      Must Go and I Must Stay; There Are Those Who
      Die; Pretty Death; The Suicide; The Broken Man;
      Enigma; Ice Age; Coronary Thrombosis;
      Preventing the Death of the Brain; Rumpled Bed;
      The Resurrection of the Dead. Part IV. Public
      Outcry: Happy Birthday; Public Outcry; American
      Independence; Gala Power Blackout of New York
      City, July '77; The Noisy Sorrowful Ones;
      Revelations; At Peace, at Rest; Wealthy Lady; He
      Traveled by Jet First Class to Tangier. Part V.
      Many Are Called: The Creation; Not-Being; Love
      Poem; That; An Infant's Song; In Medias Res;
      Earth-Rituals; Fertilizing the Continent; Many Are
      Called.

832. "Wonder." *Sage*, 12, i (Spring 1968): 15.

833. "Wonderland." See "Iris into Eye" (# 601).

834. "Wonders of the Invisible World." *Beloit Poetry
      Journal*, 24, iv (Summer 1974): 14-15.
      Repr. in *The Fabulous Beasts* (# 523), p. 7.

835. *Wooded Forms.* [New York]: Albondocani Press &
      Ampersand Books, 1972. [n.p.] (limited edition)
      and in *Modern Poetry Studies*, 3, vi (1972):
      260-261.
      Repr. in *The Fabulous Beasts* (# 523), p. 81.

836. "A World of Other People." *Epos*, 20 (Summer 1969): 10.

837. "Wounds" in *Love and Its Derangements* (# 624), p. 21.
     Repr. in *Love and Its Derangements and Other Poems* (# 623), p. 91.

838. "The Wren's Hunger." *Southern Review* (Baton Rouge), n.s., 19, ii (Spring 1983): 354-355.

839. "You/Your." *Connexion*, 1, iii (Nov. 1969): [n.p.]
     Repr. in *Southern Review* (Baton Rouge), n.s., 6, iii (Summer 1970): 726.
     and in *Love and Its Derangements* (# 624), p. 24.
     Repr. in *Love and Its Derangements and Other Poems* (# 623), p. 95.

840. "A Young Wife." *Antioch Review*, 31, iv (Winter 1971-72): 476.
     Repr. in *Angel Fire* (# 439), p. 25.
     Repr. in *Love and Its Derangements and Other Poems* (# 623), p. 156.

PLAYS

841. *Miracle Play*. Los Angeles: Black Sparrow Press, 1974.
     87p.
     Repr. in *Three Plays* (# 845), pp. 53-99.
     Premiered: New York City: Playhouse II Theatre,
     1973.

842. "Ontological Proof of My Existence." *Partisan Review*,
     37, iv (1970): 471-497.
     Repr. in *Three Plays* (# 845), pp. 11-49.
     Premiered: New York City : Cubiculo Theatre, 1972.

843. *Sunday Dinner*. Premiered: New York City: St.
     Clement's Church, 1970.

844. *The Sweet Enemy*. Premiered: New York City: Actors
     Playhouse, 1965.

845. *Three Plays*. Princeton: Ontario Review Press, 1980.
     157p.
     Contains: Ontological Proof of My Existence;
     Miracle Play; The Triumph of the Spider Monkey.

846. "The Triumph of the Spider Monkey" in *Three Plays*
     (# 845), pp. 103-157.

ANTHOLOGIES

847. *The Best American Short Stories 1979: Selected from US and Canadian Magazines*, by Joyce Carol Oates with Shannon Ravenel, eds. Boston, MA: Houghton Mifflin, 1979. 352p.

848. *Night Walks: A Bedside Companion*, Joyce Carol Oates, comp. Princeton, NJ: Ontario Review Press, 1982. 287p.

849. *Scenes from American Life: Contemporary Short Fiction*, Joyce Carol Oates, ed. New York: Random House, 1973. 271p.
New York: Vanguard Press, 1973. 271p.

ESSAYS AND OTHER NON-FICTION

850. "The Trilogy of Samuel Beckett." *Renascence*, 14 (Spring 1962): 160-165.
    Repr. under title "Anarchy and Order in Beckett's Trilogy" in *New Heaven, New Earth* (# 928), pp. 83-95.

    Although an early essay, the article is important as an indication of how far back Oates's quarrel with Postmodern might go. Beckett's fiction is treated here as a brilliantly constructed terminal moraine, the last reach of a certain kind of thinking: "His style is a triumph in a vacuum, and it is inconceivable elsewhere, that is, in the novelist's usual rich, vibrant, and varied world of experience. Beckett's immense introspction [sic] perhaps had to be done; once done, it need not be imitated...."

851. "Melville and the Manichean Illusion." *Texas Studies in Literature and Language*, 4 (Spring 1962): 117-129.
    Repr. under title "Melville and the Tragedy of Nihilism" in *The Edge of Impossibility* (# 894), pp. 59-84 (revised version).

    An attempt to "undercut the general tone of simplicity in which Melville is often discussed." Published while Oates was a student at Wisconsin, the essay tends towards truisms and shows only a sketchy awareness of the ongoing conversation on Melville. It is a preliminary indication of a recurring critical strategy by Oates: to try to locate the rarely-questioned assumptions about a major writer and subject them to rigorous thought.

852. "The 'Fifth Act' and the Chorus in the English and Scottish Ballads." *Dalhousie Review*, 42, iii (Autumn 1962): 329-340 (signed J. Oates Smith).
    Repr. under title "The English and Scottish Traditional Ballads" in *Southern Review* (Baton

Rouge), n.s., 15, iii (Summer 1979): 560-566
(revised version).
Repr. under title "In the Fifth Act: The Art of
the English and Scottish Traditional Ballads" in
Contraries (# 1019), pp. 116-140 (expanded version).

At their best the ballads "demonstrate an insight which
is artistically conscious of itself. It is this 'doubling
back' upon the narrative situation ... which gives to
the superior ballads their ageless value." Important
connections can be made between this essay, (which
was revised and republished in the *Southern Review*
and much expanded for *Contraries*) and several of the
short stories and novels, which likewise call attention
to themselves as artistic creations and challenge
modern ideas both of tragedy and of the integrity and
consequence of the individual. In its final version,
this constitutes one of Oates's most original and
thoughtful essays.

853.   "The Comedy of Metamorphosis in 'The Revenger's
       Tragedy.'" *Bucknell Review*, 11, i (Dec. 1962):
       38-52.

       "There is universality in *The Revenger's Tragedy* but
       not for the reasons one might think--that the
       disintegration of values results in the defeat,
       ultimately, of the single person who loathes vice with
       an active, compelling consciousness ...; the univer-
       sality of the work is a result of its penetration into
       the psychology of the 'revenger,' the malcontent who
       as much desires to see in the world the horror he sees
       as he desires to exorcise it." Oates may not sustain
       her thesis that the play is a masterpiece, but she
       offers insights into her own fascination with the
       grotesque, and with the idea of transforming per-
       sonalities.

854.   "The Existential Comedy of Conrad's 'Youth.'"
       Renascence, 16 (Fall 1963): 22-28 (signed J.
       Oates Smith).

       "What is notable about the existential comedy of
       'Youth' is its skillful fusion of the absurd and the
       traditionally heroic, the grotesque and the touching,
       the bitter and the comic."

855.   "The Alchemy of 'Antony and Cleopatra.'" *Bucknell
       Review*, 12, i (Mar. 1964): 37-50 (signed J. Oates
       Smith).

Repr. under title "The Tragedy of Imagination: Shakespeare's 'Antony and Cleopatra'" in *The Edge of Impossibility* (# 894), pp. 37-57 (revised version).

Oates's thesis here is that language and passion provide a stay against dissolution; but the essay becomes an appearance-reality discussion that shows little awareness of other reviews. Written in an earnest, humorless tone, it shows Oates's fearlessness at trying her hand as a critic.

856. "Henry James and Virginia Woolf: The Art of Relationships." *Twentieth Century Literature*, 10 (Oct. 1964): 119-129 (signed J. Oates Smith). Repr. under title "The Art of Relationships: Henry James and Virginia Woolf" in *New Heaven, New Earth* (# 928), pp. 9-35.

Remarkable as a discussion of the idea of the self in both writers, Oates's thesis is that in James more than Woolf, individuals transform into social roles, that they are created by their partially-ritualized relationships with one another. The article gives further insight into Oates's unconventional thinking about the nature of the personality and its portrayal in literature.

857. "Porter's 'Noon Wine': A Stifled Tragedy." *Renascence*, 17 (Spring 1965): 157-162 (signed J. Oates Smith).

Porter's "moral demands are such that she will not distort her character, will not contrive his salvation or forgive him as a Steinbeck might.... Man as man begins precisely where living on the natural or animalistic level leaves off." "The secret theme of most of Porter's writing seems to be the tragic isolation of the human heart."

858. "Masquerade and Marriage: Fielding's Comedies of Identity." *Ball State University Forum*, 6, iii (Autumn 1965): 10-21 (signed J. Oates Smith).

The essay somewhat hesitantly proposes that for Fielding, social identity is a masquerade, and that "real" identity is problematic. Covers too much ground in too little space to be totally convincing although it constitutes an important indication as to Oates's evolution as a critic.

859. "Ionesco's Dances of Death." *Thought*, 40 (Autumn
      1965): 415-431 (signed J. Oates Smith).
      Repr. in *The Edge of Impossibility* (# 894), pp.
      223-249.

      Oates has never accepted any doctrine of the essential
      incoherence or illusoriness of the self; but this essay
      suggests that she has been provoked and shaken by
      such ideas. Oates argues that for Ionesco, as for
      Lawrence, identity is bound up with passion, with the
      ability to feel, and mystery. Ionesco "is able ... to
      create in the spectator ... the unforgettable feeling of
      the absurdity of life; spiritual longings in a
      time-locked body, a mind hopelessly divided and
      warring against itself."

860. "The Ambiguity of Troilus and Cressida." *Shakespeare
      Quarterly*, 17 (Spring 1966): 141-150.

      and

      "Essence and Existence in Shakespeare's 'Troilus and
      Cressida.'" *Philological Quarterly*, 46 (Apr. 1967):
      167-185 (signed J. Oates Smith).

      A two-part essay repr. under title "The Tragedy
      of Existence: Shakespeare's 'Troilus and
      Cressida'" in *The Edge of Impossibility* (# 894),
      pp. 9-36.

      No annotation.

861. "Building Tension in the Short Story." *Writer*, 79
      (June 1966): 11-12, 44.

      "If violence erupts in fiction, it should be the outcome
      of tension; it should not come first, nor should it be
      accidental." Oates also states, "Technique is only a
      means to an end" and suggests "the stress placed
      today on technique is misleading."

862. "Heritage of Doom." Review of "Pursuit" by Berry
      Morgan. *New York Times Book Review*, 71
      (Oct. 16, 1966): 66-67.
      (*)

      No annotation.

863. "Chekhov and the Theater of the Absurd." *Bucknell
      Review*, 14, iii (Dec. 1966): 44-58 (signed J.
      Oates Smith).

Repr. in *The Edge of Impossibility* (# 894), pp. 115-137.

"Chekhov's stage 'looks' real enough and his characters speak a language that has the surface formlessness of that of real life, but in essence his conception of drama is more complex and more iconoclastic than that of the absurdists whose revolt is characterized by a simplification of life and an attendant exaggeration of limited experiences." Oates suggests, "The vision of man in absurdist drama and in Chekhov is similar, if not identical."

864. "Ritual and Violence in Flannery O'Connor." *Thought*, 41 (Winter 1966): 545-560 (signed J. Oates Smith).

In O'Connor's world, man can see "only through an initiation by violence." Oates also states, "There is no pragmatic answer to the main question O'Connor raises--which is like Kafka's before her, How must life be lived? No solution is offered to the mystery; her writings are celebrations of the fact of mystery, that is all."

and

"The Visionary Art of Flannery O'Connor." *Southern Humanities Review*, 7, iii (Summer 1973): 235-246.

"O'Connor's writing is stark and, for many readers, difficult to absorb into a recognizable world, because it insists upon a brutal distinction between what Augustine would call the City of Man and the City of God. One can reject O'Connor's fierce insistence upon this separation--as I must admit I do--and yet sympathize with the terror that must be experienced when these two 'realms' of being are imagined as distinct."

A two-part essay repr. under title "The Visionary Art of Flannery O'Connor" in *New Heaven, New Earth* (# 928), pp. 141-176.

865. "Background and Foreground in Fiction." *Writer*, 80 (Aug. 1967): 11-13.

"A failure to understand the relationship between the 'background' (overall rhythm or structure, and theme) and the 'foreground' (each sentence of each paragraph) of literature accounts for much unpublishable fiction." She also states, "A writer is not just someone who writes, but someone who reads and who writes intelligently."

866. "Man under Sentence of Death: The Novels of James M. Cain" in *Tough Guy Writers of the Thirties*, David Madden, ed. Carbondale, IL: Southern Illinois University Press, 1968, pp. 110-128.
(*)

"Though he deals constantly with the Artistic, Cain, it will be said, never manages to become an artist; there is always something sleazy, something eerily vulgar and disappointing in his work." However, Oates also suggests that no writer is "more faithful to the mythologies of America than Cain, for he writes of its ideals and hatreds without obscuring them in the difficulties of art."

867. "The Double Vision of 'The Brothers Karamazov.'" *Journal of Aesthetics and Art Criticism*, 27 (Winter 1968-69): 203-213.
Repr. under title "Tragic and Comic Visions in 'The Brothers Karamazov'" in *The Edge of Impossibility* (# 894), pp. 85-113.

"Two visions--one existential and tragic, the other Christian and comic--are unequally balanced in this novel and do not in my opinion resolve themselves." According to Oates, "Certain contemporary works, in refusing to grant readers the conventional moral protection provided by the double ... upset our sensibilities; we want the release of a consummation of violence but we are frightened at having it offered so bluntly to us." She suggests Dostoyevsky is so highly esteemed a writer because of "his fluid demonstration of the art of writing--the splendid unpredictability of the writer as writer, *who can leave nothing unsaid.*" (Emphasis Oates's)

868. Review of "Yellow Flowers in the Antipodean Room" by Janet Frame. *New York Times Book Review*, 74 (Feb. 9, 1969): 5, 46.
(*)

No annotation.

869. "Life in a Low Key." Review of "In and Out of Never-Never Land" by Maeve Brennan. *Saturday Review*, 52 (Mar. 22, 1969): 65-66.

" ... one does expect from fiction something more than the carefully controlled, 'cute' dullness of *In and Out of Never-Never Land*. It is as false to life as its opposite, the crudest kind of pornography, and, like pornography, it is disappointing in its failure of imagination."

870. "Please Tell Me It's Just a Story." Review of "The Stories of James Stern" by James Stern; "Going Places" by Leonard Michaels. *Washington Post Book World* (Mar. 30, 1969): 6.

Stern is at his best when "faithful to the details of both superficial and complex life." Michaels's "sustained interest in ... wacky dialogue and wackier activities" takes a toll: the stories "become largely tedious and unconvincing as the volume goes on and we realize that nothing, nothing is impossible because there is nothing on the page except words."

871. "The Art of Eudora Welty." *Shenandoah*, 20, iii (Spring 1969): 54-57.
(*)

"Our natural instinct is to insist that horror be emphasized, underlined, somehow exaggerated so that we may absorb it in a way satisfying to sensibilities." Oates is impressed that Welty can write a story, such as "The Demonstrators," about "nothing" and "make it mean very nearly everything."

872. "Art at the Edge of Impossibility: Mann's 'Dr. Faustus.'" *Southern Review* (Baton Rouge), n.s. 5, ii (Spring 1969): 375-397.
Repr. in *The Edge of Impossibility* (# 894), pp. 189-221.

"*Dr. Faustus* repays many readings and in its ingenious artlessness forces the reader to become a creator himself, a kind of secondary novelist." According to Oates, this novel "concerns itself with form and formlessness, the discipline of living and the temptation of dying, attempting in its very pages a synthesis of the two which cannot come about except through art, that is, through artifice."

873. "Finding Again the World." Review of "The Blue Swallows" by Howard Nemerov. *University of Windsor Review*, 6, ii (Spring 1969): 70-76.

Oates begins by faulting criticism of Nemerov as typically "inadequate and often irrelevant," but she doesn't manage to get much farther here. This short review is a summary of major themes in Nemerov: the collision of substance and shadow, time and timelessness, stasis and change. "Poetry, like magic, seeks analogy and identity: it does not simply want to imitate the magic of the world, but to name it, to fix it utterly." The review does not succeed in setting Nemerov off from his contemporaries.

874. "Speaking of Books: The Formidable W.B. Yeats." *New York Times Book Review*, 74 (Sept. 7, 1969): 2.

Introductory-level overview of Yeats, emphasizing the resistance his temperament puts up to the contemporary mind, and the process of reading him as a test of wills. "It is natural, even necessary, to resist him, because to experience Yeats deeply is perhaps to lose oneself, or to experience a weakening of one's contained self, which the greatest writers of tragedy cause us to experience." "He makes us realize, tragically, that we too desire a fantastic personal deification but that we are too modest, too embarrassed to make our claim."

875. "Fiction Chronicle." [Review of "This Is Moscow Speaking" by Yuli Daniel; "The Four Gated City" by Doris Lessing; "Into a Neutral Country" by Hugo Wolfram; "The New Yorker" by Hortense Calisher; "Slaughterhouse-Five" by Kurt Vonnegut, Jr.; "National Anthem" by Richard Kluger; "Two Days, Two Nights" by Per Olof Sundman; "Night Watch" by Stephen Koch; "An American Marriage" by Hilary Masters; "Without a City Wall" by Melvyn Bragg; "In the Midst of Earth" by Marilyn Harris; "A Set of Variations" by Frank O'Connor; "Tike and Other Stories" by Jonathan Strong; "Come Back if It Doesn't Get Better" by Penelope Gilliatt.] *Hudson Review*, 22, iii (Autumn 1969): 531-539.
      (*)

No annotation.

876. "Dreams without Substance." Review of "A Special Providence" by Richard Yates. *Nation*, 209 (Nov. 10, 1969): 512-513.
      (*)

No annotation.

877. "Yeats: Violence, Tragedy, Mutability." *Bucknell Review*, 17, iii (Dec. 1969): 1-17.
Repr. in *The Edge of Impossibility* (# 894), pp. 139-161.

Yeats's genius lies not in his ability to hammer his multiple thoughts into unity, but rather in his faithful accounting of the impossibility--which may lead one to the edge of madness--of bringing together aesthetic theory and emotional experience."

878. "Tragic Rites in Yeats' 'A Full Moon in March.'" *Antioch Review*, 29, iv (Winter 1969-70): 547-560.
Repr. in *The Edge of Impossibility* (# 894), pp. 163-187.

A Full Moon in March is obviously "not a realistic drama, yet it is surprising to see how totally Yeats has abandoned the most basic desire of the imagination--to be lied to in a realistic manner. Like contemporary dramatists of the 'absurd,' Yeats refuses to sustain an illusion." Oates also suggests that this play "is probably Yeats' only play for dancers in which music accomplishes what language could not."

879. Remarks by Joyce Carol Oates Accepting the 1970 National Book Award in Fiction for *them*. *December Magazine*, 12, i-ii (1970): 215.

Brief remarks from Oates's most intense Cassandra period: novelists, as the true historians of our time, must observe a "deathly" nihilism and obsession with sensation as they take root in American culture.

880. "The Nature of Short Fiction; or, The Nature of My Short Fiction" in *Handbook of Short Story Writing*, Frank A. Dickson and Sandra Smythe, eds. Cincinnati: Writer's Digest, [1970], pp. XI-XVIII.

"I am obsessed with the deeps of the mind, of the imagination, particularly of the semi-conscious imagination." Oates also notes, "We write for the same reasons we dream--because we cannot not dream, because it is in the nature of the human imagination to dream." As to where she finds her materials, she admits to sources in "ordinary life." She also states that she is "conventional" and "old-fashioned" because she is "less interested in technical gimmicks" than she is in attempting to understand human emotions.

881. "The World of Moderation." Review of "A Horse and
      Two Goats" by R.K. Narayan; "Blind Love" by
      V.S. Pritchett. *Washington Post Book World*
      (Jan. 18, 1970): 6.

      Brief reviews of two collections, with kind words for
      two writers who, Oates says, resist fashionable
      extremism, and whose stories are "absolutely unam-
      bitious" yet "worthy of our attention."

882. "Miss Brophy's Probing Pen." Review of "In Transit"
      by Brigid Brophy. *Washington Post Book World*
      (Jan. 25, 1970): 4-5.

      Negative satiric review. After a brief parody of
      Brophy's style, Oates observes: "Perhaps because of
      the deterioration of words in the twentieth century we
      are being treated to extremely dull novels and plays
      that celebrate such deterioration ... as if a natural
      ineptness for language, for the beauty of language,
      were a prerequisite for this serious and profound good
      news."

883. "Private and Public Lives." Review of "Love Poems" by
      Anne Sexton; "A Short History of the Fur Trade"
      by Adrien Stoutenburg. *University of Windsor
      Review*, 5, ii (Spring 1970): 107-110.

      Brief recommendations of both volumes.

884. "Eudora's Web." Review of "Losing Battles" by Eudora
      Welty. *Atlantic*, 225 (Apr. 1970): 118-120, 122.
      Repr. in *Contemporary Women Novelists: A Collec-
      tion of Critical Essays*, Patricia Meyer Spacks.
      Englewood Cliffs: Prentice-Hall, 1977, pp. 167-172.

      According to Oates, the "concerns of *Losing Battles*
      are extinct" because Welty wrote about "a world that
      has vanished from literature, and yet one which will
      remain, most beautifully and paradoxically, only in
      literature. To know our own origins, or to know
      alternate possibilities for our own lives, we must study
      Miss Welty's fiction, for we will not get this kind of
      knowledge from life."

885. "The Fact Is: We Like to Be Drugged." *McCall's*, 97
      (June 1970): 69.

      No annotation.

886. Review of "The Perfectionists" by Gail Godwin. *New York Times Book Review*, 75 (June 7, 1970): 5, 51.
     (*)

     "Truly unconventional writing has nothing to do with hallucinatory prose adventures, or tricks of style, or self-conscious appearances by the writer in his own work; it is only a matter of discovery or rediscovery, a revelation of surprising and therefore 'unconventional' emotions within a framework that may appear absolutely ordinary. What point is there to 'experimental' writing when it reveals to us familiar ideas, familiar faces ?"

887. "Drama of Limitations." *Saturday Review*, 53 (July 25, 1970): 24-25.
     (*)

     Oates agrees in this letter to the *Saturday Review* with John Aldridge's assessment of much academic criticism but disagrees with his remarks on Updike's *Bech: A Book*. She states that Updike's book is clever, "warm and engaging and deeply cynical" and "treats the life of the imagination and the intellect with great respect."

888. "Love on Film." *McCall's*, 97 (Oct. 1970): 14, 138.

     Oates expresses alarm at the glib nihilism turning up in Hollywood films. She mentions "Easy Rider," "Bob & Carol & Ted & Alice," "Alice's Restaurant," and "They Shoot Horses, Don't They ?"

889. "Evolutions." Review of "The Will to Change, Poems 1968-1970" by A. Rich. *Modern Poetry Studies*, 2, iv (1971): 190-191.

     "Miss Rich's poetry has evolved into a rather tough, intellectually combative work, less sensuous and less personal than it was in earlier collections.... This will probably result in Miss Rich's being unjustly slighted, for in the din of much of contemporary poetry--even that poetry concerned with 'poetics'--her clear, calm, intelligent voice may be too quiet."

890. "An American Tragedy." Review of "The Dollmaker" by Harriette Arnow. *New York Times Book Review*, 76 (Jan. 24, 1971): 2, 12, 14, 16.
     Repr. under title "The Nightmare of Naturalism:

Harriette Arnow's 'The Dollmaker'" in *Rediscoveries*, David Madden, ed. New York: Crown Publishers, 1971, pp. 57-66.
Repr. in *New Heaven, New Earth* (# 928), pp. 97-110.
(*)

"Because Harriette Arnow's people are not articulate, we are anxious to give their confusion a recognizable order, to complete them with language." She also states, "Tragedy does not seem to me to be cathartic, but to deepen our sense of the mystery and sanctity of the human predicament." For her, "the greatest works of literature deal with the human soul caught in the stampede of time, unable to gauge the profundity of what passes over it."

891. "The Short Story." *Southern Humanities Review*, 5, iii (Summer 1971): 213-214.
Repr. in *What Is the Short Story ?*, Eugene Current-Garcia and Welton R. Patrick, eds. Glenview: Scott Foresman, 1974, pp. 138-139.

"The short story is a dream verbalized, arranged in space and presented to the world, imagined as a sympathetic audience." Although Oates believes "that the basis of the writing of fiction is the unconscious, that oceanic, ungovernable, unfathomable reservoir of human energy, it is still my deepest certainty that art, if not life, requires intelligence and discretion and transcendence, that we must take the choice of living or telling if what we have to tell is worth anyone else's concern."

892. "With Norman Mailer at the Sex Circus: II, Out of the Machine." *Atlantic*, 228 (July 1971): 42-45.
Repr. under title "Male Chauvinist ?: Out of the Machine" in *Will the Real Norman Mailer Please Stand Up ?*, Laura Adams, ed. Port Washington, NY: Kennikat Press, 1974, pp. 216-223.
(*)

"There will be a place in our society for Mailer's heroic mysticism, at the point in history at which women can afford the same mysticism. Until then, it is better for us to contemplate the blank-faced horror of Melville's pulp factory, rather than the dreamy illogic of Mailer's 'ovum-as-artistic-creation.'"

893. "Realism of Distance, Realism of Immediacy." [Review of "Mystery and Manners" by Flannery O'Connor; "The Collected Stories of Peter Taylor"; "We Have Seen the Best of Our Times" by Nancy A.J. Potter; "Selected Stories of Roald Dahl"; "Twenty-Eight Stories" by Frances Gray Patton; "Pricksongs and Descants" by Robert Coover; "A Sea Change" by J.R. Salamanca; "Cassandra Singing" by David Madden; "What I'm Going to Do, I Think" by L. Woiwode; "The Waterfall" by Margaret Drabble; "This Is Not for You" by Jane Rule; "Bad Debts" by Geoffrey Wolff; "The Perfectionists" by Gail Godwin.] *Southern Review* (Baton Rouge), n.s., 7, i (Winter 1971): 295-313. (*)

"In these days much of our literature is apocalyptic and hurried; it is a literature in which the cartoon--like exaggerations of the dream (particularly the American Dream) are given freedom, breaking out from the gentlemanly confines of the well-made work of art. The people who inhabit our literature are not 'people' in the old, predictable sense--they do not have 'families,' they do not have permanent egos--they do not have time, above all, for subtleties of expression. If they participate in their culture it is likely to be negatively, reacting against, destroying."

894. *The Edge of Impossibility: Tragic Forms in Literature.* New York: Vanguard Press, 1972. 259p. Greenwich, CT: Fawcett, [1973]. 224p. London: Gollancz, 1976. 259p. Contains: Introduction: 'Forms of Tragic Literature'; The Tragedy of Existence: Shakespeare's 'Troilus and Cressida'; The Tragedy of Imagination: Shakespeare's 'Antony and Cleopatra'; Melville and the Tragedy of Nihilism; Tragic and Comic Visions in 'The Brothers Karamazov'; Chekhov and the Theater of the Absurd; Yeats: Violence, Tragedy, Mutability; Tragic Rites in Yeats' 'A Full Moon in March'; Art at the Edge of Impossibility: Mann's 'Dr. Faustus'; Ionesco's Dances of Death.

A collection of nine articles covering works by Shakespeare, Melville, Dostoyevsky, Chekhov, Yeats, Mann, and Ionesco.
All have been annotated as single articles.

895.   Review of "Knots" by R.D. Laing. *Modern Poetry Studies*, 3, iii (1972): 141-144.

No annotation.

896.   "In the Heart of the Heart of the Country." Review of "The Promisekeeper" by Charles Newman. *Partisan Review*, 39, i (1972): 118-120.
(*)

No annotation.

897.   "Going Places." Review of "Wolf" by Jim Harrison; "Going Nowhere" by Alvin Greenberg; "The Jane Castle Manuscript" by Philip Greene. *Partisan Review*, 39, iii (1972): 162-164.
(*)

No annotation.

898.   "So Many People." Review of "An Accidental Man" by Iris Murdoch. *Washington Post Book World* (Jan. 23, 1972): 3.
(*)

"Iris Murdoch's energy is such that she seems unable to resist inventing more and [more] characters, though, in any given novel, she does not really have enough interest in them to go around. *An Accidental Man* would have been an intense, rather suspenseful and entertaining novel, if it had not been stretched out to such lengths."

899.   Review of "The Savage God; A Study of Suicide" by A. Alvarez. *New York Times Book Review*, 77 (Apr. 16, 1972): 1, 28.

No annotation.

900.   "'Real' People or Characters ?" Review of "The Devastating Boys and Other Stories" by Elizabeth Taylor. *Washington Post Book World* (Apr. 30, 1972): 6.
(*)

Oates criticizes Taylor for dealing with characters, not people, in her fiction. She questions the absence of "all the 'real' people, all the passionate, sometimes brutal, always unpredictable people who refuse to be contained within the delicate confines of the old-fashioned *New Yorker* story."

901. "Whose Side Are You On ?" *New York Times Book Review*, 77 (June 4, 1972): 63.

    "Writers who limit themselves to fragments do not elude identity. They are, simply, *writers-who-limit-themselves-to-fragments.*" Oates disagrees with Nabokov's assertion that literature has no purpose and insists that it should alter the reader as he is in the process of reading. She suggests that "we must reject only the 'pure' literature, the antiseptic 'purity' of the literature [Sartre] scorns, and commit ourselves to literature itself, which doesn't simply belong to any era but which helps create it."

902. Review of "The Needle's Eye" by Margaret Drabble. *New York Times Book Review*, 77 (June 11, 1972): 23.
    (*)

    "Our yearning for meaningful novels, for novels that will truly change us for the better, is so constantly thwarted that when we come upon the work of a contemporary who has written such a work our first reaction is astonishment." She applauds Drabble's presentation of "characters who are not passively witnessing their lives" and also her attempt to re-create "a set of values by which human beings can live."

903. "'The Hostile Sun': The Poetry of D.H. Lawrence." *Massachusetts Review*, 13, iv (Autumn 1972): 639–656.

    "A reading of all Lawrence's poems, the worst as well as the best, gives one a sensation of having observed Lawrence from the inside, the Lawrence of the famous novels, here revealing himself in spurts of lyric poetry, in which a single poem flashes with an insight dramatized in one of the novels at great length. It is a kind of autobiography of a novelist at work, a poetic journal of his consciousness." She also suggests that "the creative artist shares to varying degrees the personalities of all his characters, even those whom he appears to detest--perhaps, at times, it is these characters he is really closest to."

    and

    "Candid Revelations: On the Complete Poems of D.H. Lawrence." *American Poetry Review*, 1 (Nov.-Dec. 1972): 11-13.

"But critics, especially 'New Critics' and 'Formalist Critics,' have not understood this: that there are many kinds of art, that there may be a dozen, a hundred ways of writing, and that no single way is perfect."

> A two-part essay repr. under title *'The Hostile Sun': The Poetry of D.H. Lawrence.* Los Angeles: Black Sparrow Press, 1973. 60p. (slightly different version).
> Repr. in *New Heaven, New Earth* (# 928), pp. 37-81.

904. "Transparent Creatures Caught in Myths." Review of "Glass People" by Gail Godwin. *Washington Post Book World* (Oct. 1, 1972): 8, 10.
      (*)

"This is a formally executed, precise, and altogether professional short novel which deepened my long-cherished belief about certain forms of art: that in exploring extremities of human behavior, in forcing us to wade through real or metaphorical blood, such art saves us from these experiences and is cathartic in the best sense of the term."

905. "So Much for the Search for Truth." Review of "The Temptation of Jack Orkney and Other Stories" by Doris Lessing. *Washington Post Book World* (Oct. 22, 1972): 4, 13.
      (*)

No annotation.

906. "New Heaven and Earth." *Saturday Review*, 55 (Nov. 4, 1972): 51-54.
      Repr. in *Arts in Society*, 10 (1973): 36-43.

"I think that art, especially prose fiction, is directly connected with culture, with society; that there is 'no art for art's sake.'" She also asserts, "All serious fictions are half-conscious dramatizations of what is going on in the world."

907. "One for Life, One for Death." Review of "Up Country" by Maxine Kumin; "Winter Trees" by Sylvia Plath. *New York Times Book Review*, 77 (Nov. 19, 1972): 7, 14.
      (*)

No annotation.

908. "Anthropology or Fiction ?" *New York Times Book Review*, 77 (Nov. 26, 1972): 41.

In a letter, Oates admits her bewilderment as to whether Castaneda's books are non-fiction or are works of art. She notes these works are "beautifully constructed," have faultless dialogue, and an unforgettable character in Don Juan, and possess a "novelistic momentum."

> Repr. in *Seeing Castaneda: Reactions to the 'Don Juan' Writings of Carlos Castaneda*, Daniel C. Noel, ed. New York: Putnam, 1976, pp. 67-69.
> (*)

Daniel C. Noel's response to the first and second letters from Oates in which she labels Castaneda's work "a hoax."

909. "Where They All Are Sleeping." Review of "Sleepers Joining Hands" by Robert Bly. *Modern Poetry Studies*, 4, iii (1973): 341-344.

Oates calls *Sleepers Joining Hands* "one of the most powerful books of any kind" that she has read lately. She notes that Bly's work is "always directed toward a moral position, yet it is curiously dramatic, mysterious, even suspenseful." Although "intellectual," his work is never argumentative or didactic.

910. "Risk-Taking." Review of "What Happens Next ?" by Gilbert Rogin; "Burning" by Diane Johnson; "The Professor's Daughter" by Piers Paul Read. *Partisan Review*, 40, i (1973): 143-146.
(*)

No annotation.

911. "Symposium: Playwriting in America." *Yale Theatre*, 4, i (1973): 23-24.

"Though I am willing to believe in the possibility of a totally intellectual drama, I think that most theatre deals with the emotions, and that these emotions must be seen to be generated out of recognizable human beings." Oates notes that "avant-garde" plays with no "underlying sense of a stable psychological reality" seem like "a purely intellectual assembling of technical tricks."

912.   "The Unique/Universal in Fiction." *Writer*, 86 (Jan.
       1973): 9-12.

       According to Oates, "All art is moral." She notes,
       "Critics who chide me for dwelling on unpleasant and
       even bloody subjects miss the point: art shows us how
       to get through and transcend pain."

913.   "A Personal View of Nabokov." *Saturday Review of the
       Arts*, 1 (Jan. 6, 1973): 36-37.
       (*)

       Oates praises *Lolita* as "one of our finest American
       novels, a triumph of style and vision" but she
       criticizes Nabokov for isolating himself from other
       human beings, for having "the most amazing capacity
       for loathing" and for having "a genius for
       dehumanizing" that is frightening.

914.   "Joyce Carol Oates on Thoreau's 'Walden.'" *Made-
       moiselle*, 76 (Apr. 1973): 96, 98.

       No annotation.

915.   Review of "Toward a Recognition of Androgyny" by
       Carolyn G. Heilbrun; "Virginia Woolf and the
       "Androgynous Vision" by Nancy Topping Bazin.
       New York Times Book Review, 78 (Apr. 15,
       1973): 7, 10, 12.

       Oates finds the word "androgyny" misleadingly
       abstract, and these studies too narrow in their
       definitions and perception of possibilities. "... even
       Heilbrun is so biased against Lawrence generally as to
       fail to recognize that "Women in Love" is exactly the
       androgynous-ideal novel she might have praised."
       Oates shows her enduring refusal here to join one
       camp or another: while she rejects as too wholesale
       Heilbrun's accusation that the American idea of
       manliness was responsible for the My Lai slaughter and
       the Kent State killings, she has her own sexual
       accusations to make: "Male critics tend to admire the
       'Woolfian' novel when it is written by women, because
       it allows them to be gentlemanly in print: to punctuate
       their reviews with the words 'exquisite, controlled,
       faultless, perfect.' Their yawns are cunning and
       malicious and always hidden."

916.   "The Myth of the Isolated Artist." *Psychology Today*,
       6 (May 1973): 74-75.

Oates argues that the "isolated artist" is an unfounded myth. She suggests that "creative work, like scientific work, should be greeted as a communal effort--an attempt by an individual to give voice to many voices, an attempt to synthesize and explore and analyze."

917. "A Cluster of Feelings: Wakoski & Levine." Review of "Smudgings" by Diane Wakoski; "Red Dust" by Philip Levine. *American Poetry Review*, 2 (May-June 1973): 55.
(*)

In reviewing poetry by Wakoski and Levine, Oates states, "My personal inclination is toward the lyrically dramatic, the poem that risks imprudence and outrage, and hints of real actions." She also prefers poetry that establishes "a genuine point of view that takes itself seriously."

918. "The Finite and the Fabulous." Review of "Rembrandt's Hat" by Bernard Malamud. *Washington Post Book World* (June 10, 1973): 3.
(*)

No annotation.

919. "The Death Throes of Romanticism: The Poems of Sylvia Plath." *Southern Review* (Baton Rouge), n.s., 9, iii (Summer 1973): 501-522.
Repr. in *Contemporary Poetry in America: Essays and Interviews*, Robert Boyers, ed. New York: Shocken Books, 1974, pp. 139-156.
and under title "The Death Throes of Romanticism: The Poetry of Sylvia Plath" in *New Heaven, New Earth* (# 928), pp. 111-140.
Repr. in *Sylvia Plath: The Woman and the Work*, Edward Butscher, ed. New York: Dodd, Mead, 1977, pp. 206-224.
Repr. under title "The Death Throes of Romanticism: The Poetry of Sylvia Plath" in *Ariel Ascending: Writings about Sylvia Plath*, Paul Alexander, ed. New York: Harper & Row, 1985, pp. 26-45.
(*)

"The artist both creates and is created by his art and ... the self--especially the 'I' of lyric poetry--is a personality that achieves a kind of autonomy, free not only of the personal life of the artist but of the part-by-part progression of individual poems as well."

920. "Art; Therapy and Magic." *American Journal*, 1 (July 3, 1973): 17-20.

No annotation.

921. "Books of Change: Recent Collections of Poems." [Review of "They Feed the Lions" by Philip Levine; "Footprints: Poems" by Denise Levertov; "A Book of Change" by Frederick Morgan; "The Lost Country" by Kathleen Raine; "Child's Play" by David R. Slavitt; "Collected Poems" by A.R. Ammons.] *Southern Review* (Baton Rouge), n.s., 9, iv (Autumn 1973): 1014-1028.

No annotation.

922. "A Visit with Doris Lessing." *Southern Review* (Baton Rouge), n.s., 9, iv (Autumn 1973): 873-882.

"Never superficially experimental, Ms. Lessing's writing is profoundly experimental--exploratory--in its effort to alter our expectations about life and about the range of our own consciousness."

923. "A Child's History of America." Review of "Some Ribs and Riffs for the Sixties" by Charles Newman. *Washington Post Book World* (Oct. 28, 1973): 10. (*)

Oates suggests that for Newman the central function of literature is a "moral, impersonal transmission of the accumulated wisdom of one individual's life in the form of literature that addresses itself to a specific historical, geographical condition--one's homeland."

924. "Written As If by People from Different Planets." Review of "A Memory and Other Stories" by Mary Lavin; "Dances of Death" by Gillian Tindall; "Summer" by Jack Ansell; "Judith and Other Stories" by James T. Farrell. *New York Times Book Review*, 78 (Nov. 25, 1973): 7, 14, 18. (*)

"It is a truth not universally acknowledged, that the short story is so subtle an art form, and at the same time so independent of its surroundings, that a reviewer does violence to any collection if he reads it straight through, as he would a novel."

925. "The Teleology of the Unconscious: The Art of Norman Mailer." *Critic* (Chicago), 32 (Nov.-Dec. 1973): 25-35.
Repr. in *New Heaven, New Earth* (# 928), pp. 177-203.

"To assert himself against the oppressive language-systems, then, the individual must be a kind of artist; he must attempt the creation of his own special language. To create a mythology in order to escape being enslaved by someone else's has been, perhaps the dynamic urge behind much art, at least art created in a time of social confusion."

926. "Kafka's Paradise." *Hudson Review*, 26, iv (Winter 1973-74): 623-646.
Repr. in *New Heaven, New Earth* (# 928), pp. 265-298.

"It is ironic that, in our time, Kafka's most fervent admirers have been men who have demonstrated, through their critical analyses of Kafka, an amazing 'identification' with Kafka's deluded heroes, and not with the vision that Kafka sets over and against these heroes."

927. "The Poet, the Self, and Nature." *Dialogue*, 7, i (1974): 73-83.
Repr. under title "Le poète, le moi et la nature" in *Dialogue*, 6, iii (1975): 115-126.

In a remarkable essay, Oates engages in an intelligent, compassionate quarrel with both halves of the Sylvia Plath legacy: the testimony of the poems and the popular and academic mythology. Oates's objections to Plath's sensibility, spread out, eventually, into a criticism of the complacencies of much contemporary thought. On Plath: "... like many who are persecuted, she identified in a perverse way with her own persecutors and not with those who, along with her, were victims. But she did not "like" other people because she did not essentially believe that they existed; she knew intellectually that they existed, of course, since they had the power to injure her, but she did not believe they existed in the way she did, as pulsating, breathing, suffering individuals. Even her own children were objects of her perception, there for the restless scrutiny of her image-making mind and not there as human beings...." And on her popularity: "It reveals much that is wrong with the contemporary intellectuals' assessment of themselves: a total failure to consider that the undeveloped (whether people or nations) are not sacred because they are undeveloped, but sacred because they are part of nature; and the role of the superior intellect is not to honor incompletion, in itself or in anything, but to help bring about the fulfillment of potentialities."

928. *New Heaven, New Earth: The Visionary Experience in Literature.* New   York: Vanguard Press, 1974. 307p.
New York: Fawcett Crest, 1975. 288p.
London: Gollancz, 1976. 307p.
Contains: The Art of Relationships: Henry James and Virginia Woolf; 'The Hostile Sun': The Poetry of D.H. Lawrence; Anarchy and Order in Beckett's Trilogy; The Nightmare of Naturalism: Harriette Arnow's 'The Dollmaker'; The Death Throes of Romanticism: The Poetry of Sylvia Plath; The Visionary Art of Flannery O'Connor; The Teleology of the Unconscious: The Art of Norman Mailer; Out of Stone, into Flesh: The Imagination of James Dickey; Kafka's Paradise.

A collection of nine essays dealing with works by James, Woolf, Lawrence, Beckett, Arnow, Plath, O'Connor, Mailer, Dickey, and Kafka.
All essays have been annotated individually.

929. Preface to *Where Are You Going, Where Have You Been ?: Stories of Young America.* Greenwich, CT: Fawcett, 1974, pp. 8-10.

Oates names the mode of the stories in this collection "psychological realism." She commends younger readers who often "intuitively" understand these stories and suggests that older readers who often see only "morbidity, absurdity, and a sense that life is meaningless" have misunderstood.

930. "Disguised Fiction." *PMLA*, 89 (May 1974): 580-581.

"Criticism is an art form--one should never forget that. It is deeply personal, always biased, sometimes eccentric and sometimes rather bland and derivative: but it is more an expression of the critic's mind than it is a description of the work of art itself."

931. "Other Celebrity Voices: How Art Has Touched Our Lives." *Today's Health*, 52 (May 1974): 31.

    Oates discusses her first experiences with *Alice in Wonderland* and *Through the Looking Glass* at "possibly" age four and her emotional response to this book.

932. Review of "If Beale Street Could Talk" by James Baldwin. *New York Times Book Review*, 79 (May 19, 1974): 1-2.
    (*)

    Oates suggests the "worst possible fate for a serious writer" is to "be praised without being read."

933. "Recent Books: Keithley, Levine, Sale, and Roth; A Column." Review of "Song in a Strange Land" by George Keithley; "1933" by Philip Levine; "Modern Heroism" by Roger Sale; "My Life As a Man" by Philip Roth. *American Poetry Review*, 3 (May-June 1974): 43-45.
    (*)

    "It has always been my belief that a good novel is read the first time for its story--for all literature, no matter how sophisticated, should be suspenseful--and the second time for its more subtle concerns."

934. "Don Juan's Last Laugh: A Novelist Looks at Carlos Castaneda's Fourth and Final Don Juan Trip and Discovers a Fellow Artist at Work." Review of "Tales of Power" by Carlos Castaneda. *Psychology Today*, 8 (Sept. 1974): 10, 12, 130.
    Repr. in *Seeing Castaneda: Reactions to the 'Don Juan' Writings of Carlos Castaneda*, Daniel C. Noel, ed. New York: Putnam, 1976, pp. 122-128.

    "Perhaps it takes a writer of fiction to intuit the work of a fellow artist: at any rate it seems to me beyond doubt that this series of books is art, not mere repertorial observation. Like all art, it is somewhat self-conscious; it resists and transcends conventional labeling."

935. "Is This the Promised End ?: The Tragedy of 'King Lear.'" *Journal of Aesthetics and Art Criticism*, 33 (Fall 1974): 19-32.
    Repr. in *Contraries* (# 1019), pp. 51-81.

"For most writers, the act of writing is itself a triumph, an affirmation, and the anguish experienced by an audience is not really in response to an emotion within the work itself ... but the artist's genius, his ability to transmute into formal images an archetypal human drama."

936. "Out of Stone into Flesh: The Imagination of James Dickey." *Modern Poetry Studies*, 5, ii (Autumn 1974): 97–144.
and in *New Heaven, New Earth* (# 928), pp. 205–263.
(*)

Although Dickey is not "popular with liberals," one can learn "as from no other serious writer, what it is like to have been born into one world and to have survived into another." In a survey of Dickey's poetry from his first book *Into the Stone* to 1970's *The Eye-Beaters*, Oates suggests that the emphasis he places in his later poems on "decay, disease, regression, and estrangement" may signal that he is ending a poetic phase and preparing "to take on newer challenges."

937. Review of "The Black House" by Paul Theroux; "Something I've Been Meaning to Tell You" by Alice Munro; "Women and Children" by Beth Harvor. *Ontario Review*, 1 (Fall 1974): 102–105.
(*)

No annotation.

938. "A Family Haunted by Death." Review of "Manual Labor" by Frederick Busch. *New York Times Book Review*, 79 (Nov. 3, 1974): 66.
(*)

No annotation.

939. Afterword to *The Poisoned Kiss and Other Stories from the Portuguese*. Fernandes / Joyce Carol Oates. New York: Vanguard Press, 1975, pp. 187–189.

Writing about the origin of the Fernandes stories, Oates states, "The only way I could accept these stories was to think of them as a literary adventure of cerebral/Gothic commentary on my own writing, or as the expression of a part of my personality that had been stifled."

940. Review of "The Awful Rowing toward God" by Anne
     Sexton. *New York Times Book Review*, 80
     (Mar. 23, 1975): 3-4.
     Repr. in *Anne Sexton: The Artist and Her
     Critics*, J.D. McClatchy, ed. Bloomington, IN:
     Indiana University Press, 1978, pp. 168-172.
     (*)

"It is probable that a serious artist exercises relatively
little control over the choice of subjects of his or her
art. The more fortunate artist is simply one who, for
reasons not known, identifies powerfully with a unit
larger than the self: Faulkner with his 'postage stamp'
of earth; Shakespeare with the glorious, astounding
variety of human personality, Dostoyevsky with all of
Russia."

941. "Updike's American Comedies." *Modern Fiction Studies*,
     21, iii (Autumn 1975): 459-472.
     Repr. in *John Updike: A Collection of Critical
     Essays*, David Thorburn and Howard Eiland, eds.
     Englewood Cliffs: Prentice-Hall, 1979, pp. 53-68
     (slightly different version).
     Repr. under title "John Updike's American
     Comedies" in *The Profane Art* (# 1039), pp.
     90-105.

"Updike exiled from America is unthinkable, and
America without Updike to record it--unthinkable as
well. His special value for us is his willingness to be
disarmed of perspective, to allow his intensely realized
worlds to flower with something of the mysterious
effortlessness of nature itself, and to attempt to
spiritualize the flesh since, for many in our time, the
'flesh' may be all that remains of religious experience."

942. "The Immense Indifference of Things: The Tragedy of
     Conrad's 'Nostromo.'" *Novel: A Forum on Fiction*,
     9, i (Fall 1975): 5-22.
     Repr. under title "The Immense Indifference of
     Things: Conrad's 'Nostromo'" in *Contraries*
     (# 1019), pp. 82-115.

"As a novelist Conrad is always superior to his ideas.
His works are most living when 'ideas' as such are set
aside, in order that his characters may bravely play
their scenes.... But, inevitably, their energies are
curtailed by the author's larger, more general, and
very restrictive consciousness." She adds, "It may be

also that great works of art are necessarily flawed or incomplete because they represent, to the artist, one of the central mysteries of his life--that which cannot be resolved but which 'must' be explored."

943.   "William Goyen's Life Rhythms." Review of "The Collected Stories of William Goyen." *New York Times Book Review*, 80 (Nov. 16, 1975): 4, 14. (*)

"In recent years many unfortunate statements have been made about the craft of serious fiction writing. There have been self-conscious, pretentious and astonishingly egotistical claims made by certain writers, each of whom imagines himself to be the finest living craftsman, the only living master of the arrangement of words known as the sentence."

944.   "Many Are Called..." in *American Poets in 1976*, William Heyen, ed. Indianapolis: Bobbs-Merrill, 1976, pp. 202-211.

"All poets are familiar with the absurdity of even the most well-intentioned critics' attempts to 'fix' them: to define them permanently. So long as we live, we cannot be defined. And when we are no longer living, it will really be the critics' own obsessions they claim to see in us: literary criticism is largely a matter of psychic projecting."

945.   "Jocoserious Joyce." *Critical Inquiry*, 2 (Summer 1976): 677-688.
       Repr. in *Contraries* (# 1019), pp. 171-187.

"Early and continued success may be the destruction of all but the most ingenious or melancholy of writers." Oates also states, "The impulse of comedy is gregarious; it is really comedy, rather than tragedy, that 'breaks down the dykes' between people ... and unlooses a communal music."

946.   "Something Transparent, Archetypal, Terrible." Review of "Lost Title." Poems by Daniel Hughes. *Modern Poetry Studies*, 7, ii (Autumn 1976): 149-151.

Hughes is "too interested in the possibilities of dramatizing various states of mind to settle for a single, static point of view." "Images of straining away, tugging to break free, wandering, stumbling,

falling characterize the poems." "Lost titles" is "one of
the most moving and realized books of poetry I have
encountered in quite a while."

947. Review of "A Girl in Winter" by Philip Larkin. *New
      Republic*, 175 (Nov. 20, 1976): 38-40.
      (*)

      "Larkin's studied nihilism is as florid in its way as the
      too-generous affirmation of a Whitman, and there is no
      reason to think that there is more 'truth' in diminished
      things than there is in inflated things: for the poet
      expresses his interior landscape primarily."

948. Review of "Separate Flights" by André Dubus; "The
      Butterfly Ward" by Margaret Gibson Gilboord;
      "The Great Sunflower" by Clifford Stone. *Ontario
      Review*, 5 (Fall-Winter 1976-77): 105-107.
      (*)

      No annotation.

949. "Desperate First-Person Characters." Review of "Re-
      member Me" by Fay Weldon. *New York Times Book
      Review*, 81 (Nov. 21, 1976): 7, 54.
      (*)

      "It is possible that feminist concerns with the
      exploitation of women by men, while still painfully
      relevant to our lives, are no longer viable as subjects
      for serious fiction ? By denying subtlety and humanity
      to roughly one-half the population, and by delineating
      Maleness in place of specific human beings who happen
      to be male, the writer with feminist interests severely
      jeopardizes her power to create imaginative literature."

950. Review of "Selected Poems" by Robert Creeley. *New
      Republic*, 175 (Dec. 18, 1976): 26-28.
      (*)

      "It was fashionable for a while in the '60s to refuse to
      revise, so that one retained the spontaneous flow of
      the mind ..., but after the passage of even a brief
      space of time such experimentation appears to have
      been merely self-indulgent.... Since Williams, the
      elevation of the presumably trivial into art has become
      fairly commonplace, and there is the danger that a
      once-revolutionary concept can become ... another
      poetic convention."

951. "Anne Sexton: A Self-Portrait in Letters." *American Book Review*, 1, i (1977): 3-4.

> "What is extraordinary about the letters, and in fact one of their redeeming features, is the tone the poet takes when she addresses correspondents who are recognizably sick." Oates admires the self-restraint in the letters; offers a long list of Sexton's correspondents; laments the necessary omission of letters of a sensitive nature.

> > Repr. under title "Anne Sexton: Self-Portrait in Poetry and Letters" in *The Profane Art* (# 1039), pp. 165-183.

> Combines review from *American Book Review* with review of Sexton's *Love Poems* and *The Awful Rowing toward God*. Sexton is praised as a poet of ephemeral moods, herself driven by artistic impulses she could not understand, could not control. "What her unsympathetic critics have charged her with--the overvaluing of her private sorrows to the exclusion of the rest of the world--seems to have been felt by Sexton herself. This sort of knowledge, however, rarely brings with it the ability to 'change.'"

952. Review of "Lancelot" by Walker Percy. *New Republic*, 176 (Feb. 5, 1977): 32-34.

> "Percy has acquired the reputation of being a 'philosophical thinker' ...; but I have never really found in his fiction much evidence to support this view, and no evidence at all that he has responded in an unusually deep or subtle way to the complex worldviews elaborated by these men." Faults, in passing, Percy's "Love among the Ruins" for being shrill, and finds "Lancelot" disappointing in its glibness and lack of conviction.

953. "The Course of True Love Never Did Run Smooth." Review of "A Very Different Love Story: Burt and Linda Pugach's Intimate Account of Their Triumph over Tragedy" by Berry Stainback. *New York Times Book Review*, 82 (Feb. 6, 1977): 5.

> Ostensibly a review of Stainback's book, Oates here retells the Pugach's story in an oddly flippant manner, apparently to stress both the perverseness of their courtship and marriage (involving, among other things, a disfiguring assault with lye) and the false

sentimentality of the book itself. The tone of the review, however, is muddled, suggesting Oates's mixed feelings about the story itself, the way it is told and its uncomfortable kinship to some of her own fictions.

954. "A Taut Novel of Disorder." Review of "A Book of Common Prayer" by Joan Didion. *New York Times Book Review*, 82 (Apr. 3, 1977): 1, 34-35.
   (*)

   Friendly review of Didion's novel: "Like her narrator [Didion] has been an articulate witness to the most stubborn and intractable truths of our time, a memorable voice, partly eulogistic, partly despairing: always in control." Many references to Didion's other novels; nothing addressed to Didion's detractors.

955. "More Lonely than Evil." Review of "The Children of Dynmouth" by William Trevor. *New York Times Book Review*, 82 (Apr. 17, 1977): 13, 36.
   (*)

   Favorable review of Trevor's novel, setting him in the Joyce tradition, and offering an aside that "it has been the case for decades that English novelists continue to work in a realistic and conventional tradition that looks back not to the great Modernists ... but to the late 19th century." Short, general essay.

956. "The Style of the 70's: The Novel." *New York Times Book Review*, 82 (June 5, 1977): 7, 40-41.

   Essay on the novel in the late seventies: passing discussion of Bellow and Cheever; briefer mention of Barth, Barthelme, Coover, and others; closing affirmation that today's general rubrics will not hold up under scrutiny.

957. Review of "The Other One" by Colette (translated by Roger Senhouse and Elizabeth Tait); "The Blue Lantern" by Colette (translated by Roger Senhouse). *New Republic*, 176 (June 11, 1977): 27-29.
   Repr. under title "Colette's Purgatory" in *The Profane Art* (# 1039), pp. 132-139.

   Praise for Colette's humble approach to her subjects, for the "seductive" charm of her prose, and for her courage in looking at the complexities of domestic life and human relationships. "The great theme of Colette's work is the tragedy of mutability: the innocent, brutal delight all lovers take in sensual pleasure, and the broken and bewildered aftermath of that pleasure when it becomes clear that what has been so passionately worshipped is, if not illusory, ruthlessly ephemeral."

958. Review of "The Simone Weil Reader" edited by George A. Panichas. *New Republic*, 177 (July 2, 1977): 33-37.

Long review essay treating Weil's life and writings; Oates shows herself fascinated and somewhat uneasy with Weil's idiosyncrasies and mystical inclinations: "It is not possible to shake off the feeling, from the very start, that Simone Weil's followers and Simone Weil herself are touched with a sort of playful madness: are they serious about these 'ideas,' are they perhaps speaking metaphorically, is the body of Weil's writings really a prose poem not meant to be taken literally ...?" The essay builds to a close with some strongly personal observations about the mystical frame of mind.

> Repr. under title "'May God Grant That I Become Nothing': The Mysticism of Simone Weil" in *The Profane Art* (# 1039), pp. 147-158 (slightly different version).

A revised and polished version of the above article, lacking the spontaneous air of the original review, and the bolder, more personal passages which close it.

959. "Four Novels." Review of "Sadler's Birthday" by Rose Tremain; "Staggerford" by Jon Hassler; "Children of the Black Sabbath" by Anne Hébert; "A Wreath of Pale White Roses" by Erika Duncan. *New York Times Book Review*, 82 (July 24, 1977): 14-15, 29. (*)

Four novels are treated in about 2000 words, very generally.

960. Review of "Over by the River and Other Stories" by William Maxwell. *New Republic*, 177 (Sept. 10, 1977): 28-29.

Short appreciative review.

961. "An Airy Insubstantial World." Review of "Falconer" by John Cheever. *Ontario Review*, 7 (Fall-Winter 1977-78): 99-101. (*)

Brief negative review of Cheever's best-seller: "its victories are far too easy, its transcendence of genuine pain and misery is glib, even crude. But one should read Cheever for the richness of his observations, perhaps, rejoicing in his capacity to see and to feel and to value."

962. "A Novice in Affliction." Review of "Eyes, etc." by Eleanor Clark. *New York Times Book Review*, 82 (Oct. 16, 1977): 11, 40.

Favorable review, praising especially the novelist's courage and candor in recording passing, unmeasured responses to contemporary life.

963. "On 'Love Poems'" in *Anne Sexton: The Artist and Her Critics*, J.D. McClatchy, ed. Bloomington, IN: Indiana University Press, 1978, pp. 143-145.

Brief comments, essentially exerpts from "Anne Sexton: Self-Portrait in Poetry and Letters" in her *Profane Art*.

964. "Picaresque Tale." Review of "Refiner's Fire: 'The Life and Adventures of Marshall Pearl, a Foundling'" by Mark Helprin. *New York Times Book Review*, 83 (Jan. 1, 1978): 7.

Praises the novel for setting "an Augie March young man into a Gabriel Garcia Marquez universe."

965. Review of "Gaudete" by Ted Hughes. *New Republic*, 178 (Jan. 28, 1978): 32-34.

Guarded discussion of a long poem: "Gaudete will probably come to be seen as the most controversial work of England's finest contemporary poet."

966. "Lawrence's 'Götterdämmerung': The Tragic Vision of 'Women in Love.'" *Critical Inquiry*, 4, iii (Spring 1978): 559-578.
Repr. under title "Lawrence's 'Götterdämmerung': The Apocalyptic Vision of 'Women in Love'" in *Contraries* (# 1019), pp. 141-170.

Lawrence's novel "celebrates love and marriage as the only possible salvation for twentieth century man and

dramatizes the fate of those who resist the aban-
donment of the ego demanded by love...." "Between
the individual and the cosmos there falls the deathly
shadow of the ego.... Where the human will is active
there is always injury to the spirit ...; that human
beings are compelled not only to assert their greedy
claims upon others but to manipulate their own lives in
accord with an absolute that has little to do with their
deeper yearnings constitutes our tragedy." A polished,
important essay for the understanding of both Oates
and Lawrence.

967.   Review of "Figures of Thought: Speculations on the
       Meaning of Poetry, and Other Essays" by Howard
       Nemerov. *New Republic*, 178 (Apr. 8, 1978):
       29-31.

Reviews the contents of major essays in the collection.
"Apart from, esthetically uninvolved in, questions of
social upheaval.... Nemerov in his poetry and essays
has insisted upon a philosophical detachment that
refines his work of the personal and allows him an
ironist's celebral authority."

968.   Review of "One Half of Robertson Davies" by
       Robertson Davies. *New Republic*, 178 (Apr. 15,
       1978): 22-25.

Hostile, condescending overview of Davies's career,
with sideline comments on the short, politicized, and
(in Oates's view) contrived heritage of Canadian
literature.

969.   "Pseudonyms Together." Review of "Nine and a Half
       Weeks" by Elizabeth McNeill; "Affair" by Antony
       Amato and Katherine Edwards. *New York Times
       Book Review*, 83 (Apr. 16, 1978): 12-13.

Satiric essay on two "true stories" about extramarital
sexual adventures. Remarkable as another of Oates's
attacks on sensationalism.

970.   "Author Joyce Carol Oates on 'Adolescent America.'"
       U.S. News and World Report, 84 (May 15, 1978):
       60.

Brief general pronouncements about America as a
young culture and the improved condition of American
women.

971. Review of "Critical Encounters: Literary Views and Reviews, 1953-1977" by Nona Balakian. *New Republic*, 178 (May 20, 1978): 33-34, 36.

Enthusiasm for Balakian's critical stance, with some opening attacks at the state of criticism in the wake of structuralism and deconstructive theory.

972. Review of "Silences" by Tillie Olsen. *New Republic*, 179 (July 29, 1978): 32-34.

"The book's strengths lie, however, in its polemical passages. Olsen asks why so many more women are silenced than men; she asks why there is only one writer 'of achievement' for every 12 men writers; why our culture continues to reflect a masculine point of view almost exclusively." "She never confronts the most troublesome question of all: What has 'creativity' as such to do with 'art' ?"

973. "A Private Dream Flashing onto an Enormous Screen." *TV Guide* (Northeastern edition), 26 (Oct. 7, 1978): 4-6, 8.

Standard comparisons of literature and film as media.

974. "The Novelists: Iris Murdoch." *New Republic*, 179 (Nov. 18, 1978): 27-31.
Repr. under title "Sacred and Profane Iris Murdoch" in *The Profane Art* (# 1039), pp. 184-194.
(*)

Discusses Murdoch essentially as a Platonist who philosophizes by means of her fiction. "The basic idea seems to be that centuries of humanism have nourished an unrealistic conception of the powers of the will: we have gradually lost the vision of a reality separate from ourselves, and we have no adequate conception of original sin."

975. "Joyce Carol Oates on Poetry." Review of "The Year of Our Birth" by Sandra McPherson; "The Dream of a Common Language" by Adrienne Rich; "The Pregnant Man" by Robert Phillips; "Tread the Dark" by David Ignatow; "The Night Traveler" by Mary Oliver; "A Call in the Midst of the Crowd" by Alfred Corn. *New Republic*, 179 (Dec. 9, 1978): 25-30.

Lengthy review essay. Opening with an attack on the vacuity of contemporary poetry criticism, with its interchangeable "superlatives and disparagements," Oates moves on to a retrospective discussion of Rich, and short friendly, carefully unsuperlative-undisparaging treatments of the other poets.

976. "Marital Crime and Punishment." Review of "Tender Mercies" by Rosellen Brown. *New York Times Book Review*, 83 (Dec. 10, 1978): 12, 52.

Raises "minor" objections to a generally "haunting novel."

977. "The Tragic Vision of 'The Possessed.'" *Georgia Review*, 32, iv (Winter 1978): 868–893.
Repr. under title "Tragic Rites in Dostoyevsky's 'The Possessed'" in *Contraries* (# 1019), pp. 17–50.

"... many of Dostoyevsky's critics are simply incapable of measuring his genius...." A wise and unusually contentious essay, treating Dostoyevsky as a prophet of social and moral breakdown, of civilization's loss of faith and various forms of mass suicide. Oates argues for the formal excellence of the novel, and is impatient with critics who find the book a "loose baggy monster."

978. Introduction to *The Best American Short Stories 1979: Selected from US and Canadian Magazines*, by Joyce Carol Oates with Shannon Ravenel, eds. Boston, MA: Houghton Mifflin, 1979, pp. XI–XXII.

Oates edited the 1979 collection, and used the occasion to make some trenchant observations about the paradoxical state of American experimental writing: "Had there been meta-fictions of comparable uniqueness among this year's published fiction I would have been grateful to reprint them, but it seems to me that meta-fictions ironies have begun to run out, or to repeat themselves with dismaying frequency. "Nearly every 'experimental' story one encounters today reads like an undergraduate imitation of Ionesco, or Beckett, or Borges, or one of their American counterparts. Post-sixties 'fictions' have dwindled into patterns as rigid as O. Henry's, in which an arbitrary proposition ... is threaded through with exotic motifs or mock symbols ... in a story of not less than five pages or more than eight. Presumably someone reads these 'fictions,' but not more than once...."

979. Preface to *Critical Essays on Joyce Carol Oates*, Linda W. Wagner. Boston, MA: G.K. Hall, 1979, pp. XI-XIII.

While friendly towards the critics collected in the book, Oates affirms that the essential "unfolding fact of the work" is always "something undefinable."

980. "The Interior Castle: The Art of Jean Stafford's Short Fiction." *Shenandoah*, 30, iii (1979): 61-64. Repr. in *The Profane Art* (# 1039), pp. 123-127.

Oates finds the stories highly controlled, "marred by an arch, over-written self-consciousness," but remarkable for their "rigorous structure" and occasionally "terrifying" themes.

981. Review of "The Coup" by John Updike. *New Republic*, 180 (Jan. 6, 1979): 32-35.
(*)

"Beneath, behind, informing every scene of this inspired novel, ... is a passionate and despairing cynicism which I take to be, for all its wit, Updike's considered view of where we are and where we are going." "Updike has grown amazingly cynical with the passage of time."

982. "Post-Borgesian." Review of "A Perfect Vacuum" by Stanislaw Lem. *New York Times Book Review*, 84 (Feb. 11, 1979): 7, 40.
(*)

"... where Borges's ingenuity is saved from meretriciousness by the master's quick, deft, poetic style and the brevity of his fictions, Stanislaw Lem draws out each of his jokes laboriously...."

983. "Full of Promising Material." Review of "I Know Your Heart, Marco Polo" by Henry Bromell. *New York Times Book Review*, 84 (Apr. 1, 1979): 15, 18.

Unfavorable review.

984. Review of "The Penguin Book of Women Poets" edited by Carol Cosman, Joan Keefe and Kathleen Weaver. *New Republic*, 180 (Apr. 21, 1979): 28-30.

"What is insulting ... is not the book itself, or even its idea, but the need for it."

985. "Honey and Bill and Dan and Celia." Review of "Only
      Children" by Alison Lurie. *New York Times Book
      Review*, 84 (Apr. 22, 1979): 7, 27.
      (*)

      Brief, favorable review.

986. "A Humane and Adventurous Art." Review of "Telling
      Lives: Essays by Leon Edel, Justin Kaplan,
      Alfred Kazin, Doris Kearns, Theodore Rosengarten,
      Barbara W. Tuchman, Geoffrey Wolff" edited by
      Marc Pachter. *New York Times Book Review*, 84
      (May 13, 1979): 3, 29.

      Finds the book unbalanced and incomplete, but
      valuable.

987. Review of "Testimony and Demeanor: Stories" by John
      Casey. *New Republic*, 180 (May 19, 1979): 34-35.

      Favorable, unincisive review of a writer characterized
      by "chaste, self-conscious prose. Each of the stories
      contains small gems...."

988. "Laughter and Trembling." Review of "The Best of
      Sholom Aleichem" edited by Irving Howe and Ruth
      R. Wisse. *New York Times Book Review*, 84
      (July 8, 1979): 1, 26-27.

      Lengthy review, emphasizing the historical context and
      the tragic colorations of the great Yiddish storyteller:
      "The only godliness in Sholom Aleichem's disintegrating
      Jewish culture belongs to the Jews themselves--and
      they are being systematically destroyed or expelled
      from the villages in which they have lived for
      centuries."

989. Review of "Sophie's Choice" by William Styron; "Music
      and Silence" by Anne Redmon. *Mademoiselle*, 85
      (Aug. 1979): 74, 76.

      No annotation.

990. Review of "C.G. Jung Word and Image" edited by
      Aniela Jaffé. *New Republic*, 181 (Aug. 4 & 11,
      1979): 39-42.
      Repr. under title "Legendary Jung" in *The
      Profane Art* (# 1039), pp. 159-164.

      Oates demonstrates her extensive, enthusiastic reading
      in Jung, and laments his dismissal by a generation of
      academics who have not actually read him.

991. Review of "Burger's Daughter" by Nadine Gordimer; "Confessions of Summer" by Phillip Lopate; "The Poems of Stanley Kunitz, 1928-1978" by Stanley Kunitz. *Mademoiselle*, 85 (Sept. 1979): 64-66.

No annotation.

992. "To Be Female Is to Die." Review of "The Basement" by Kate Millett. *New York Times Book Review*, 84 (Sept. 9, 1979): 14, 24, 26.

Millett's account is of a true-life horror story; while admiring Millett's courage in taking on such intractable material, Oates suggests that Millett never achieved symbolic mastery of it: "Sympathy and identification are two different responses, and violent identification-- a psychological projection over which the subject has little control--may sometimes obscure understanding."

993. Review of "On Not Being Good Enough: Writings of a Working Critic" by Roger Sale. *New Republic*, 181 (Sept. 15, 1979): 31-32.

A ferocious attack on an influential reviewer. "Ineptitude and malice frequently dovetail in Sale, and inspire him to a schoolmasterish crankiness...." "One would not trouble to examine Roger Sale ... except for the fact that Sale has made his reputation in some quarters as a hatchet-man, and that the type he represents ... is general in literary hack journalism."

994. "Bleak Craft." Review of "Collected Stories of Paul Bowles, 1939-1976." *New York Times Book Review*, 84 (Sept. 30, 1979): 9, 29.
    Repr. under title "Before God Was Love: The Short Stories of Paul Bowles" in *The Profane Art* (# 1039), pp. 128-131.
    (*)

Cautious praise for a writer who regularly out-gothics Oates herself: "Too much has been made, perhaps, of the dream-like brutality of Bowles's imagination, which evokes a horror far more persuasive than anything in Poe, or in Gide.... But the stories, like fairytales, tend to dissolve into their elements because so little that is human in a psychological sense is given." "Even in Lawrence's coldest, most 'legendary' tales, one confronts and, to some extent, enters into the lives of recognizable human beings whose personalities are always convincing; and this is not true in

Bowles." An important review for those interested in
Oates's ideas on the importance and limits of the gothic
mode.

995. Review of "The Beggar Maid" by Alice Munro; "Endless
      Love" by Scott Spencer; "The Mangan Inher-
      itance" by Brian Moore. *Mademoiselle*, 85 (Oct.
      1979): 72, 74.

No annotation.

996. Review of "The Obstacle Race: The Fortunes of Women
      Partners and Their Work" by Germaine Greer;
      "Problems and Other Stories" by John Updike;
      "The Old Patagonian Express: By Train through
      the Americas" by Paul Theroux. *Mademoiselle*, 85
      (Dec. 1979): 44, 48.

No annotation.

997. Review of "Darkness Visible" by William Golding. *New
      Republic*, 181 (Dec. 8, 1979): 32-34.
      (*)

"An author's strategic superiority to his subject is not
so self-evident as one might think, for though he
appears to be inventing his work he is really
discovering it; the 'superiority' of his puppet-master
position should not delude him into thinking that he is
necessarily superior to his characters."

998. "The Canadian Inheritance: Engel, Munro, Moore."
      Review of "The Glassy Sea" by Marian Engel;
      "The Beggar Maid" by Alice Munro; "The Mangan
      Inheritance" by Brian Moore. *Ontario Review*, 11
      (Winter 1979-80): 87-90.
      (*)

Brief reviews of novels of three writers, each
"obsessed--with the problem of individual identity."

999. Review of "Hans Christian Anderson [sic]" by Bo
      Grønbech. *American Book Review*, 3, vi (1980):
      20.

"Though innumerable studies have been done of
Andersen, and the prominent facts of his life are well
known, Bo Grønbech has been particularly successful
in weaving together, often with dramatic subtlety,
events and observations from Andersen's life, and
their analogous or metaphorical expression of his
work." Conventionally favorable review.

1000. "On Editing 'The Ontario Review'" by J.C. Oates and Raymond Smith in *The Art of Literary Publishing*, Bill Henderson, ed. Wainscott: Pushcart, 1980, pp. 142–150.

Light observations on the joys and troubles of editing.

1001. "A Special Message to the Members of the First Edition Society" in *Bellefleur* (# 3).

In a brief introduction, Oates mentions the "haunting image" from which the novel eventually grew, and offers some observations on Gothic fiction: "If Gothicism has the power to move us ... it is only because its roots are in psychological realism. Much of *Bellefleur* is a diary of my own life, and the lives of people I have known." The novel is also, she claims, "a critique of America; but it is in the service of a vision of America that stresses, for all its pessimism, the ultimate freedom of the individual."

1002. "Is There a Female Voice ? Joyce Carol Oates Replies" in *Gender and Literary Voice*, Janet Todd, ed. New York: Holmes & Meier, 1980, pp. 10–11. (Women and Literature; n.s., 1)

In a brief response to a question posed by the editor, Oates affirms that a feminist theme doesn't confer distinction upon a literary work, that "content is simply raw material." She says, however, that she prefers, as a reviewer, to keep silent when she runs into "amateurish and stereotypical works by women"; and that she resents critics who group "women writers" into some special category in their overviews of contemporary literature.

1003. Review of "A Writer's Britain: Landscape in Literature" by Margaret Drabble; "Beecher" by Dan McCall; "A Game Men Play" by Vance Bourjaily. *Mademoiselle*, 86 (Jan. 1980): 30, 32, 38.

No annotation.

1004. Review of "The Life of Katherine Mansfield" by Antony Alpers; "Women on Love: Eight Centuries of Feminine Writing" by Evelyne Sullerot (translated by Helen R. Lane); "Views and Spectacles: New and Selected Shorter Poems" by Theodore Weiss. *Mademoiselle*, 86 (Feb. 1980): 80, 82.

No annotation.

1005.   Review of "Popism: The Warhol 60's" by Andy Warhol
        and Pat Hackett. *New Republic*, 182 (Feb. 2,
        1980): 31-34.

        Lengthy review essay, not only about the book but
        about Oates's "Modernist" uneasiness about Warhol
        and an art that professes to express nothing.

1006.   Review of "Plains Song" by Wright Morris; "Female
        Sexual Slavery" by Kathleen Barry; "Death
        Mother and Other Poems" by Frederick Morgan.
        Mademoiselle, 86 (Mar. 1980): 108, 110.

        No annotation.

1007.   Review of "Morgan's Passing" by Anne Tyler; "The
        Open Cage: An Anzia Yezierska Collection" and
        "Bread Givers" by Anzia Yezierska; "Signs of
        Spring" by Laurel Lee. *Mademoiselle*, 86 (Apr.
        1980): 50, 54.

        No annotation.

1008.   Review of "Prize Stories 1980: The O. Henry Awards"
        edited by William Abrahams. *New Republic*, 182
        (Apr. 5, 1980): 35-36.

        Praises Abrahams for a fine collection and a long
        record of resisting the "experimental work of the
        less-than-first-rate."

1009.   "The Authority of Timelessness." Review of "I,
        Vincent: Poems from the Pictures of Van Gogh"
        by Robert Fagles; "Agadir" by Arthur Lundkvist;
        "Under Stars" by Tess Gallagher; "Rounding the
        Horn" by David R. Slavitt. *Ontario Review*, 12
        (Spring-Summer 1980): 100-105.

        Imprecise, laudatory review of four books of poetry
        which "deserve more readers than they are likely to
        get."

1010.   Review of "Portrait of an Artist" by Laurie Lisle;
        "Falling in Place" by Ann Beattie. *Mademoiselle*,
        86 (May 1980): 76, 82.

        No annotation.

1011. Review of "The Magician's Garden and Other Stories" by Géza Csáth. *New Republic*, 182 (May 17, 1980): 36-38.

> Repr. under title "Géza Csáth's Garden: The Contours of Surrealism" in *The Profane Art* (# 1039), pp. 140-146.

> Remarkable for an opening discussion of the power and pitfalls of surrealism, and its important variations from allegory.

1012. Review of "Smile Please" by Jean Rhys; "Diana and Nikon" by Janet Malcolm; "(W)holes" by Cynthia Macdonald. *Mademoiselle*, 86 (June 1980): 50, 52.

> No annotation.

1013. "People Have Always Hated Me." Review of "Asylum Piece and Other Stories" and "Sleep Has His House" by Anna Kavan. *New York Times Book Review*, 85 (June 1, 1980): 14, 30-31.

> "... the challenge of transforming an intensely private, subjective vision into art has not been consistently met by Kavan in the books under review." "Kafka's influence was deleterious on Kavan ... for the misty, fuzzy, featureless Allegory of Dread quickly becomes tiresome when language is not finely honed."

1014. Review of "At Odds: Women and the Family in America from the Revolution to the Present" by Carl N. Degler; "Crashing" by Enid Harlow; "Rough Strife" by Lynne Sharon Schwartz. *Mademoiselle*, 86 (July 1980): 48, 50.

> No annotation.

1015. Review of "Disturbing-Convincing"; "He-She" by Herbert Gold; "Imagining America" by Peter Conrad; "Quarterly Review of Literature Poetry Series, vol. 2" edited by Theodore Weiss and Renée Weiss. *Mademoiselle*, 86 (Aug. 1980): 64, 68.

> No annotation.

1016. Review of "A Glass of Blessings" by Barbara Pym; "Robert Penn Warren Talking: Interviews 1950-1978" by Floyd C. Watkins and John T. Hiers; "Stories" by Doris Lessing; "The Catfish Man: A

Conjured Life" by Jerome Charyn. *Mademoiselle*, 86 (Sept. 1980): 62, 65.

No annotation.

1017.   "Triumphant Tales of Obsession." Review of "A Change of Light and Other Stories" by Julio Cortázar (translated by Gregory Rabassa). *New York Times Book Review*, 85 (Nov. 9, 1980): 9, 34-35.

Long enthusiastic review, noting Cortázar's conservative critical temperament and the general lack of concern, in the fiction, for political issues. "... the actual reading of "A Change of Light" is an invariable pleasure. And the incursion of fantasy, of improbability, and nightmare, do not deflect from the stories' 'realist' emotional authority: several stories in this collection have the power to move us as Kafka's stories do."

1018.   "'The Picture of Dorian Gray': Wilde's Parable of the Fall." *Critical Inquiry*, 7, ii (Winter 1980): 419-428.
        Repr. in *Contraries* (# 1019), pp. 3-16.

"Wilde's novel must be seen as a highly serious meditation upon the moral role of the artist--and interior challenge, in fact, to ... the famous pronouncements that would assure us that there is no such thing as a moral or an immoral book." "Wilde's genius was disfigured by his talent: he always sounds much more flippant, far more superficial, than he really is." Gray's quest for sensations is a version of quest for meaning. Once more, Oates demonstrates her skill at seeing undertones, countermovements in fiction and in taking intelligent exception to critical consensus.

1019.   *Contraries: Essays.* New York: Oxford University Press, 1981. XI, 187p.
        Contains: 'The Picture of Dorian Gray': Wilde's Parable of the Fall; Tragic Rites in Dostoyevsky's 'The Possessed'; Is This the Promised End ?: The Tragedy of 'King Lear'; The Immense Indifference of Things: Conrad's 'Nostromo'; In the Fifth Act: The Art of the English and Scottish Traditional Ballads; Lawrence's 'Götterdämmerung': The Apocalyptic Vision of 'Women in Love'; Jocoserious Joyce.

All essays have been annotated individually.

1020. "Imaginary Cities: America" in *Literature and the Urban Experience: Essays on the City and Literature*, Michael C. Jaye and Ann Chalmers Watts, eds. New Brunswick: Rutgers University Press, 1981, pp. 11-33. Repr. in *The Profane Art* (# 1039), pp. 9-34.

A meandering essay, treating the place of the city in the imaginative life of American writers, and offering little that surprises: cities are places of social turbulence, of challenge; they are hellish; they offer the virtue of both anonymity and the chance of self-creation, especially for women. Much attention given to Chicago and New York as they appear in Saul Bellow's novels.

1021. "Many Stories." Review of "The Lone Pilgrim" by Laurie Colwin; "A Gift Horse and Other Stories" by Kate Cruise O'Brien; "Naming Things" by H.E. Francis; "The Calling" by Mary Gray Hughes; "Transports and Disgraces" by Robert Henson; "Desirable Aliens" by John Bovey. *New York Times Book Review*, 86 (Jan. 25, 1981): 12, 21.
(*)

Brief reviews, arguing for no particular strategy in short fiction, but rather for the diversity and flexibility of the form: "In actual practice, as opposed to theory, the short-story form is elastic enough, and democratic enough, to accommodate any number of competing esthetic theories. Riddling skeins of words by Samuel Beckett are as rightfully 'stories' as the beautifully but conventionally crafted short fictions of Hemingway. There are stories that read as plays, consisting only of dialogue; there are stories that are exclusively and obsessively interior; there are 'formula' stories that, executed with sufficient skill, are as impressive as more original works."

1022. "Why Is Your Writing So Violent ?" *New York Times Book Review*, 86 (Mar. 29, 1981): 15, 35.

Oates takes on the frequently-asked question about her writing: she calls the question "always insulting," "always ignorant," and "always sexist." Her answer makes reference to the tradition of realism and the realities of the 20th century; it lambasts traditional ideas about what kinds of fiction women should properly write. It does not, however, address the

style or the patterns of the violence in her fiction, or
make comparisons to violence in the novels of other
American writers of either sex.

1023.   "Portrait of the Artist As Son, Lover, Elegist."
        Review of "The Source of Light" by Reynolds
        Price. *New York Times Book Review*, 86
        (Apr. 26, 1981): 3, 30.

Price's novel is "richly detailed and intensely
romantic"; his best works are "lyric, brooding,
meditative, obsessive, and possess ... the clarity of
a vast tapestry in which action is necessarily arrested
and individual figures exist only in their relationship
to one another and to the design." Generic
enthusiasm, ultimately finding fault, however, with
the inadequate realization of two of the major
characters.

1024.   "A Tale of Love and Idolatry." Review of "The
        Temptation of Eileen Hughes" by Brian Moore.
        New York Times Book Review, 86 (Aug. 2,
        1981): 3.

Objects to inadequate characterization in the novel,
which is "as skeletal as a television or film script, in
which background footage (in this case, of London)
compensates for the foreground anemia."

1025.   "The Rise and Fall of a Poet." Review of "The
        Complete Poems" by Anne Sexton. *New York
        Times Book Review*, 86 (Oct. 18, 1981): 3, 37.

"The emotions are flicked before us like playing
cards, and we are invited to think that the
instruction of her poetry lies in its examination, as if
unconsciously, of the tragic limitations of this kind of
life-in-poetry: a curious failure not of 'feeling' but of
'imagination.'"

1026.   "A Man Who Became His Own Grandfather." Review of
        "Poppa John" by Larry Woiwode. *New York
        Times Book Review*, 86 (Nov. 15, 1981): 11, 24.

Favorable review, though Oates finds the ending
"weak and contrived."

1027.   Review of "Alice in Wonderland" by Lewis Carroll. *TV
        Guide*, 30 (Jan. 16, 1982): 22, 24.

"Background" for understanding an upcoming television musical.

1028. Review of "Sounding the Territory" by Laurel Goldman. *New York Times Book Review*, 87 (Feb. 21, 1982): 1, 29-30.

   Again Oates praises a first novel, while finding fault with characterization.

1029. "Two Poets." Review of "The Chinese Insomniacs" by Josephine Jacobsen; "The Country between Us" by Carolyn Forché. *New York Times Book Review*, 87 (Apr. 4, 1982): 13, 28-29.

   Brief general praise for both Jacobsen and Forché. Jacobsen is "characteristically understated"; Forché "might be considered a poet's poet."

1030. "Luxury of Being Despised." *Bennington Review*, 13 (June 1982).
   Repr. in *First Person Singular* (# 1077), pp. 194-197 (slightly different version).

   No annotation.

1031. "Notes on Failure." *Hudson Review*, 35, ii (Summer 1982): 231-245.
   Repr. in *The Profane Art* (# 1039), pp. 106-120.
   and in *Pushcart Prize VIII: Best of the Small Presses, 1983-84*, vol. 7, Bill Henderson, ed. Wainscott: Pushcart Press, 1983, pp. 194-208.

   "One is born not to suffer but to negotiate with suffering, to choose or invent forms to accommodate it." The article discusses Henry and Alice James, Conrad, and other 19th century writers, and does so in a late Victorian style, with many assertions of what is not, and allusions to what a mystery it is. An important essay for its suggestions of Oates's sense of herself at this stage in her career.

1032. "Stories That Define Me: The Making of a Writer." *New York Times Book Review*, 87 (July 11, 1982): 1, 15-16.

   Autobiographical vignettes--about her childhood, her years at Syracuse, the impact of Lewis Carroll and Hemingway, about feminism--interspersed with ideas about literature and confessions that ultimately no one can know or explain herself. The essay, an important one, gains conviction and intensity in its latter half, and the last two paragraphs help clarify her "melancholy" vision of reality.

1033.   "Family   Portrait.   Father   and   Son."   Review   of
        "Unframed Originals" by W.S. Merwin. *New York
        Times Book Review*, 87 (Aug. 1, 1982): 7, 29.

        "Only as the narrator matures and detaches himself
        from childhood scenes does the book lose its quirky,
        obsessive quality and become, by its end, a nostalgic
        reverie of a more conventional sort."

1034.   "A Child with a Cold, Cold Eye." Review of "Novel on
        Yellow   Paper",   "Over   the   Frontier"   and   "The
        Holiday" by Stevie Smith. *New York Times Book
        Review*, 87 (Oct. 3, 1981): 11, 26-27.

        "Stevie Smith wrote novels with the left hand and
        made no claims otherwise." No doubt the narrator's
        claims for strong emotion are authentic ..., but they
        are not dramatized within the fictional context ...
        they fall flat indeed." There is praise here, however,
        for Smith as a poet in volumes not under review.

1035.   "The Magnanimity of 'Wuthering Heights.'" *Critical
        Inquiry*, 9, ii (Dec. 1982): 435-449.
        Repr. in *The Profane Art* (# 1039), pp. 63-81.

        "The great theme of *Wuthering Heights*, perversely
        overlooked by many of its admiring critics as well as
        by its detractors, is precisely this 'inevitability': how
        present-day harmony, in September, 1802, has come
        about." Again Oates is working against the prevailing
        critical wind, asserting here that the novel is about
        the natural re-establishment of balance, order, and
        sanity. Well-written, well-argued, and provocative
        both as criticism and as possible light on Oates's own
        gothic romances.

1036.   "Dodgson's Golden Hours." *English Language Notes*,
        20, ii (Dec. 1982): 109-118.
        and in *Soaring with the Dodo: Essays on Lewis
        Carroll's Life and Art*, Edward Guiliano and
        James R. Kincaid, eds. Charlottesville: distr. by
        University Press of Virginia, 1982, pp. 109-118.
        (Carroll Studies; 6)
        Repr. under title "Charles Dodgson's Golden
        Hours" in *The Profane Art* (# 1039), pp. 82-89.

        Ostensibly a review of two new Lewis Carroll editions,
        Oates meditates here on the mysterious relationship of
        Carroll to Dodgson, of a literary work to the author's
        inmost self.

1037. "Books I Enjoyed." *New York Times Book Review*, 87 (Dec. 5, 1982): 62.

Oates briefly mentions *Wuthering Heights* and *Wide Sargrasso Sea*, making some comparisons between the two.

1038. "(Woman) Writer" in *First Person Singular* (# 1077), pp. 190-197.

A keynote address to the Twentieth Century Woman Writer's Conference in 1983. "The luxury of being despised is an embittered and satirical one, yet it allows for a certain energizing of forces, away from the self, perhaps, and into the work: away from the distractions and the immediate gratifications of visibility, and toward the semipermanence of art."

1039. *The Profane Art: Essays and Reviews*. New York: Dutton, 1983. 212p.
Contains: I. Essays: Imaginary Cities: America; At Least I Have Made a Woman of Her: Images of Women in Yeats, Lawrence, Faulkner; The Magnanimity of 'Wuthering Heights'; Charles Dodgson's Golden Hours; John Updike's American Comedies; Notes on Failure. II. Reviews: The Interior Castle: The Art of Jean Stafford's Short Fiction; Before God Was Love: The Short Stories of Paul Bowles; Colette's Purgatory; Géza Csath's Garden: The Contours of Surrealism; "May God Grant That I Become Nothing": The Mysticism of Simone Weil; Legendary Jung; Anne Sexton: Self-Portrait in Poetry and Letters; Sacred and Profane Iris Murdoch; Flannery O'Connor: A Self-Portrait in Letters.

Individual annotation under each title.

1040. "Flannery O'Connor: A Self-Portrait in Letters" in *The Profane Art* (# 1039), pp. 195-203.

In a review article, Oates dwells here on the difference that O'Connor's letters seem to show between the writer and the private woman, "the highly complex woman artist whose art was, perhaps, too profound for even the critic in her to grasp."

1041. "From England to Brooklyn to West Virginia." Review of "The Stories of Breece D'J Pancake." *New York Times Book Review*, 88 (Feb. 13, 1983): 1, 24-25.

Favorable review of *The Stories of Breece D'J Pancake*.

1042. "A Fable of Innocence and Survival." Review of "Tzili" by Aharon Appelfeld. *New York Times Book Review*, 88 (Feb. 27, 1983): 9.

"It is a measure of Aharon Appelfeld's uncanny skill that a narrative so deliberately shorn of familiar human relations and emotions should bear so much power."

1043. "Assorted Stories." Review of "The Man Who Sold Prayers" by Margaret Creal. *New York Times Book Review*, 88 (Mar. 13, 1983): 10.

Unfavorable review: "Situation allegory, one might call it--brisk, amusing but so lightweight it's impossible to believe in Saintly's existence from one page to another."

1044. "At Least I Have Made a Woman of Her: Images of Women in Twentieth-Century Literature." *Georgia Review*, 37, i (Spring 1983): 7-30.
       and under title "At Least I Have Made a Woman of Her: Images of Women in Yeats, Lawrence, Faulkner" in *The Profane Art* (# 1039), pp. 35-62.

A major article, revealing a stridently feminist Oates; she attacks Yeats for the sentiments of "A Prayer for My Daughter," and expresses dismay at Lawrence as "one of those 'liberators' of the twentieth century whose gospel, as applied to and experienced by women, may in fact constitute a more insidious--precisely 'because' iconoclastic-imprisonment." Oates also grapples here with a definition of the Modern: "it is not an exaggeration to argue that Modernist fiction carries over deep-rooted nineteenth-century prejudices of a distinctly bourgeois sort."

1045. "Love in an Old-Age Home." Review of "In the Palomar Arms" by Hilma Wolitzer. *New York Times Book Review*, 88 (June 5, 1983): 14, 25.

"'In the Palomar Arms'" is a gentle, unpretentious novel populated by well-meaning people who cause one another harm out of ignorance rather than cruelty." Mild praise for a modest work.

1046. "People to Whom Things Happen." Review of "The Times Are Never So Bad" by André Dubus. *New York Times Book Review*, 88 (June 26, 1983): 12, 18.

Cautiously appreciative review: "André Dubus's fiction is perhaps an acquired taste, for his characters are resolutely ungiving and uncharming." "Where another writer might dramatize his characters' plights in order to reveal and exorcise their strategies of delusion, Mr. Dubus has other intentions. ... he has learned 'of how often memory lies, and how often the lies are good ones.'"

1047. "Love and Other Illusions." Review of "The Philosopher's Pupil" by Iris Murdoch. *New York Times Book Review*, 88 (July 17, 1983): 1, 20-21.

Uneasy enthusiasm for Murdoch, whose fiction Oates finds to be growing steadily more rarified and idiosyncratic. "The early novels seem quintessentially English, the later self-consciously 'Russian.'"

1048. "Monet, Summer, 1900." Review of "Light" by Eva Figes. *New York Times Book Review*, 88 (Oct. 16, 1983): 11, 30-33.

Favorable, general review of a work "clearly descended from Woolf's great experimental novels." "... that *Light* is self-consciously derivative in technique does not detract from the beauty of its images or its prose."

1049. "The Citizen Courier in Outer Space." Review of "Mysteries of Motion" by Hortense Calisher. *New York Times Book Review*, 88 (Nov. 6, 1983): 7, 26.

Praises a new novel for its "scrupulous attention to details" connected to space flight, and for its attempts to be prophetic.

1050. "A Special Message to the Members of the First Edition Society" in *Mysteries of Winterthurn* (# 12).

Oates briefly described the novel, and the quartet of which it is a part, as an elaborate exercise within the "formal discipline of 'genre.'" Xavier Kilgarvan, the protagonist, is "thoroughly American," and the murder cases in the novel are "dream-like" variations on "old favorites" in the tradition of American crime.

1051. "Frankenstein's Fallen Angel." *Critical Inquiry*, 10, iii
      (Mar. 1984): 543-554.

      Oates tours through some of the archetypes suggested
      to her by Mary Shelley's *Frankenstein*. She refers to
      the protagonist-scientist variously as a version of
      Milton's Satan, a "demonic parody of Milton's God," of
      Shakespeare's Edmund, and finally "a finite and flawed
      god at war with, and eventually overcome by, his
      creation." The creature is a "Doppelganger--the
      nightmare that is deliberately created by man's
      ingenuity" [Oates's emphasis], an Adamic and Satanic
      figure, a "shadow self locked within consciousness." A
      strong loosely-structured introduction to the novel.

1052. "Does the Writer Exist?" *New York Times Book
      Review*, 89 (Apr. 22, 1984): 1, 17.

      The essay picks up on an idea broached earlier in her
      essays on Lewis Carroll, of a marked and widening
      separation between the established "writer" and the
      human being. Oates does not confess anything here
      about her personal life and its disconnections from her
      public self; her approach instead recalls the episte-
      mological distinctions favored by Roland Barthes, or
      Jorge Luis Borges (whose sketch "Borges and I" she
      mentions). Also discussed is James's tale "The Private
      Life."

1053. "The Union Justified the Means." Review of "Lincoln"
      by Gore Vidal. *New York Times Book Review*, 89
      (June 3, 1984): 1, 36-37.

      Favorable review of *Lincoln*.

1054. "Wonderlands." *Georgia Review*, 38, iii (Fall 1984):
      487-506.

      Major essay on gothic and fantastic literature, covering
      material from Mary Shelley and Poe through Lewis
      Carroll and Oscar Wilde: its major emphasis is on the
      paradoxes at the heart of the gothic mode: that in
      true gothic fantasy our "shadow selves" are gratified,
      souls are at once fulfilled and disintegrated. The
      loathsome becomes desirable, the unholy sanctified.
      Because it considers connections of fantastic literature
      to the idea of the self, the essay seems to lie at a
      nexus point in understanding Oates's quest in fiction,
      even though here, as in most of her writing about
      literary history, she does not mention her own work.

1055. "Novel in Movieland." Review of "The Talisman" by Stephen King. *Vogue*, 174 (Nov. 1984): 271, 274.

Playful review of a pop-novel by two American gothicists, asserting that the book was contrived with movie-rights in mind.

1056. "Ernest Hemingway: Man's Man ? Woman-Hater ? Our Greatest Writer ?" *TV Guide* (Northeastern edition), 32 (Dec. 8, 1984): 4-6, 8.

General introductory discussion of Hemingway and *The Sun Also Rises*, occasioned by the broadcast of a "Made-for TV" movie.

1057. "The English Secret Unveiled ?" Review of "Ivy: The Life of I. Compton-Burnett" by Hilary Spurling. *New York Times Book Review*, 89 (Dec. 9, 1984): 7, 9.

General discussion of Burnett's career, with passing assessments of her importance: "What struck readers in the 1920's as savagely witty--because so persistently unsentimental--sounds painfully dated today, and many of the exchanges in the novels are of the forced quality of television situation comedy. The use of puppet characters in sketchily realized settings suggests an imaginative deficiency, rather than the unique genius proclaimed by Compton-Burnett's early supporters. "

1058. "Best of TV. [Hill Street Blues.] *TV Guide* (Northeastern edition), 33 (June 1, 1985): 5, 7.

"*Hill Street Blues* is most moving when it deals directly with conflicts rising out of personal rather than social (or even criminal) issues. "

1059. "On Boxing." *New York Times Magazine* (June 16, 1985): 28-32, 34, 37-38.

With passing references to boxing as "a dramatic story" and "America's tragic theater," Oates writes a conventional and expert article on the sport's history and appeal: indicating that she inherited her interest in it from her father, Oates gives a portrait of the atmosphere at ringside at Madison Square Garden, and weaves in anecdotes about Marciano, Joe Louis, and fighters long before her time. The essay often emulates Hemingway, Pete Axthelm, Norman Mailer and the better writers in the American sports magazines.

1060. "A Terrible Beauty Is Born. How ?" *New York Times Book Review*, 90 (Aug. 11, 1985): 1, 27, 29.

Anecdotal essay (on Joyce, Lawrence, Updike, Godwin, Woolf, Yeats, Didion--but not actually herself), treating the mysterious mixture of coincidence and intuition from which major literature has sprung. Essentially an unsophisticated and somewhat oblique answer to a standard question--how do writers get those great ideas ? Oates reveals a rather traditional belief in inspiration and fate as the source of worthy fiction.

(*) Reprinted or partly reprinted in *Contemporary Literary Criticism*, vol. 3, Carolyn Riley, ed. Detroit: Gale Research, 1975 (# 1126).

INTERVIEWS WITH JOYCE CAROL OATES

ON HERSELF AND OTHERS

1061. Avant, John Alfred. "An Interview with Joyce Carol Oates." *Library Journal*, 97 (Nov. 15, 1972): 3711-3712.

1062. Batterberry, Michael & Batterberry, Ariane, eds. "Focus on Joyce Carol Oates." *Harper's Bazaar*, 106 (Sept. 1973): 159, 174, 176.

1063. Bellamy, Joe David. "The Dark Lady of American Letters: An Interview with Joyce Carol Oates." *Atlantic*, 229 (Feb. 1972): 63-67. Repr. in *The New Fiction: Interviews with Innovative American Writers*, Joe David Bellamy. Urbana: University of Illinois Press, 1974, pp. 19-31.

1064. Boesky, Dale. "Correspondence with Miss Joyce Carol Oates." *International Review of Psychoanalysis*, 2 (1975): 481-486.

1065. Franks, Lucinda. "The Emergence of Joyce Carol Oates." *New York Times Magazine* (July 27, 1980): 22, 26, 30, 32, 43-44, 46.

1066. "How Is Fiction Doing ?" [An Interview with Joyce Carol Oates and Others.] *New York Times Book Review*, 85 (Dec. 14, 1980): 3.

1067. Kuehl, Linda, ed. "An Interview with Joyce Carol Oates." *Commonweal*, 91 (Dec. 5, 1969): 307-310.

1068. Lask, Thomas. "Publishing: Joys of Rewriting." *New York Times*, 82 (July 22, 1977), sect. 3: 18.

1069. Oates, Joyce Carol. "The Books That Made Writers." *Writer*, 93 (Oct. 1980): 24.

1070. ———. "A Conversation with Colin Wilson." *Ontario Review*, 4 (Spring-Summer 1976): 7-15.

1071. ———. "A Conversation with Margaret Atwood." *Ontario Review*, 9 (Fall-Winter 1978): 5-18. Repr. in *First Person Singular* (# 1077), pp. 84-94.

1072. ———. "A Conversation with Philip Roth." *Ontario Review*, 1 (Fall 1974): 9-22.

1073. ———. "Conversations with Dan Berrigan on Detroit, Survival and Hope." *Detroit Free Press*, Detroit Section (Apr. 6, 1975): 17-21.

1074. ———. "Conversations with John Gardner on Writers and Writing." *Detroit Free Press Sunday Magazine* (Mar. 23, 1975): 20.

1075. ———. "Face to Face: Joyce Carol Oates in Conversation with Graeme Gibson." *Maclean's*, 87 (Apr. 1974): 42-43, 56-58, 60.

1076. ———. "Margaret Atwood: Poems and Poet." *New York Times Book Review*, 83 (May 21, 1978): 15, 43-45. Repr. in *First Person Singular* (# 1077), pp. 84-94.

1077. ———, comp. *First Person Singular. Writers on Their Craft*. Princeton, NJ: Ontario Review Press, 1983. 280p.

1078. Parini, Jay. "A Taste of Oates." *Horizon*, 26 (Nov.-Dec. 1983): 50-52.

1079. Phillips, Robert. "Joyce Carol Oates: The Art of Fiction." *Paris Review*, 20 (Fall-Winter 1978): 199-226. Repr. in *Writers at Work. The Paris Review Interviews; Fifth Series*, George Plimpton, ed. New York: Viking Press, 1981, pp. 359-384.

1080. Pinsker, Sanford. "Speaking about Short Fiction: An Interview with Joyce Carol Oates." *Studies in Short Fiction*, 18, iii (Summer 1981): 239-243. Repr. in *Conversations with Contemporary American Writers,* Sanford Pinsker. Amsterdam: Rodopi, 1985, pp. 36-42 (Costerus, n.s.; 50)

1081. Sjöberg, Leif. "Samtal med Joyce Carol Oates." *Artes*, 3 (1980): 13-32.

1082. ⸻. "An Interview with Joyce Carol Oates." *Contemporary Literature*, 23, iii (Summer 1982): 267-284 (expanded version).
        Repr. in *Interviews with Contemporary Writers; Second Series, 1972-1982*, L.S. Dembo, ed. Madison, WI: University of Wisconsin Press, 1983, pp. 348-365.

1083. "Transformations of Self: An Interview with Joyce Carol Oates." *Ohio Review*, 15, i (Autumn 1973): 50-61.

1084. Z[immerman], P[aul] D. "Hunger for Dreams." *Newsweek*, 75 (Mar. 23, 1970): 109A.

II. SECONDARY SOURCES

CRITICISM ON JOYCE CAROL OATES

AND HER WORK

BIBLIOGRAPHIES

1085. McCormick, Lucienne P. "A Bibliography of Works by and about Joyce Carol Oates." *American Literature*, 43, i (Mar. 1971): 124-132.

1086. Catron, Douglas M. "A Contribution to a Bibliography of Works by and about Joyce Carol Oates." *American Literature*, 49, iii (Nov. 1977): 399-414.

1087. Dickinson, Donald C., comp. "Joyce Carol Oates: A Bibliographical Checklist." *American Book Collector*, Section A: Primary Publications, (Nov.-Dec. 1981): 26-38; Section B: Secondary Publications, n.s., 3, i (Jan.-Feb. 1982): 42-48.

1088. Coven, Brenda. *American Women Dramatists of the 20th Century: A Bibliography.* Metuchen: Scarecrow Press, 1982, pp. 163-164.

BOOKS

1089. Grant, Mary Kathryn. *The Tragic Vision of Joyce Carol Oates*. Durham, NC: Duke University Press, 1978. 167p.

Grant's is a persuasive and provocative if somewhat single-minded book; running counter to DeMott and others who find in Oates a kind of labile nihilism, Grant contends that Oates's vision is genuinely tragic, that beneath the horror and the grotesque and the surreal in the fiction there is a passionate moralist at work, a didacticist, working constantly to "voice a celebrative sense of life," to express an "ever-developing sense of affirmation." There are problems of course in making such a case; but Grant does a better job than any other critic to date in venturing towards the heart of Oates's fiction, and along the way she offers insights which any reader can welcome, regardless of one's view of these works as genuinely tragic or not. Grant is good at making distinctions: between Oates and Lawrence on the possibility of Tragedy, between Oates and O'Connor on lessons and the impact of violence, between Oates and her contemporaries on the dangers and possibilities of life in the city. A reader might do well to read the final chapter of Grant, "The Tragic Vision," before launching into the close studies in the middle of the book, as that last chapter makes clear the special kind of post-Nietzschean tragedy that she finds in play in Oates. In sum, Grant has a balanced, sensible view of Oates, and her volume is of real help to anyone considering the larger questions raised by her writings.

1090. Creighton, Joanne V. *Joyce Carol Oates*. Boston, MA: Twayne, 1979. 173p. (TUSAS; 321)

Creighton's book is the best comprehensive study to date of Oates's fiction, because it avoids conventional labelings, looks carefully into not only the fiction

itself but also the clues to its intentions which turn
up in Oates's critical writings and interviews, and
solicits some telling comments from Oates herself by
way of interviews and correspondence. The first
chapter, which explores Oates's idea of the self, her
indebtedness to Thomas Mann and D.H. Lawrence,
and her quarrel with modern and Postmodern
conceptions of identity, is essential, and a good place
for the lay reader to start in investigating Oates's
fiction. Subsequent chapters are close readings of
major novels and stories through 1975.

1091. Wagner, Linda W. *Critical Essays on Joyce Carol
       Oates*. Boston, MA: G.K. Hall, 1979, 180p.
       (Critical Essays on American Literature)

Wagner's collection is a good place to begin in
reviewing the variety of responses Oates's work has
provoked, and some of the most provocative ideas
about her to date. Wagner's 12-page introduction
gives a good overview by itself, stressing the abrupt
shifts in Oates's career and major concerns, the
inadequacy of any of the labels commonly assigned
her, the ups and downs of her fortunes among the
reviewers. Avoiding any strong pronouncements of
her own, Wagner collects seventeen reviews
(remarkable more as specimens than as revelations)
and eleven essays, including two (Bender and
Stevens) written expressly for this collection and
unavailable anywhere else. The highlight of the book
is Walter Sullivan's "The Artificial Demon: Joyce Carol
Oates and the Dimensions of the Real," which opens
with real insight and boldness several of Oates's
central ideas, and the formal and aesthetic problems
which result. The understanding in Benjamin DeMott's
"The Necessity in Art of a Reflective Intelligence" is
less compassionate, but eloquent in its objections to
the writings before 1970, and to the high-cult
ideology which welcomed them:

> Those who praise Miss Oates ... do so in a vein
> that encourages her to regard an inability to
> perceive or create meaning as a virtue--a
> "courageous" eschewal of judgment, a new foray
> into the meaning of meaninglessness. And this
> "critical line" is but part of a wider body of
> conviction throughout the culture at
> large--conviction hostile to the sequential and
> the reflective, impatient with effort at

discriminating the quality of this or that response to life on the ground that such effort is un-involved, secondary, less like an action than an imitation of an action, hence unproductive of excitement or profit or pleasure.

Bender's essay treats *Childwold:* its variations on Nabokov's *Lolita*, its friendly quarrel with trendy literary ideas. Oates, says Bender, "sees the literary tradition not as a 'trap' to be skirted but as a realm of reality open to infinite revision and counter-statement, a realm of play and illusion. Her imitations are thus not the parodic acts of the fabulator; they are serious and even passionate responses to other fictive worlds." The Stevens essay, on the poetry before 1978, is very general, concerning itself chiefly with the recurring theme of the "remorseless insignificance of life," and how a nihilistic mood is counteracted here and there in the verse. "The poems," says Stevens, offer a "core of realistic detail"; the Oates poem ultimately demands "to be read on its own terms."

Also among the essays are excerpts from the then-forthcoming books by Creighton, Grant, Friedman, and Waller.

1092. Waller, G[ary] F. *Dreaming America: Obsession and Transcendence in the Fiction of Joyce Carol Oates.* Baton Rouge: Louisiana State University Press, 1979. 224p.

Discussing major themes in Oates's fiction through 1976, Waller has gone thoroughly into Oates's own critical writings and offers one of the first solid discussions of their connections to the fiction. He extensively documents Oates's long concern with the central ideas of the Postmodern period in American fiction, demonstrates the importance of her abiding interest in D.H. Lawrence, and draws widely but thoughtfully from Oates's writings in tracing her headiest ideas about the revolution now underway in the idea of the individual consciousness. In a book loaded with provocative quotations, Oates is portrayed as a kind of prophet of social and psychological upheaval, a writer as erudite and genuinely experimental as any other now working, with especially unsettling ideas to offer about where, as a people, we are going; but Waller's studies of the

major novels tend only to reiterate these big-scale
themes, rather than consider the artistic challenges
they must pose and how Oates, in each case, has
faced them. "Oates's basic problem as a novelist,"
says Waller, is "how to combine her intellectual
intentions with the suggestiveness of her world of
surging and unpredictable emotions." Beyond
combining, however, there is the problem of how the
intellectual intention or the surging emotion can make
for a successful novel--a matter understandably
beyond the reach of this study, and of most criticism
on Oates at the moment. Waller is invaluable,
however, for establishing that something of real
consequence is working itself out in Oates, and that
she is in tune with our times in every important way.

1093.   Friedman, Ellen G. *Joyce Carol Oates*. New York:
        Ungar, 1980. 238p. (Modern Literature Mono-
        graphs)

Friedman provides useful summaries and interpretations
of eight novels through 1978. Focusing at the start,
as Creighton does, on Oates's concern with modern
definitions of identity, Friedman's book soon dilutes
itself by trying to discuss too much in too short a
space: romanticism, realism, myth, naturalism, the
individual and society, Faustian and Freudian heroes,
the surreal, fairy-tales, irony and satire are all
touched upon here, commonly in terms too
loosely-defined to provide much insight. The readings
are useful in their meticulousness, but they are
neither balanced nor evaluative: emphasis is put so
strongly on grandiose themes, and on plot as a
vehicle for themes, that Oates comes off
(unintentionally, it would seem) as a writer of prolix,
lurid, heavily-moralizing fables laden with familiar
symbolism and pretentious messages.

1094.   Bastian, Katherine. *Joyce Carol Oates's Short Stories*
        between Tradition and Innovation. Frankfurt
        a.M.: Bern, Lang, 1983. 173p. (Neue Studien
        zur Anglistik und Amerikanistik; 26)

Bastian has made the best foray to date into the
complex, important problem of Oates's response to
literary tradition, her adaptations, variations, and
echoings of major writers of the last two centuries.
Bastian begins conservatively, dealing with a
sequence of stories which flatly announce themselves

as paying homage of some sort to specific ancestors (Joyce's "The Dead," Kafka's "The Metamorphosis," James's "The Turn of the Screw," and so on), and describing the intent of the adaptation and the large scale differences between the original and the Oates tale. The book expands its reach later, as Bastian takes on the whole issue of Oates as a contemporary force in literature and the heritage she has proven so conscious of: dividing the stories into three sub-genres (the extraordinary, recognition, initiation) Bastian seeks to describe the old and the new in Oates's handling of each. Anyone who finds the short stories exceptionally thoughtful--and many critics apparently do--ought to begin with Bastian, for guidance in organizing their thinking about this highly-involved topic, perhaps the most difficult of all in understanding the place Oates seeks to take in her own time and in the lineage of fiction. Printed in Germany as part of an academic series, this is a hard book to find in the United States: it is well worth the extra trouble to secure.

1095. Norman, [K.] Torborg [M.]. *Isolation and Contact: A Study of Character Relationships in Joyce Carol Oates's Short Stories 1963-1980*. Göteborg: Acta Universitatis Gothoburgensis, 1984. 261p. (Gothenburg Studies in English; 57)

Written as a thesis, Norman's book has the virtue of a precise strategy: Oates's major short story collections are intensively studied in light of speech act theory, to observe how both character and context are revealed through dialogue. Writing a clean, straightforward prose, Norman does very close readings of a number of the stories, intending "to show how Oates's characters in their opposition to isolation and in their striving towards affirmative contact are on the move from a traditionally prevalent individual outlook towards a dynamic community of interrelationships." The weakness of the book has to do with its proportions: Norman does not permit herself much discrimination among the stories or the collections, and the large-scale findings she offers are something less than astounding. She observes that the conversations of characters reflect their social circumstances, their interlocutors, their inner lives, their sense of isolation, their wish to transcend it; that men and women frequently cannot communicate; that individuality is both a boon and an entrapment. The detailed readings, therefore, some-times seem more of a workout for speech act theory than an opening-up of the given tale. But Norman has paid unprecedentedly close attention to some of these stories, and subsequent critics would do well to consult her before offering minute readings of their own.

CRITICISM ON JOYCE CAROL OATES

IN PERIODICALS AND BOOKS

1096. Oates, Joyce Carol. "Building Tension in the Short Story." *Writer*, 79 (June 1966): 11-12, 44.

For annotation, see # 861.

1097. Bower, Warren. "Bliss in the First Person." *Saturday Review*, 51 (Oct. 26, 1968): 34-35.

In a short biographical piece, Bower reports on a conversation with Oates who states that she is "obsessed with the mysteries of human relationships." Oates thinks her writing has "no 'ideas' in it at all only human emotions."

1098. Clemons, Walter. "Joyce Carol Oates at Home." *New York Times Book Review*, 74 (Sept. 28, 1969): 4-5, 48.

Oates explains to Clemons that her writing is "mainly daydreaming." She admits she does not do much rewriting and very little research. She thinks that striving for the right brand of cigarettes or the correct things on the radio for the time is "stagey and irrelevant."

1099. "Writing As a Natural Reaction." *Time*, 94 (Oct. 10, 1969): 8.

Biographical sketch with critical commonplaces, a few good quotations from an interview: "'The greatest realities are physical and economic, all the subtleties of life come afterward,' she says. 'Intellectuals have forgotten, or else they never understood, how difficult it is to make one's way up from a low economic level, to assert one's will in a great crude way. It's so difficult. You have to go through it. You have to be poor.'"

1100.   Oates, Joyce Carol. "The Nature of Short Fiction; or,
        The Nature of My Short Fiction" in *Handbook of
        Short Story Writing*, Frank A. Dickson and
        Sandra Smythe, eds. Cincinnati: Writer's Digest,
        [1970], pp. XI-XVIII.

        For annotation, see # 880.

1101.   Dalton, Elizabeth. "Joyce Carol Oates: Violence in the
        Head." *Commentary*, 49 (June 1970): 75-77.

        In a very negative review of Oates's work, Dalton
        states that Oates's stories have a "workshop
        correctness of structure and development that makes
        the violence seem all the more deliberate and unreal."
        She asserts that them is a "failure of literary
        intelligence, of structure and style."

1102.   Mazzaro, Jerome. "Feeling One's Oates." *Modern
        Poetry Studies*, 2, iii (1971): 133-137.
        (*)

        Mazzaro particularly notes Oates's preoccupation with
        intersubjectivity in *Love and Its Derangements*. This
        intersubjectivity "has little if anything to do with the
        mere articulation of language" but is instead the "felt
        osmotic processes which are suggested by the book's
        merging fluids of birth and death." Oates attacks not
        only the misuses of language but also the subjugation
        of women by men because "it is not only the language
        that has failed but man."

1103.   Kazin, Alfred. "Heroines." *New York Review of
        Books*, 16 (Feb. 11, 1971): 32-34.

        Kazin calls Oates "a novelist of her own mind, playing
        this mind out now well, now badly, but playing it out
        to the farthest boundary of social upheaval." He
        suggests she is "empathically related to the flow of
        [her characters'] consciousness, but with no more
        emphasis of sympathy than there is rejection." He
        rejects ordinary people because he asserts "satire is
        no more her thing than a short book is."

1104.   Oates, Joyce Carol. "The Short Story." *Southern
        Humanities Review*, 5, iii (Summer 1971): 213-214.
        Repr. in *What Is the Short Story ?*, Eugene
        Current-Garcia and Welton R. Patrick, eds.
        Glenview: Scott Foresman, 1974, pp. 138-139.

        For annotation, see # 891.

1105. Kazin, Alfred. "Oates." *Harper's*, 243 (Aug. 1971): 78-82.

Kazin suggests that Oates writes "the way Mozart wrote down the score already written out in his head." He criticizes her for writing "to relieve her mind of the people who haunt it, not to create something that will live." Much of the critical commentary in this article has been reprinted (see # 1112).

1106. Cornillon, Susan Koppelman. "The Fiction of Fiction" in *Images of Women in Fiction; Feminist Perspectives*, Susan Koppelman Cornillon, ed. Bowling Green, OH: Bowling Green University Popular Press, 1972, pp. 117-124.

As part of a larger discussion of women's fiction, Cornillon uses Oates, particularly *them*, to illustrate the mistake of perceiving a cultural stereotype as one's self. She faults Oates for not clearly separating "her own attitudes and opinions on the issue of sex role from her characters." She also criticizes Oates for not allowing the reader "to share the experiencing of any of the physical phenomena that are uniquely female." She tentatively attributes this failure to Oates finding "the sordid realities of female life, for females in our culture dwell in the slums of personhood, too unbearable to record."

1107. Ivanescu, Mircea. "Un Profil: Joyce Carol Oates." *Secolul XX*, 15, v (1972): 140-142.

No annotation.

1108. Ditsky, John. "The Man on the Quaker Oats Box: Characteristics of Recent Experimental Fiction." *Georgia Review*, 26 (Fall 1972): 297-301.

According to Ditsky, Oates is only "superficially similar" to the realists. He suggests that tonally she is more aligned with the experimentalists because she shares their concern with "inner states" and their "shattered vision." Although her form is more realistic, he suggests her spirit is experimental.

1109. Oates, Joyce Carol. "New Heaven and Earth." *Saturday Review*, 55 (Nov. 4, 1972): 51-54. Repr. in *Arts in Society*, 10 (1973): 36-43.

For annotation, see # 906.

1110. Sullivan, Walter. "The Artificial Demon: Joyce Carol
       Oates and the Dimensions of the Real." *Hollins
       Critic*, 9, iv (Dec. 1972): 1-12.
       Repr. in *Critical Essays on Joyce Carol Oates*,
       Linda W. Wagner. Boston, MA: G.K. Hall, 1979,
       pp. 77-86.

       Sullivan states that Oates is one of the most talented
       writers in this country today and credits her with
       "an unerring eye and an infallible ear." However, he
       feels she is a short story writer, not a novelist. Even
       in what he considers her best novels--*A Garden of
       Earthly Delights* and *them*, he faults her for a lack
       of focus and a failure to identify her main characters.
       He also suggests that she writes the "same story over
       and over--a chroniclo whcrc violcnce is a prelude to
       total spiritual disintegration and the only freedom is
       the total loss of self."

1111. Clemons, Walter. "Joyce Carol Oates: Love and Vio-
       lence." *Newsweek*, 80 (Dec. 11, 1972): 72-74, 77.

       In a "feature" story on Oates, Clemons suggests that
       she is "non-Gothic, and original, in her tenacious
       adherence to the humble ordinariness that surrounds
       violence." He places her in the "tradition of insight
       and imagination."

1112. Kazin, Alfred. "Cassandras: Porter to Oates" in
       *Bright Book of Life: American Novelists and
       Storytellers from Hemingway to Mailer*, Alfred
       Kazin. Boston, MA: Little, Brown, 1973, pp.
       198-205.
       Repr. as [On Joyce Carol Oates] in *Critical
       Essays on Joyce Carol Oates*, Linda W. Wagner.
       Boston, MA: G.K. Hall, 1979, pp. 157-160.
       (*)

       Kazin is critical of Oates's lack of "right and
       well-fitting structure" and feels that she devotes too
       much space, even in *them* "her best novel to date,"
       to emotion and the depiction of "teeming private
       consciousness." He calls her work "haunting" rather
       than "successful."

1113. Hicks, Jack. *Cutting Edges: Young American Fiction
       for the '70s*. New York: Holt, Rinehart &
       Winston, 1973, pp. 542-543.

       A brief biographical sketch including a long quotation
       from Oates in which she articulates the aim of serious

art--"to externalize personal, private, shapeless fantasies into structures that are recognizable to other people."

1114. Oates, Joyce Carol. "The Unique/Universal in Fiction." *Writer*, 86 (Jan. 1973): 9-12.

For annotation, see # 912.

1115. Pinsker, Sanford. "Isaac Bashevis Singer and Joyce Carol Oates: Some Versions of Gothic." *Southern Review* (Baton Rouge), n.s., 9, iv (Autumn 1973): 895-908. Repr. in *Between Two Worlds: The American Novel of the 1960's*, Sanford Pinsker. Troy, NY: Whitston Publ., 1980, 115-127.

Pinsker labels both Oates and Singer as gothic--as writers of "darkly serious fiction."

1116. Lundkvist, Arthur. "Mardrömmar och spex." *Bonniers Litterära Magasin*, 42, v (Dec. 1973): 276-281.

No annotation.

1117. Mulyarchik, A. "Dzhois Kerol Outs ishchet vykhod" (Joyce Carol Oates Looks for a Way Out). *Literaturnaya Gazeta* (Dec. 26, 1973): 5.

No annotation.

1118. Oberg, Arthur. "Deer, Doors, Dark." *Southern Review* (Baton Rouge), n.s., 9, i (Winter 1973): 243-256.

Brief, kind, unfavorable review of *Love and Its Derangements*. Oates, for Oberg, "has not settled on what kind of poem she wishes to make into her own." "That there is 'a landscape of love' in these poems I never doubt. But it is commonly obscured or hidden by what is less immediate and vague."

1119. Dike, Donald A. "The Aggressive Victim in the Fiction of Joyce Carol Oates." *Greyfriar*, 15 (1974): 13-29.

Dike sees escape, as opposed to quest, as the main goal of most of Oates's characters. He also notes that any complex character is likely to be both victim and aggressor or may move from one role to the other. "Between people who love each other ... occur the most brutal exacerbations. Intimacy is the greatest opportunity and also the most dangerous."

1120. DeRamus, Betty. "Peeking into the Very Private World of Joyce Carol Oates." *Detroit Free Press Sunday Magazine* (Mar. 3, 1974): 13-15. Repr. in *Authors in the News*, vol. 1, Barbara Nykoruk, ed. Detroit: Gale Research, 1976, pp. 365-366. (Biography News Library)

Playful but respectful biographical sketch, centered on a brief letter from Oates declining to be interviewed for fear of uncomfortable local publicity. DeRamus instead interviews people around Oates, and reports what they think of her as a colleague and friend.

1121. Oates, Joyce Carol. "Disguised Fiction." *PMLA*, 89 (May 1974): 580-581.

For annotation, see # 930.

1122. Pickering, Samuel F., Jr. "The Short Stories of Joyce Carol Oates." *Georgia Review*, 28, ii (Summer 1974): 218-226.

Pickering concedes that many of Oates's stories are "well-written and provocative"; nevertheless he finds her Catholic stories "one-dimensional," her academic stories "her weakest tales," and her love stories "Verdiesque with melodramatic and sentimental rhythms." In her later stories, he finds that "the body, then sentence structures, finally words themselves, become too subjective to convey meaning to a wide audience."

1123. Denne, Constance Ayers. "Joyce Carol Oates's Women." *Nation*, 219 (Dec. 7, 1974): 597-599.

According to Denne, Oates's own consciousness as a woman is the subject of *Do with Me What You Will*. Denne suggests that "Elena represents the logical culmination of an artistic interest in the lives and consciousness of women" which Oates has been exploring for more than a decade. Elena finds a "way out, not through the law or any of our present institutions but through awakened human consciousness."

1124. Sullivan, Walter. "Old Age, Death, and Other Modern Landscapes: Good and Indifferent Fables for our Time." *Sewanee Review*, 82, i (Winter 1974): 138-140.

Sullivan thinks Oates is "enormously talented" and is at her best writing dialogue, but he advises her to "stop writing for a while and seriously consider what she has been doing." He complains that not only has he seen all her characters before but "each of her novels seems a little less exciting, a little more repetitive."

1125. Peden, William. *The American Short Story: Continuity and Change 1940-1975.* Boston, MA: Houghton Mifflin, 1975, pp. 88-97.

Although Peden does praise Oates's narrative pace in his survey of her short story collections, he also states, "Joyce Carol Oates's house of fiction at times becomes a windowless tomb without an exit, a contemporary House of Usher, in which her people fall upon the thorns of life and bleed, bleed, bleed."

1126. Riley, Carolyn, ed. "Joyce Carol Oates" in *Contemporary Literary Criticism*, vol. 3. Detroit: Gale Research, 1975, pp. 359-364.

These sixteen excerpts from critical reviews of Oates's work contain opinions ranging from "superb writer with a perfect eye and ear" to a writer of poetry that is not memorable.

1127. Oates, Joyce Carol. Afterword to *The Poisoned Kiss and Other Stories from the Portuguese.* Fernandes/Joyce Carol Oates. New York: Vanguard Press, 1975, pp. 187-189.

For annotation, see # 939.

1128. Quinn, Sally. "Joyce Carol Oates: A Life Within." *Washington Post* (Apr. 30, 1975): B1, B11.

Celebrity-sketch of Oates, especially amusing for her bored resistance to Quinn's questions, and for Quinn's failure to notice it.

1129. Fossum, Robert H. "Only Control: The Novels of Joyce Carol Oates." *Studies in the Novel*, 7, ii (Summer 1975): 285-297.
Repr. in *Critical Essays on Joyce Carol Oates*, Linda W. Wagner. Boston, MA: G.K. Hall, 1979, pp. 49-60.

According to Fossum, Oates "may be the finest American novelist, man or woman, since Faulkner and

surely the best to appear in the past decade." He
credits her with "brilliantly illuminating the emotional
lives of her characters" but notes that each of her
novels deals with fundamentally the same emotions and
conflicts. Although Oates and her characters seem
preoccupied with control and order, "in her world,
the only order is that of art, the only one in control
the artist herself."

1130. Neubacher, Jim. "Violence: Some Sadism in 2 Cool
       Novels." *Detroit Free Press Sunday Magazine*
       (Dec. 28, 1975): 5-B.

No annotation.

1131. Oates, Joyce Carol. "Many Are Called ..." in
       American Poets in 1976, William Heyen, ed.
       Indianapolis: Bobbs-Merrill, 1976, pp. 202-211.

For annotation, see # 944.

1132. Janssens, G.A.M. *De Amerikaanse roman 1950-1975.*
       Amsterdam: Athenaeum-Polak & Van Gennep,
       1976, pp. 239-241.

A short overview of Oates's career which mentions
only two of her novels. *A Garden of Earthly Delights*
and *Do with Me What You Will.* The ingredients of
Oates's fiction are an intuitive, non-selective use of
language, melodramatic effects, pathological behavior
and violence, and a realistic, detailed rendering of
the world. This writer notes that Oates has improved
technically between the two novels.

1133. Silva, Fred. In *Contemporary Novelists*, 2nd ed.,
       James Vinson, ed. New York: St. Martin's
       Press, 1976, pp. 1046-1049.

Although Silva praises Oates for writing excellent
short stories, he finds fault with each of her novels.
For example, he considers *them* her best novel, but
feels it is uneven because of "fragmentary structure
and unclear motivation." He criticizes her other
novels for having "arbitrary violence," uncertain
characterization, and contrived plot twists, and
suggests that she has yet to write a "truly unified
novel."

1134. Allen, Mary Inez. "The Terrified Women of Joyce Carol Oates" in *The Necessary Blankness: Women in Major American Fiction of the Sixties.* Urbana: University of Illinois Press, 1976, pp. 133-159.

Allen's work is polemical: the book is about the misogyny she finds in male-dominated contemporary American fiction, and the ways in which American women writers portray the predicament of women in a sexist world. Her point about Oates is simple: Oates is "a master at depicting women's anxieties of many sorts, and she makes a striking contribution to our understanding of contemporary America as seen by women. Here is an author to read if one dares to know the particular fear there is in being a woman--here and now--even when the surface of life may appear as familiar and safe as a supermarket on a sunny day." The bulk of the essay is a review of Oates's women and the internal and external miseries they face: a sense of emptiness and intellectual inadequacy, the sexual repression or indifference, the threat of violence against them, their manipulation by the world. Nothing surprising is said about any of these characters: the object is to note a bold pattern in Oates's fiction by looking at many of them at once.

1135. Harter, Carol. "America As 'Consumer Garden': The Nightmare Vision of Joyce Carol Oates." Paper presented at Ohio-Indiana American Studies Meeting, Spring 1974. *Revue des Langues Vivantes*, Bicentennial Issue (1976): 171-187.

According to Harter, "Oates's milieu is 'Everywhere U.S.A.'" with the "American landscape often manifest[ing] itself as grotesque." Harter suggests Oates has developed a mythic mode for *them* and *Wonderland* and has become "a creator of modern fable and a shaper of twentieth century American myth."

1136. Basney, Lionel. "Joyce Carol Oates: Wit and Fear." *Christianity Today*, 20 (June 18, 1976): 13-14 and (July 2, 1976): 20-21.

In a two-part article, Basney labels Oates as "clearly high brow" but not "an academic writer." Her criticism is that of a working artist "as she tends to find in her subjects the ways in which they bear a vision like her own." He suggests she is a wit, but a "wit of the nerves, and not of words" and thinks her style is "disquieting and creative," although it often becomes rhetorical.

1137. Greenwalt, Julie. "Joyce Carol Oates Leads Two
      Lives: Dark Lady of U.S. Fiction and Shy
      Faculty Wife." *People*, 6 (Nov. 15, 1976): 66, 68.

      Chatty and obsolete biographical sketch.

1138. Kraus, Siegfried Erich. "Joyce Carol Oates in Search
      of the Sense of Human Life." *Arbeiten aus
      Anglistik und Amerikanistik*, 3 (1977): 39-65.

      According to Kraus, Jules in *them* is "perhaps Oates's
      heroic ideal" because he is "on the verge of
      transcending the old, egocentered man." Kraus
      suggests Oates offers three complex issues as
      alternatives to existentialism: hope, "homelife in a
      peaceful secure domain," and the "means of
      communication between men to overcome dangerous
      conflicts."

1139. Hollowell, John. *Fact and Fiction: The New Journalism
      and the Nonfiction Novel*. Chapel Hill: University
      of North Carolina Press, 1977, p. 17.

      Very brief mention.

1140. Goodman, Charlotte. "Women and Madness in the
      Fiction of Joyce Carol Oates." *Women and
      Literature*, 5, ii (1977): 17-28.

      Goodman suggests that Oates's fiction deserves more
      attention from the feminist critics because "it
      dramatizes forcefully some of the factors that
      contribute to the despair and psychological
      disintegration of contemporary women." Oates explores
      the question "What does it mean to be a woman?" and
      illustrates the harmful effects of marriage, children,
      and sexual relationships.

1141. Petite, Joseph. "Out of the Machine: Joyce Carol
      Oates and the Liberation of Women." *Kansas
      Quarterly*, 9, ii (Spring 1977): 75-79.

      Petite calls Oates a "liberationist" because "she
      rejects all stereotyping that destroys individuality."
      However, Petite finds it odd that so few of Oates's
      women characters "break out of the machine of
      femaleness" and become individuals.

1142. Jeannotte, M. Sharon. "The Horror Within: The Short
      Stories of Joyce Carol Oates." *Sphinx*, 2, iv
      (Summer 1977): 25-36.

Jeannotte sees Oates's fiction as part of the evolution of the Gothic/Romantic genre. However, Oates's characterization is not traditional Gothic in that she "never allows her characters to escape unscathed or to profit from their experiences by becoming 'better' persons."

1143. Leff, Leonard J. "The Center of Violence in Joyce Carol Oates's Fiction." *NMAL: Notes on Modern American Literature*, 2, i (Winter 1977): item 9.

Two-page Freudian reading of Oates: women cause all the trouble. "Oates depicts women who disown their biological heritage--their power to give man not only life but succor." The point is too broad and too briefly discussed to be sustained.

1144. Joslin, Michael. "Joyce Carol Oates" in *American Novelists Since World War II*, Jeffrey Hetterman and Richard Layman, eds. Detroit: Gale Research, 1978, pp. 371-381. (Dictionary of Literary Biography; 2)

This biographical, critical, and bibliographical survey of Oates contains many quotations from her own commentary. Joslin provides short summaries of each novel's plot and structure, its critical reception, and its autobiographical connections, but he includes few of his own perceptions. He devotes only one paragraph to her short stories, which he considers "her finest works," and a paragraph each to her poetry, "shorthand, instantaneous accounts of a state of mind that might have been treated in a 400-page work," and her critical writing, which while not 'careful, exhaustive scholarship,' is erudite and fresh."

1145. Creighton, Joanne V. "Unliberated Women in Joyce Carol Oates's Fiction." *World Literature Written in English*, 17, i (Apr. 1978): 165-175.
Repr. in *Critical Essays on Joyce Carol Oates*, Linda W. Wagner. Boston, MA: G.K. Hall, 1979, pp. 149-156.

Creighton notes that recurrent female types in Oates are Mothers and Daughters, with more attention paid to the Daughters who have "little resilience and are incapable of dealing with the unexpected." Oates presents women as "locked into the destructive form of Kali, unliberated into the totality of female

selfhood." Although the vast majority of Oates's
women do not have careers, those who do "pay for
their professional success with precious coin, their
stifled sexual identities." Oates explores "the sexual
roots of female non-liberation."

1146. Waller, G.F. "Through Obsession to Transcendence:
       The Recent Work of Joyce Carol Oates." *World
       Literature Written in English*, 17, i (Apr. 1978):
       176-180.
       Repr. in *Critical Essays on Joyce Carol Oates*,
       Linda W. Wagner. Boston, MA: G.K. Hall, 1979,
       pp. 161-173.

In reviewing Oates's work between 1975-78, Waller
notes a "more radically apocalyptic strain" in which
obsessive violence becomes a means for transcendence.
He sees Oates "moving closer to an Eastern doctrine
of "annatta" or "niratina" (non-ego) where negation
becomes the means to overcoming the bondage of
desire and egocentricity." He calls this period a
transitional stage and notes that her style is uneven
and experimental.

1147. Grant, Mary Kathryn. "The Language of Tragedy and
       Violence" in *Critical Essays on Joyce Carol
       Oates*, Linda W. Wagner. Boston, MA: G.K.
       Hall, 1979, pp. 61-76.

Grant's essay is a chapter excerpted from her volume
The Tragic Vision of Joyce Carol Oates. She argues
that Oates uses a variety of rhetorical strategies to
create "a fiction permeated with violence and
tragedy," and concerns herself with the details of
that technique in *them, A Garden of Earthly Delights*,
and *Do with Me What You Will*.

1148. Stevens, Peter. "The Poetry of Joyce Carol Oates" in
       Critical Essays on Joyce Carol Oates, Linda W.
       Wagner. Boston, MA: G.K. Hall, 1979, pp.
       123-147.

A diffident, impressionistic piece which at crucial
moments flees into platitudes. Oates's poetry is "a
picture of modern meaninglessness" punctuated with
"flashes of hope; "she offers "details of this
remorseless insignificance of life;"and although the
poetry "falls into prosiness with lines that display
flabby rhythms, with images that remain vague, with

structures too jagged to reveal the ideas," it "expresses a consistent vision," and demands "to be read on its own terms."

1149. Wagner, Linda W. "Joyce Carol Oates: The Changing Shapes of Her Realities" in *Critical Essays on Joyce Carol Oates*, Linda W. Wagner. Boston, MA: G.K. Hall, 1979, pp. xvii-xxxi. Repr. in *Great Lakes Review*, 5, ii (Winter 1979): 15-23. Repr. in *American Modern: Essays in Fiction and Poetry*, Linda W. Wagner. Port Washington, NY; London: Kennikat Press, 1980, pp. 67-75. (National University Publications)

Wagner notes that in Oates's fiction the "assumption that the artist is in control is absent." The artist is seen as recorder, not judge. Oates's world view "recognizes the primacy of emotion over reason [and] emphasizes the reality of human passion." Her point of view, however, often distances the reader, especially in her early fiction. In a survey of Oates's critical reception, Wagner traces the uneven response from the early enthusiastic praise to the present trend of "faint praise."

1150. Van Heerswynghels, Judith. "Le discours de la violence dans la fiction de Joyce Carol Oates" in *Le discours de la violence dans la culture américaine*, ouvrage dirigé par Régis Durand. Lille: Publications de l'Université de Lille III, 1979, pp. 49-70.

Commonplaces about the violence in Oates's fiction, with extravagant claims for its proportions in the fiction, and for its consequence. The violence is "of cosmic dimensions"; everything, including "the most banal experience" constitutes "menace"; violence, "inseparably linked" to language, suffuses Oates's fiction, her "personal vision," and her conception of "real America."

1151. Tucker, Jean M. "The American Mother in 3 Stories: Freeman, Cather and Oates." *Doshisha Literature*, 29 (1979): 116-133.

In a comparison of three short stories about mothers, Tucker notes that there is very little real difference in the mothers depicted by Cather and Oates, although the experiences of American women have certainly changed in the thirty years separating the stories. Each mother is "still shut up in the house with the children, still feeling strangely cheated."

1152. Lundkvist, Arthur. *Fantasi med Realism: om nutida utländsk skönlitteratur* (Realistic Imagination: On Presentday Foreign Literature). Stockholm: Liber Förlag, 1979, pp. 143-156.

No annotation.

1153. Janeway, Elizabeth. "Women's Literature" in *Harvard Guide to Contemporary American Writing*, Daniel Hoffman, ed. Cambridge; London: Belknap Press, 1979, pp. 377-381.

Janeway sees Oates's assessment of humankind as being part of the same tradition as Dostoyevsky. Her characters are constantly torn between achieving success, which in Oates's world becomes equated with sickness, and wanting a stable identity, which she implies must be sacrificed to achieve success. The main difference between Oates and Dostoyevsky is that she "adds the flavor of women's testimony." She tries to explain how and why women become hysterical. Oates, typical of many women writers, analyzes what male writers have considered only "feminine traits of character" by "splitting open the atom to show us the mechanism inside."

1154. Mickelson, Anne Z. "Sexual Love in the Fiction of Joyce Carol Oates" in *Reaching Out: Sensitivity and Order in Recent American Fiction by Women*, Anne Z. Mickelson. Metuchen: Scarecrow Press, 1979, pp. 15-34.

Mickelson views the "Oedipal Conflict" as the fundamental theme in Oates's fiction. She criticizes Oates for her lack of "psychic development" of her women characters who often exist as "a peg on which to hang a concept, for example, sexual warfare." She blames Oates's problems as a writer on her "working out her own fears and obsessions through the medium of fiction."

1155. Freese, Peter. "Ueber die Schwierigkeiten des Erwachsenwerdens: Amerikanische 'Stories of Initiation' von Nathaniel Hawthorne bis Joyce Carol Oates" in *Die Short Story im Englisch-*

unterricht der Sekundarstufe II: Theorie und Praxis, Peter Freese, Horst Groene, Liesel Hermes, hrsg. Paderborn: Schöningh, 1979, pp. 206-255.

Very brief mention of Oates in a long and astoundingly schematic study of the structure of initiation stories: Freese mentions only *Where Are You Going, Where Have You Been?*, with a suggestion as to which of his archetypes it resembles.

1156. Barza, Steven. "Joyce Carol Oates: Naturalism and the Aberrant Response." *Studies in American Fiction*, 7 (1979): 141-151.

Although Barza states that Oates "is faithful to the spirit of Naturalism," he asserts that she "radically disrupts their assumption of normal stimulus-response connections." He suggests her most prevalent "stimulus-response dysfunction" is one involving a strong response with negligible or no stimulus.

1157. Pinsker, Sanford. "Joyce Carol Oates and the New Naturalism." *Southern Review* (Baton Rouge), n.s., 15, i (Winter 1979): 52-63.

Pinsker notes that Oates has certain "affinities" with both a "Naturalistic aesthetic" and contemporary writers such as Heller and Pynchon. He thinks she achieves a hypnotic effect by blending naturalistic detail and melodramatic atmosphere. Her stated ambition of writing "the socio-moral history of every person now living in the United States" places her "squarely in Zola's company."

1158. Batman, Alex. "Joyce Carol Oates" in *American Poets Since World War II*, Donald Greiner, ed. Detroit: Gale Research, 1980, pp. 99-102. (Dictionary of Literary Biography; 5)

Although Batman finds that Oates's poetry is not the "strength of her canon," he sees the same themes operating here as in her fiction, especially the "existence of savagery in civilized society." He calls *The Fabulous Beasts* Oates's "most accomplished work," and *Women Whose Lives Are Food, Men Whose Lives Are Money* the darkest.

1159.   Oates, Joyce Carol. "A Special Message to the
        Members of the First Edition Society" in
        Bellefleur (# 3).

        For annotation, see # 1001.

1160.   Manske, Eva. "Individual and Society in Contemporary
        American Fiction." *Zeitschrift für Anglistik und
        Amerikanistik*, 4 (1980): 321.

        A dozen novels, including Oates's *them*, are cursorily
        dealt with as attacking contemporary American
        society. A reductive reading, endlessly and predicta-
        bly belabored.

1161.   Bender, Eileen T. "Between the Categories: Recent
        Short Fiction by Joyce Carol Oates." *Studies in
        Short Fiction*, 17, iv (Fall 1980): 415-423.

        According to Bender, a "continuing concern" in
        Oates's short fiction is the "predicament of the artist"
        who is seen as a "medium for both the voiceless and
        the articulate." Bender considers two collections--
        The Poisoned Kiss and *The Hungry Ghosts*--as
        "fragmented novels" unified in theme and setting and
        offering a coherent vision.

1162.   Dong, Stella. "Five Bestselling Writers Recall Their
        First Novels." *Publishers' Weekly*, 218 (Oct. 10,
        1980): 47-48.

        Oates reports that she wrote *By the North Gate* while
        feeling lonely and cut off in Bowmar, Texas.

1163.   Friedman, Ellen G. "Joyce Carol Oates" in *American
        Women Writers*, vol. 3, Lina Mainiero, ed. New
        York: Ungar, 1981, pp. 281-285.

        In a brief survey of Oates's life and fiction with
        emphasis on the plots and themes of each novel,
        Friedman argues that in Oates's later fiction (after
        1973) "form is theme." For example, she feels the
        isolated consciousness in *The Assassins* reflects each
        character's isolation "from the living totality of
        being." She feels more critical attention should be
        given to Oates's "careful structure" and "moral
        vision."

1164.   Tolomeo, Diane. "Joyce Carol Oates" in *American
        Writers*, A. Walton Litz, ed. Suppl. 2, part 2.
        New York: Scribner's, 1981, pp. 503-527.

Tolomeo notes that the tension between body and spirit "rages" through most of Oates's novels, although there is "no glaring dichotomy" between the two. In fact, a character's physical state often reflects the state of his soul. She feels Oates's most durable theme is "the corruption of our world and the plea that we open our eyes to what we are destroying." She also suggests that Oates's later stories and characters "often serve as glosses on each other."

1165. Labrie, Ross. "Love and Survival in Joyce Carol Oates." *Greyfriar*, 22 (1981): 17-26.

Although Labrie labels Oates a naturalist, he sees several differences. For example, violence is not only an "inevitable catastrophe," it is an affirmation in her work. Also Oates "is impressed with the need for values within the natural world." For her, survival is both a biological and a spiritual triumph.

1166. Yamamoto, Tetsu. "Joyce Carol Oates no 10 nenkan: Sono Higeki no Shūen (Ten Years of Oates: Surroundings of Her Tragedy) in *Yamakawa Kōzō Kyōju Taikan Kinen Ronbunshū*. Toyonaka: [n.pub.] 1981, pp. 547-560.

No annotation.

1167. Oates, Joyce Carol. "Why Is Your Writing So Violent?" *New York Times Book Review*, 86 (Mar. 29, 1981): 15, 35.

For annotation, see # 1022.

1168. Griffin, Bryan F. "Panic Among the Philistines: The Collapse of the Literary Establishment." *Harper's*, 263 (Aug. 1981): 48.

Griffin's major objection to contemporary writers seem to be the overuse of superlatives in referring to themselves, each other, and the times. He finds and quotes, out of context, a few awkward encomiums from Oates; but Bryan is after whole legions of writers--Irving, Doctorow, Barth, Styron, Mailer, Capote, Updike--any point he might have to make gets lost in such generalizations.

1169. Oates, Joyce Carol. "Luxury of Being Despised." *Bennington Review*, 13 (June 1982).

Repr. in *First Person Singular* (# 1077),   pp.
194–197 (slightly different version).

No annotation.

1170. Oates, Joyce Carol. "Stories That Define Me: The
Making of a Writer." *New York Times Book
Review*, 87 (July 11, 1982): 1, 15–16.

For annotation, see # 1032.

1171. Donoghue, Denis. "Wonder Woman." *New York Review
of Books*, 29 (Oct. 21, 1982): 14, 16–17.

In a very negative review, Donoghue labels Oates "a
Gothic romancer," a "psychological novelist," and an
"essentialist." He suggests the Gothic element is her
substitute for tragedy. He criticizes her tor
producing "characters who have no responsibility for
the objective world, having no relation to it." He
asserts he doesn't trust the teller's "hope of altering
the world" because her tales say that "life is so
appalling, it exhilarates." He also criticizes Oates for
forcing "words into the pretense of being feelings."

1172. Robison, James C. In *The American Short Story:
1945–1980: A Critical History*, Gordon Weaver,
ed. Boston, MA: Twayne, 1983, pp. 86–89.
(Twayne's Critical History of the Short Story)

In this brief survey of her short stories, Weaver
applauds Oates's skillful use of dialogue and setting.
However, he criticizes her for raising issues which
she seldom probes or clarifies and for not offering a
"clear distinction between what her characters see
and what their creator sees."

1173. Oates, Joyce Carol. "(Woman) Writer" in *First Person
Singular* (# 1077), pp. 190–197.

For annotation, see # 1038.

1174. van Boheemen, Christel. "Joyce Carol Oates en de
droom van Amerika." *De Gids*, 146, i (1983):
71–78.

General discussion of Oates's achievement up to 1981,
stressing her mediumistic sensibility, her contribution
to the American Gothic tradition (especially in
Bellefleur) and her peculiar blending of facts and
fantasy to convey the psychological essence of

American dreams and nightmares (focusing on *Angel of Light*).
(Annotation by Joris Duytschaever)

1175. Reed, J.D. "Postfeminism: Playing for Keeps." *Time*, 121 (Jan. 10, 1983): 60.

Reed reports Oates "outdistanced feminism long before it was fashionable to do so, taking her themes from headlines." Oates explains her lack of identification with feminine fantasy: "I learned long ago that being Lewis Carroll was infinitely more exciting than being Alice."

1176. Oates, Joyce Carol. "A Special Message to the Members of the First Edition Society" in *Mysteries of Winterthurn* (# 12).

For annotation, see # 1050.

(*) Reprinted or partly reprinted in *Contemporary Literary Criticism*, vol. 3, Carolyn Riley, ed. Detroit: Gale Research, 1975 (# 1126).

REVIEWS AND REVIEW ESSAYS

ACCOMPLISHED DESIRES (# 19)

1177. Evans, Elizabeth. "Joyce Carol Oates' 'Patient Griselda.'" *Notes on Contemporary Literature*, 6, iv (1976): 205.

ALL THE GOOD PEOPLE I'VE LEFT BEHIND (# 23)

1178. *Choice*, 16 (July–Aug. 1979): 670.

ANGEL FIRE (# 439)

1179. *Library Journal*, 97 (Dec. 1, 1972): 3936.

1180. *Publishers' Weekly*, 203 (Feb. 19, 1973): 78.

1181. Vendler, Helen. "The Ideas and Words, but Not the Surfaces and Cadences." *New York Times Book Review*, 78 (Apr. 1, 1973): 7-8.

1182. Marvin, Patricia H. *Library Journal*, 98 (Apr. 15, 1973): 1290.

1183. Kameen, Paul. *Best Sellers*, 33 (May 15, 1973): 82-83.

1184. *Choice*, 10 (June 1973): 622.

1185. *Virginia Quarterly Review*, 49, iii (Summer 1973): cx.

1186. Perloff, Marjorie. "Floral Decorations for Bananas." *Parnassus*, 2, i (Fall-Winter 1973): 133-138.

1187. Young, Vernon. *Hudson Review*, 26, iv (Winter 1973-74): 726-727.

1188. Cotter, James Finn. *America*, 130 (Feb. 2, 1974): 78.

ANGEL OF LIGHT (# 1)

1189. *Kirkus Reviews*, 49 (June 15, 1981): 758.

1190. *Publishers' Weekly*, 219 (June 19, 1981): 94.

1191. *Booklist*, 77 (July 1, 1981): 1369.

1192. W[illiamson], C[hilton, Jr.]. *National Review*, 33 (July 24, 1981): 850.

1193. Hobson, Laura Z. *Saturday Review*, 8 (Aug. 1981): 44-45.

1194. *Washingtonian*, 16 (Aug. 1981): 17.

1195. Edwards, Thomas R. "The House of Atreus Now." *New York Times Book Review*, 86 (Aug. 16, 1981): 1, 18.

1196. Wood, Susan. "Vengeance in Washington." *Washington Post Book World* (Aug. 16, 1981): 5, 10, 12.

1197. Clemons, Walter. "Wild Oates." *Newsweek*, 98 (Aug. 17, 1981): 74.

1198. Skow, John. "Deafening Roar." *Time*, 118 (Aug. 17, 1981): 83.

1199. Clapperton, Jane. *Cosmopolitan*, 191 (Sept. 1981): 24.

1200. *Saturday Review*, 8 (Sept. 1981): 79.

1201. Soete, Mary. *Library Journal*, 106 (Sept. 1, 1981): 1648.

1202. Phillipson, John. *Best Sellers*, 41 (Oct. 1981): 248.

1203. "When Will There Be a DC Novel That Shows What This City Is ?" *Washingtonian*, 17 (Oct. 1981): 19.

1204. Croghan, L.A. *Wilson Library Bulletin*, 56, ii (Oct. 1981): 145.

1205. *New Yorker*, 57 (Oct. 5, 1981): 192.

1206. Coale, Samuel [C.]. *America*, 145 (Nov. 21, 1981): 325.

1207. Stuewe, Paul. "Imports: Sex in Venice, Essays from Bloomsbury and Uris's Jerusalem." *Quill and Quire*, 48 (Jan. 1982): 39.

1208. Kemp, Peter. "Rottenness Abounding." *Times Literary Supplement*, 4113 (Jan. 29, 1982): 105.

1209. Greenwell, Bill. "Black Cackling." *New Statesman*, 103 (Feb. 5, 1982): 25-26.

1210. Moorehead, Caroline. "Wild Oates." *Spectator*, 248 (Feb. 6, 1982): 26.

1211. Lee, Hermione. "In the Land of the Dead." *Observer* (Feb. 7, 1982): 28.

1212. Mellors, John. "Versions of Hell." *Listener*, 107 (Feb. 11, 1982): 24.

1213. Brittain, Victoria. "Recent Fiction." *Illustrated London News*, 270 (Mar. 1982): 51.

1214. Poland, Lynn M. *Christian Century*, 99 (Mar. 3, 1982): 248.

1215. Farnsworth, Jane. *Quarry* (Kingston, ON), 31, ii (Spring 1982): 83-86.

1216. Curran, Ronald. *World Literature Today*, 56, ii (Spring 1982): 339.

1217. *Publishers' Weekly*, 222 (July 16, 1982): 77.

1218. *New York Times Book Review*, 87 (Aug. 29, 1982): 19.

1219. Arnow, Harriette Simpson. "Families without Heroes or Heroines." *Michigan Quarterly Review*, 21, iv (Fall 1982): 677-679.

1220. Roberts, Audrey. *National Forum*, 63 (Winter 1983): 42.

1221. Halio, Jay L. "Contemplation, Fiction, and the Writer's Sensibility." *Southern Review* (Baton Rouge), n.s., 19, i (Winter 1983): 209-210.

ANONYMOUS SINS AND OTHER POEMS (# 441)

1222. Publishers' Weekly, 196 (Aug. 18, 1969): 69.

1223. Avant, John Alfred. Library Journal, 94 (Dec. 1, 1969): 4440.

1224. Bedient, Calvin. "Vivid and Dazzling." Nation, 209 (Dec. 1, 1969): 610.
       Repr. in Critical Essays on Joyce Carol Oates, Linda W. Wagner. Boston, MA: G.K. Hall, 1979, pp. 24-26.

1225. Ratti, John. "In the American Idiom." New Leader, 52 (Dec. 8, 1969): 10-11.

1226. Mazzaro, Jerome. "Oh Women, Oh Men." Modern Poetry Studies, 1, i (1970): 39-41.

1227. Stevens, Peter. Canadian Forum, 49 (Jan. 1970): 243-244.

1228. Walsh, Chad. "'Lyrical Sanity' and Some Other Styles of Poetry." Washington Post Book World (Mar. 8, 1970): 7.

1229. Carruth, Hayden. Hudson Review, 23, i (Spring 1970): 182.

1230. French, Roberts W. "The Novelist-Poet." Prairie Schooner, 44, ii (Summer 1970): 177-178.

1231. Choice, 7 (July-Aug. 1970): 686.

1232. McGann, Jerome. "Poetry and Truth." Poetry, 118, iii (Dec. 1970): 195-203.

1233. Virginia Quarterly Review, 46, i (Winter 1970): xiii.

THE ASSASSINS: A BOOK OF HOURS (# 2)

1234. Kirkus Reviews, 43 (Sept. 15, 1975): 1084.

1235. Publishers' Weekly, 208 (Sept. 29, 1975): 42.

1236. Prescott, Peter S. "Varieties of Madness." Newsweek, 86 (Oct. 27, 1975): 99B, 100, 100D.

1237. *Booklist*, 72 (Nov. 1, 1975): 350.

1238. Juhasz, Suzanne. *Library Journal*, 100 (Nov. 15, 1975): 2174.

1239. O'Hara, J.D. *New York Times Book Review*, 80 (Nov. 23, 1975): 10, 14, 18.

1240. Klausler, Alfred P. *Christian Century*, 92 (Dec. 17, 1975): 1164-1165.

1241. Cushman, Kathleen. "The Assassins: A Novel of Murder Probes Three Lives." *National Observer*, 15 (Jan. 10, 1976): 19.

1242. Weiss, Brian. *Best Sellers*, 35 (Feb. 1976): 334.

1243. Thurman, Judith. "Joyce Carol Oates: Caviar and a Big Mac." *Ms.*, 8 (Feb. 1976): 42-43.

1244. *Time*, 107 (Feb. 23, 1976): 65.
      Repr. in *Critical Essays on Joyce Carol Oates*, Linda W. Wagner. Boston, MA: G.K. Hall, 1979, p. 38.

1245. Kramer, Hilton. "Naipaul's 'Guerrillas' and Oates's 'Assassins.'" *Commentary*, 61, iii (Mar. 1976): 54-57.

1246. Grosskurth, Phyllis. "In Extremis." *Canadian Forum*, 56 (May 1976): 33-34.

1247. *Choice*, 13 (May 1976): 370.

1248. *Publishers' Weekly*, 210 (Aug. 30, 1976): 336.

1249. Coyne, Patricia S. "Thinking Man's Breakfast." *National Review*, 28 (Sept. 3, 1976): 965-966.

1250. Cooke, Michael G. "Recent Novels: Women Bearing Violence." *Yale Review*, 66, i (Autumn 1976): 148-150.

1251. McLellan, Joseph. *Washington Post Book World* (Nov. 14, 1976): L5.

1252. *Kliatt Paperback Book Guide*, 11 (Winter 1977): 7.

1253. Sullivan, Walter. "Gifts, Prophecies and Prestidigita-
      tions: Fictional Frameworks, Fictional Modes."
      Sewanee Review, 85, i (Winter 1977): 116-117.

1254. *Virginia Quarterly Review*, 53, i (Winter 1977): 17.

1255. Pollock, John. "The Nouveau-Lipsian Style of Joyce
      Carol Oates." *San Jose Studies*, 4, ii (1978):
      32-40.

1256. *Thought*, 55 (Dec. 1980): 478-479.

AT THE SEMINARY (# 35)

1257. Fowler, Doreen A. "Oates's 'At the Seminary.'"
      Explicator, 41, i (Fall 1982): 62-64.

BELLEFLEUR (# 3)

1258. *Kirkus Reviews*, 48 (June 1, 1980): 733.

1259. *Booklist*, 76 (June 15, 1980): 1464.

1260. *Publishers' Weekly*, 217 (June 20, 1980): 72.

1261. Soete, Mary. *Library Journal*, 105 (July 1980): 1541.

1262. Gardner, John. "The Strange Real World." *New York
      Times Book Review*, 85 (July 20, 1980): 1, 21.

1263. Leonard, John. "Books of the Times." *New York
      Times*, 129 (July 21, 1980), sect. 3: 15, 436-438.

1264. Batchelor, John Calvin. "Hot News: Funny Oates."
      Village Voice, 25 (July 30-Aug. 5, 1980): 34.

1265. *Mademoiselle*, 86 (Aug. 1980): 64.

1266. Banks, Russell. "Joyce Carol Oates: In a Gothic
      Manor." *Washington Post Book World* (Aug. 17,
      1980): 4, 8, 14.

1267. *Time*, 116 (Aug. 25, 1980): 67.

1268. Milder, Phyllis. *Best Sellers*, 40 (Sept. 1980): 202.

1269. Leonard, John. "Bellefleur." *Books of the Times*, 3
      (Sept. 1980): 436.

1270. Cheesewright, Gordon. "Oates' Gothic Epic: Strange, Oppulent [sic]." *Christian Science Monitor*, 72 (Sept. 8, 1980): 16.

1271. Jackson, Marni. "Staring into the Shadows." *Maclean's*, 93 (Sept. 8, 1980): 56.

1272. *People*, 14 (Sept. 8, 1980): 8.

1273. Hill, Douglas. "Creative Tic Douloureux." *Books in Canada*, 9 (Oct. 1980): 18-19.

1274. Taliaferro, Frances. "Literary Gluttony." *Harper's*, 261 (Oct. 1980): 91.

1275. *Los Angeles*, 25 (Oct. 1980): 237.

1276. Stuewe, Paul. "American Thrillers: Firestarter, Brass, Diamonds, Brain 2000." *Quill and Quire*, 46 (Oct. 1980): 40.

1277. Murray, James G. *Critic* (Chicago), 39 (Dec. 1980): 4.

1278. Brady, Charles A. "Fantasy Represents an Escape into Reality: The Jam Pot & the Lembas." *Commonweal*, 107 (Dec. 5, 1980): 692-693.

1279. du Plessix Gray, Francine. *Commonweal*, 107 (Dec. 5, 1980): 696.

1280. Cooke, Judy. "Losing Innocence." *New Statesman*, 101 (Mar. 6, 1981): 22-23.

1281. Ackroyd, Peter. "A Family and Its Fortunes." *Sunday Times* (Mar. 8, 1981): 42.

1282. Wilson, A.N. "Gothic Pose." *Spectator*, 246 (Mar. 14, 1981): 19.

1283. Sage, Lorna. "Across the Gothic Drawbridge." *Observer* (Mar. 15, 1981): 33.

1284. Cunningham, Valentine. "Counting up the Cost." *Times Literary Supplement*, 4068 (Mar. 20, 1981): 303.

1285. Kemp, Peter. "The Damaged Planet." *Listener*, 105 (Apr. 23, 1981): 549.

1286.   Clifford, Gay. "Magical Realism." *Quarto*, 18 (June 1981): 10-11.

1287.   *Publishers' Weekly*, 220 (July 10, 1981): 90.

1288.   *Observer* (July 19, 1981): 29.

1289.   *New York Times Book Review*, 86 (Sept. 6, 1981): 19.

1290.   *Changing Times*, 35 (Dec. 1981): 62.

1291.   *Virginia Quarterly Review*, 57, i (Winter 1981): 18.

1292.   Baroche, C. "Ça fait bien du monde la famille Bellefleur." *Quinzaine Littéraire*, 364 (1-15 févr. 1982): 8-9.

1293.   Lapierre, R. *Liberté*, 24, iv (juil.-août 1982): 94.

1294.   *Kliatt Paperback Book Guide*, 16 (Winter 1982): 14.

1295.   Curran, Ronald. *World Literature Today*, 56, i (Winter 1982): 114.

1296.   Karl, Frederick R. *American Fictions, 1940-1980.* New York: Harper & Row, 1983, pp. 546-549.

1297.   Gellerfelt, M. *Bonniers Litterära Magasin*, 52, i (Feb. 1983): 64.

1298.   Coale, Samuel C. "Marriage in Contemporary American Literature: The Mismatched Marriages of Manichean Minds." *Thought*, 58 (Mar. 1983): 116-117.

THE BEST AMERICAN SHORT STORIES 1979: SELECTED FROM US AND CANADIAN MAGAZINES (Joyce Carol Oates, ed.) (# 847)

1299.   Burke, Jeffrey. "Ineffable Pleasures." *Harper's*, 259 (Sept. 1979): 99-100.

1300.   *Publishers' Weekly*, 216 (Sept. 3, 1979): 89.

1301.   Price, R. *New York Times Book Review*, 84 (Nov. 4, 1979): 14, 49.

1302.   Gullason, Thomas A. *Studies in Short Fiction*, 18, i (Winter 1981): 89-90.

A BLOODSMOOR ROMANCE (# 4)

1303. *Booklist*, 78 (July 1982): 1395.

1304. *Kirkus Reviews*, 50 (July 15, 1982): 819.

1305. *Publishers' Weekly*, 222 (July 30, 1982): 61.

1306. Mitchell, Sally. *Library Journal*, 107 (Aug. 1982): 1482.

1307. Wolcott, James. "Stop Me Before I Write Again: Six Hundred More Pages by Joyce Carol Oates." *Harper's*, 265 (Sept. 1982): 67-69.

1308. Johnson, Diane. "Balloons and Abductions." *New York Times Book Review*, 87 (Sept. 5, 1982): 1, 15-16.

1309. Disch, Thomas M. "Joyce Carol Oates' Three-Quarter-Mile Antimacassar." *Washington Post Book World* (Sept. 12, 1982): 3-4.

1310. *People*, 18 (Sept. 13, 1982): 12.

1311. Broyard, Anatole. "Elegant Balloon." *New York Times*, 132 (Sept. 18, 1982): 12.

1312. *Los Angeles Times Book Review* (Sept. 19, 1982): 1.

1313. Prescott, Peter S. "Romantic Agony." *Newsweek*, 100 (Sept. 20, 1982): 91-92.

1314. *New Yorker*, 58 (Sept. 27, 1982): 145-146.

1315. Bosworth, Patricia. "Another Wonderland." *Working Woman*, 7 (Oct. 1982): 138-139.

1316. Blake, Patricia. "Antimacassar." *Time*, 120 (Oct. 4, 1982): 78-79, 81.

1317. *West Coast Review of Books*, 8 (Nov. 1982): 31.

1318. *Best Sellers*, 42 (Dec. 1982): 330.

1319. *New York Times Book Review*, 87 (Dec. 5, 1982): 36.

1320. Glastonbury, Marion. "Tableaux." *New Statesman*, 105 (Jan. 28, 1983): 26.

1321. Mars-Jones, Adam. "Gilding the Unmentionables." *Times Literary Supplement*, 4165 (Jan. 28, 1983): 79.

1322. King, Francis. "Melodrama." *Spectator*, 250 (Jan. 29, 1983): 24.

1323. Sage, Lorna. "Spoils of Erotic Parody." *Observer* (Jan. 30, 1983): 47.

1324. Cadogan, Mary. *Books and Bookmen*, 28 (Feb. 1983): 33.

1325. Dillin, Gay Andrews. *Christian Science Monitor*, 75 (Feb. 11, 1983): B3.

1326. *Virginia Quarterly Review*, 59, ii (Spring 1983): 58.

1327. Curran, Ronald. *World Literature Today*, 57, ii (Spring 1983): 290.

1328. *Publishers' Weekly*, 224 (Aug. 5, 1983): 90.

1329. *New York Times Book Review*, 88 (Aug. 21, 1983): 27.

BY THE NORTH GATE (# 61)

1330. Frankel, Haskel. *Saturday Review*, 46 (Oct. 26, 1963): 45.

1331. Kauffmann, Stanley. "Violence amid Gentility." *New York Times Book Review*, 68 (Nov. 10, 1963): 4, 61.

1332. Spector, Robert Donald. "The Chin Stays Up." *Book Week* (Nov. 17, 1963): 32.

1333. *Library Journal*, 88 (Dec. 15, 1963): 4873.

1334. Duus, Louise. "The Population of Eden: J.C. Oates' 'By the North Gate.'" *Critique*, 7, ii (1964): 176-177.

1335. Ylvisaker, Miriam. *Library Journal*, 89 (Jan. 1, 1964): 135.

1336. *Time*, 83 (Jan. 3, 1964): 80.

1337. Copeland, Edith. *Books Abroad*, 38 (Summer 1964): 313.

1338. McConkey, James. *Epoch*, 13, ii (Winter 1964): 171-172.
    Repr. in *Critical Essays on Joyce Carol Oates*, Linda W. Wagner. Boston, MA: G.K. Hall, 1979, pp. 3-4.

1339. *Publishers' Weekly*, 200 (Aug. 23, 1971): 82.

CHILDWOLD (# 5)

1340. *Publishers' Weekly*, 210 (Sept. 6, 1976): 57.

1341. *Booklist*, 73 (Nov. 1, 1976): 392.

1342. Pearson, Carol. *Library Journal*, 101 (Nov. 15, 1976): 2394-2395.

1343. Z[immerman], P[aul] D. "Blurred Vision." *Newsweek*, 88 (Nov. 15, 1976): 115.

1344. Hendin, Josephine. *New York Times Book Review*, 81 (Nov. 28, 1976): 8, 30.

1345. Rubenstein, Roberta. "In 'Childwold' Art Imitates Life All Too Well." *National Observer*, 15 (Dec. 11, 1976): 18.

1346. Lardner, Susan. "Oracular Oates." *New Yorker*, 52 (Jan. 3, 1977): 74, 76.

1347. *Virginia Quarterly Review*, 53, ii (Spring 1977): 62.

1348. Wright, Helen. *Best Sellers*, 37 (Apr. 1977): 5.

1349. *Choice*, 14 (Apr. 1977): 202.

1350. Chayes, Irene H. *New Republic*, 176 (May 28, 1977): 36-37.

1351. Allen, Bruce. "Dream Journeys." *Sewanee Review*, 85, iv (Fall 1977): 693-694.

1352. Miller, Jane. "Speech for the Speechless." *Times Literary Supplement*, 3942 (Oct. 14, 1977): 1185.

1353.   Sage, Lorna. "The Pleasures of Betrayal." *Observer*
        (Oct. 23, 1977): 29.

1354.   *Publishers' Weekly*, 212 (Dec. 26, 1977): 66.

1355.   Hepburn, Neil. "Liaisons Curieuses." *Listener*, 99
        (Jan. 19, 1978): 94.

1356.   *New York Times Book Review*, 83 (Feb. 5, 1978): 41.

1357.   *Glamour*, 76 (Apr. 1978): 76.

1358.   *Kliatt Paperback Book Guide*, 12 (Fall 1978): 13.

1359.   Bender, Eileen T. "'Paedomorphic' Art: Joyce Carol
        Oates' 'Childwold'" in *Critical Essays on Joyce
        Carol Oates*, Linda W. Wagner. Boston, MA:
        G.K. Hall, 1979, pp. 117-122.

1360.   Cartano, Tony. "Joyce Carol Oates contre les
        'erreurs courantes.'" *Quinzaine Littéraire*, 298
        (16-31 mars 1979): 9.

CONTRARIES: ESSAYS (# 1019)

1361.   *Kirkus Reviews*, 49 (Jan. 1, 1981): 64.

1362.   *Publishers' Weekly*, 219 (Jan. 9, 1981): 68.

1363.   Flores, Ralph. *Library Journal*, 106 (Feb. 15, 1981):
        454.

1364.   *Booklist*, 77 (Mar. 1, 1981): 912-913.

1365.   Phillipson, John S. *Best Sellers*, 41 (June 1981): 110.

1366.   Kirby, David. *Dalhousie Review*, 61, ii (Summer 1981):
        384-386.

1367.   Phillips, Robert. "Overview of an Extraordinary Mind."
        Commonweal, 108 (Aug. 28, 1981): 475-476.

1368.   Earnshaw, Doris Smith. *World Literature Today*, 56, ii
        (Spring 1982): 342-343.

1369.   Woodcock, George. "Various Occasions." *Sewanee
        Review*, 90, iii (Summer 1982): 466-470.

CROSSING THE BORDER: FIFTEEN TALES (# 77)

1370. *Publishers' Weekly*, 209 (June 21, 1976): 86.

1371. Tyler, Anne. "Fiction-Trouble." *New York Times Book Review*, 81 (July 18, 1976): 8, 10.

1372. McLellan, Joseph. "Briefly Noted." *Washington Post Book World* (July 18, 1976): G4.

1373. Zimmerman, Paul D. "Stormy Passage." *Newsweek*, 88 (July 26, 1976): 74.

1374. Pearson, Carol. *Library Journal*, 101 (Aug. 1976): 1659.

1375. *Booklist*, 73 (Sept. 15, 1976): 122.

1376. Johnson, Greg. "Metaphysical Borders." *Southwest Review*, 61, iv (Autumn 1976): 438-441.

1377. *Choice*, 13 (Nov. 1976): 1139.

1378. Halewood, William H. "An American in Windsor." *Canadian Forum*, 56 (Dec. 1976-Jan. 1977): 55.

1379. Uphaus, Suzanne Henning. "Boundaries: Both Physical and Metaphysical." *Canadian Review of American Studies*, 8, ii (Fall 1977): 236-242.

1380. Garrett, George. "Fables and Fabliaux of Our Time." *Sewanee Review*, 85, i (Winter 1977): 106-107.

1381. Treglown, Jeremy. "Snob Story." *New Statesman*, 96 (July 7, 1978): 27.

1382. Hope, Mary. *Spectator*, 241 (July 8, 1978): 26.

1383. Beaver, Harold. "Heroes of Marriage." *Times Literary Supplement*, 3980 (July 14, 1978): 789.

1384. Lee, Hermione. "Desperate Women." *Observer* (July 30, 1978): 26.

1385. *Publishers' Weekly*, 214 (Oct. 2, 1978): 132.

1386. Mellors, John. "Irish Times." *Listener*, 101 (Jan. 4, 1979): 30-31.

1387. Michaelis, Rolf. "Lautlose Schreie, Joyce Carol Oates: 'Grenzüberschreitungen.'" *Die Zeit*, 10 (2. März 1979): 49.

1388. Heuff, Elsje. *Literair Paspoort*, 289 (juli-aug. 1979): 317.

1389. *Kliatt Paperback Book Guide*, 13 (Winter 1979): 27.

1390. Brown, Russell M. "Crossing Borders." *Essays on Canadian Writing*, 22 (Summer 1981): 154-168.

1391. Carrington, Ildikó de Papp. "The Emperor's New Clothes: Canadians through American Eyes." *Essays on Canadian Writing*, 22 (Summer 1981): 136-153.

CYBELE (# 7)

1392. Soete, Mary. *Library Journal*, 107 [i.e. 105] (Mar. 15, 1980): 745.

1393. *Booklist*, 76 (May 15, 1980): 1348.

1394. Wagner, Linda W. "Oates' 'Cybele.'" *Notes on Contemporary Literature*, 11, v (1981): 2-8.

DAISY (# 83)

1395. Steiner, Dorothea. "'Daisy': Woman As Oatesian Prototype and Persona" in *Die englische und amerikanische Kurzgeschichte*, Hans Bungert, ed. Darmstadt: Wissenschaftliche Buchgesellschaft, forthcoming.

THE DEAD (# 87)

1396. Taylor, Gordon O. "Joyce 'after' Joyce: Oates's 'The Dead.'" *Southern Review* (Baton Rouge), n.s., 19, iii (Summer 1983): 596-605.

DO WITH ME WHAT YOU WILL (# 8)

1397. Avant, John Alfred. *Library Journal*, 98 (Aug. 1973): 2336.

1398. *Kirkus Reviews*, 41 (Aug. 1, 1973): 833.

1399. *Publishers' Weekly*, 204 (Aug. 20, 1973): 83-84.

1400. Breslin, John B. *America*, 129 (Oct. 6, 1973): 250.

1401. Johnson, Diane. "Full of the Dickens." *Washington Post Book World* (Oct. 7, 1973): 3.

1402. Bedient, Calvin. "The Story of Sleeping Beauty and a Love That Is Like Hatred." *New York Times Book Review*, 78 (Oct. 14, 1973): 1, 18.

1403. Lehmann-Haupt, Christopher. "Stalking the Eternal Feminine." *New York Times*, 123 (Oct. 15, 1973): 35.

1404. [Graham, Don.] "Briefly Noted." *New Yorker*, 49 (Oct. 15, 1973): 185-186.

1405. Clemons, Walter. "Sleeping Princess." *Newsweek*, 82 (Oct. 15, 1973): 107.

1406. Duffy, Martha. "Power Vacuum." *Time*, 102 (Oct. 15, 1973): E3-E4.

1407. Shapiro, Charles. "Law and Love." *New Republic*, 169 (Oct. 27, 1973): 26-27.

1408. Sweeney, Gail White. "Mind-Rape." *Ms.*, 2 (Nov. 1973): 39-40, 42-43.

1409. Phillipson, John S. *Best Sellers*, 33 (Nov. 1, 1973): 339-340.

1410. Hill, W[illiam]. *America*, 129 (Nov. 17, 1973): 382.

1411. Cook, Bruce. "The Latest Oates: Entirely Too Much of a Good Thing." *National Observer*, 12 (Nov. 24, 1973): 25.

1412. DeMott, Benjamin. "'Now' Rituals." *Atlantic*, 232 (Dec. 1973): 127.

1413. *New York Times Book Review*, 78 (Dec. 2, 1973): 76.

1414. *Saturday Evening Post*, 246 (Jan. 1974): 72.

1415. Sanborn, Sara. "Two Major Novelists All by Herself." *Nation*, 218 (Jan. 5, 1974): 20-21.

Repr. in *Critical Essays on Joyce Carol Oates*, Linda W. Wagner. Boston, MA: G.K. Hall, 1979, pp. 32-35.

1416. Blythe, Ronald. "Spellbound." *Listener*, 91 (Jan. 10, 1974): 56.

1417. "The Heavy Mob." *Times Literary Supplement*, 3749 (Jan. 11, 1974): 25.

1418. Sage, Lorna. "Monstruous Intimacies." *Observer* (Jan. 13, 1974): 25.

1419. *Booklist*, 70 (Jan. 15, 1974): 517.

1420. Ackroyd, Peter. "A Modern Romance." *Spectator*, 232 (Jan. 19, 1974): 75.

1421. Ellmann, Mary. "Nolo Contendere." *New York Review of Books*, 20 (Jan. 24, 1974): 36-37.

1422. Colegate, Isabel. "A Year's Grief." *New Statesman*, 87 (Jan. 25, 1974): 121-122.

1423. *Choice*, 10 (Feb. 1974): 1868.

1424. Stanbrough, Jane. "Joyce Carol Oates' Carnal Transcendentalism." *Denver Quarterly*, 9, i (Spring 1974): 84-89.

1425. Allen, Bruce. *Hudson Review*, 27, i (Spring 1974): 122-124.

1426. Lemon, Lee T. "Eight Novels." *Prairie Schooner*, 48, i (Spring 1974): 77-78.

1427. *Contemporary Review*, 224 (Apr. 1974): 218.

1428. *New York Times Book Review*, 79 (Nov. 10, 1974): 38.

1429. Sullivan, Walter. "Old Age, Death, and Other Modern Landscapes: Good and Indifferent Fables for Our Time." *Sewanee Review*, 82, i (Winter 1974): 138-140.

1430. Burwell, Rose Marie. "The Process of Individuation As Narrative Structure: Joyce Carol Oates' 'Do with Me What You Will.'" *Critique*, 17, ii (1975): 93-106.

1431. Detweiler, Robert. "Jüngste Entwicklungen in der amerikanischen Erzählliteratur" in *Die amerikanische Literatur der Gegenwart*, Hans Bungert, ed. Stuttgart: Reclam, 1977, p. 222.

1432. Masinton, Martha & Masinton, Charles G. "Second-Class Citizenship: The Status of Women in Contemporary American Fiction" in *What Manner of Woman: Essays on English and American Life and Literature*, Marlene Springer, ed. New York: New York University Press, 1977, p. 312.

1433. Karl, Frederick R. *American Fictions, 1940-1980.* New York: Harper & Row, 1983, p. 420.

THE EDGE OF IMPOSSIBILITY (# 894)

1434. *Kirkus Reviews*, 40 (Mar. 1, 1972): 306-307.

1435. *Publishers' Weekly*, 201 (Mar. 6, 1972): 58-59.

1436. Park, Clara Claiborne. "A Dead Serious Vision." *Washington Post Book World* (Apr. 23, 1972): 10.

1437. Adams, Phoebe. *Atlantic*, 229 (May 1972): 112.

1438. Avant, John Alfred. *Library Journal*, 97 (May 1, 1972): 1718-1719.

1439. Weber, Brom. *Saturday Review*, 55 (June 10, 1972): 63-64.

1440. Balakian, Nona. "The Tragedy of Delusion." *New York Times*, 121 (June 12, 1972): 33.

1441. Sale, Roger. "A High Intelligence at Work Carelessly." *New York Times Book Review*, 77 (July 9, 1972): 23-24.

1442. *Booklist*, 69 (Oct. 1, 1972): 123.

1443. Goldman, Michael. "The Destructive Element." *Partisan Review*, 40, iii (1973): 529-533.

1444. *Choice*, 9 (Feb. 1973): 1585.

1445. McLellan, Joseph. *Washington Post Book World* (Dec. 16, 1973): 6.

1446. L[emon], L[ee] T. *Prairie Schooner*, 48, iv (Winter 1974-75): 368-369.

1447. Tanner, Tony. "Panic Stations." *New Statesman*, 91 (Mar. 12, 1976): 332.

1448. Carey, John. "Lucid Intervals." *Listener*, 95 (Mar. 25, 1976): 372-373.

1449. Chapman, Robert. *Books and Bookmen*, 21 (Sept. 1976): 61-62.

EXPENSIVE PEOPLE (# 9)

1450. *Publishers' Weekly*, 194 (Aug. 12, 1968): 47.

1451. *Kirkus Reviews*, 36 (Aug. 15, 1968): 929.

1452. Hoagland, Joan M. *Library Journal*, 93 (Oct. 15, 1968): 3800.

1453. Hicks, Granville. "What Is Reality?" *Saturday Review*, 51 (Oct. 26, 1968): 33-34.
    Repr. in *Critical Essays on Joyce Carol Oates*, Linda W. Wagner. Boston, MA: G.K. Hall, 1979, pp. 13-15.

1454. Bailey, J.E. "The Doomed and the Damned." *Time*, 92 (Nov. 1968): 102.

1455. Knowles, John. "Nada at the Core." *New York Times Book Review*, 73 (Nov. 3, 1968): 5.

1456. Cassill, R[onald] V[erlin]. "Journey to the End of Suburban Night." *Washington Post Book World* (Nov. 3, 1968): 5.

1457. Grant, Louis T. "A Child of Paradise." *Nation*, 207 (Nov. 4, 1968): 475.

1458. Archer, William H. *Best Sellers*, 28 (Nov. 15, 1968): 335.

1459. Lask, Thomas. "Open Season on Suburbia." *New York Times*, 118 (Dec. 7, 1968): 45.

1460. Bergonzi, Bernard. "Truants." *New York Review of Books*, 11 (Jan. 2, 1969): 40-41.

1461. L'Heureux, John. "Something New, Something Blue." *Critic* (Chicago), 27 (Feb.-Mar. 1969): 83-85.

1462. Cotter, James F[inn]. *America*, 120 (Mar. 22, 1969): 340.

1463. *Antioch Review*, 29, i (Spring 1969): 109-110.

1464. Price, Martin. "Reason and Its Alternatives: Some Recent Fiction." *Yale Review*, 58, iii (Spring 1969): 468-469.

1465. Morse, J. Mitchell. *Hudson Review*, 22, ii (Summer 1969): 324-325.

1466. Raban, Jonathan. "Fictive Games." *New Statesman*, 78 (Oct. 3, 1969): 467.

1467. Tomalin, Claire. "An Intruder in Dublin." *Observer* (Oct. 5, 1969): 34.

1468. Morgan, Edwin. "Imperfect Communication." *Listener*, 82 (Oct. 9, 1969): 493.

1469. "American Nightmares." *Times Literary Supplement*, 3529 (Oct. 16, 1969): 1177.

1470. Strating, J.J. "Amerikaans romannieuws." *Litterair Paspoort*, 235 (Jan. 1970): 29.

1471. *Publishers' Weekly*, 197 (Jan. 12, 1970): 66.

1472. Petersen, Clarence. "Perverse Pros." *Washington Post Book World* (Mar. 15, 1970): 13.

1473. "Shooting Wars." *Times Literary Supplement*, 3603 (Mar. 19, 1971): 313.

1474. Mudrick, Marvin. "Fiction and Truth." *Hudson Review*, 25, i (Spring 1972): 146-150.

1475. Pinsker, Sanford. "Suburban Molesters: Joyce Carol Oates' 'Expensive People.'" *Midwest Quarterly*, 19 (Autumn 1977): 89-103.
Repr. in *Critical Essays on Joyce Carol Oates*, Linda W. Wagner. Boston, MA: G.K. Hall, 1979, pp. 93-101.

1476. Little, Judy. "Satirizing the Norm: Comedy in Women's Fiction." *Regionalism and the Female Imagination*, 3, ii–iii (Fall 1977–Winter 1978): 43–44.

1477. Coale, Samuel C. "Marriage in Contemporary American Literature: The Mismatched Marriages of Manichean Minds." *Thought*, 58 (Mar. 1983): 117.

THE FABULOUS BEASTS (# 523)

1478. *Kirkus Reviews*, 43 (Oct. 1, 1975): 1161.

1479. *Publishers' Weekly*, 208 (Nov. 3, 1975): 67.

1480. Juhasz, S[uzanne]. *Library Journal*, 101 (Jan. 15, 1976): 343.

1481. Fletcher, Connie. *Booklist*, 72 (Mar. 15, 1976): 1016.

1482. Herrington, Neva Johnson. "Holding on to a Robin's Egg." *Southwest Review*, 61, ii (Spring 1976): 213–214.

1483. *Choice*, 13 (Apr. 1976): 226.

1484. Frost, Kenneth. "Searching for Symbols." *Book Forum*, 2 (Summer 1976): 403–404.

1485. Ramsey, Paul. "Image and Essence: Some American Poetry of 1975." *Sewanee Review*, 84, iii (Summer 1976): 536–537.

1486. Martz, Louis L. "Recent Poetry: Mending Broken Connections." *Yale Review*, 66, i (Autumn 1976): 114–118.

1487. Siegel, Robert. "Emerson's Smile." *Poetry*, 130 (May 1977): 107–110.

1488. Cotter, James Finn. "Poetry Is Dead, Long Live, Poetry." *America*, 137 (Aug. 20, 1977): 81.

1489. *Kliatt Paperback Book Guide*, 11 (Fall 1977): 15.

FIRST PERSON SINGULAR: WRITERS ON THEIR CRAFT (Joyce Carol Oates, comp.) (# 1077)

1490. *Kirkus Reviews*, 51 (Oct. 15, 1983): 1126.

1491. Kakutani, Michiko. *New York Times*, 133 (Dec. 13, 1983), sect. 3: 21.

1492. Atlas, James. "Writers on How It's Done." *Atlantic*, 253 (Jan. 1984): 96-98.

1493. Smith, Starr E. *Library Journal*, 109 (Feb. 1, 1984): 181.

1494. *Chatelaine*, 57 (Apr. 1984): 4.

FOUR SUMMERS (# 136)

1495. Cushman, Keith. "A Reading of Joyce Carol Oates's 'Four Summers.'" *Studies in Short Fiction*, 18, ii (Spring 1981): 137-146.

A GARDEN OF EARTHLY DELIGHTS (# 10)

1496. *Kirkus Reviews*, 35 (Apr. 15, 1967): 525.

1497. *Publishers' Weekly*, 191 (May 29, 1967): 62.

1498. Lacey, Maybelle. *Library Journal*, 92 (June 1, 1967): 2180.

1499. Hicks, Granville. "Fiction That Grows from the Ground." *Saturday Review*, 50 (Aug. 5, 1967): 23-24.

1500. Lask, Thomas. "The Sins of the Parents." *New York Times*, 116 (Sept. 5, 1967): 41.

1501. Janeway, Elizabeth. "Clara the Climber." *New York Times Book Review*, 72 (Sept. 10, 1967): 5, 63.

1502. "Hardscrabble Heroine." *Time*, 90 (Sept. 22, 1967): 106.

1503. S[okolov], R[aymond] A. "Tobacco Boulevard." *Newsweek*, 70 (Oct. 2, 1967): 93-94.

1504. Nelson, Elizabeth. *America*, 117 (Oct. 21, 1967): 448.

1505. Long, Robert Emmet. *Commonweal*, 87 (Feb. 23,
        1968): 630- 631.

1506. Doyle, James. "Cather in the Raw." *Critic* (Chicago),
        26 (Feb.-Mar. 1968): 75-76.

1507. Sterne, Richard Clark. "Versions of Rural America."
        Nation, 206 (Apr. 1, 1968): 448, 450.
        Repr. in *Critical Essays on Joyce Carol Oates*,
        Linda W. Wagner. Boston, MA: G.K. Hall, 1979,
        pp. 11-12.

1508. Hicks, Granville. "What Is Reality ?" *Saturday
        Review*, 51 (Oct. 26, 1968): 33-34.
        Repr. in *Critical Essays on Joyce Carol Oates*,
        Linda W. Wagner. Boston, MA: G.K. Hall, 1979,
        pp. 13-15.

1509. *Publishers' Weekly*, 195 (Jan. 6, 1969): 55.

1510. *Saturday Review*, 52 (Mar. 22, 1969): 61.

1511. Quirino, Leonard. *Novel: A Forum on Fiction*, 2
        (Winter 1969): 188-190.

1512. Stegner, Page. "Stone, Berry, Oates--and Other
        Grist from the Mill." *Southern Review* (Baton
        Rouge), n.s., 5, i (Winter 1969): 278-279.

1513. "Spanned and Splayed." *Times Literary Supplement*,
        3562 (June 4, 1970): 601.

1514. Jebb, Julian. "An American Nightmare." *Observer*
        (June 7, 1970): 31.

1515. Reynolds, Stanley. "Being Young." *New Statesman*,
        79 (June 19, 1970): 892.

1516. Shrapnel, Norman. "Grand Tour." *Guardian Weekly*,
        102 (June 20, 1970): 19.

1517. Cole, Barry. "Invisible Man." *Spectator*, 224 (June 20,
        1970): 823.

1518. "Shooting Wars." *Times Literary Supplement*, 3603
        (Mar. 19, 1971): 313.

1519. Mudrick, Marvin. "Fiction and Truth." *Hudson Review*, 25, i (Spring 1972): 146-150.

1520. Burwell, Rose Marie. "Joyce Carol Oates and an Old Master." *Critique*, 15, i (1973): 48-58.

1521. Goodman, Charlotte. "Images of American Rural Women in the Novel." *University of Michigan Papers in Women's Studies*, 1 (June 1975): 63-64.

THE GODDESS AND OTHER WOMEN (# 156)

1522. *Kirkus Reviews*, 42 (Oct. 1, 1974): 1076.

1523. *Publishers' Weekly*, 206 (Oct. 7, 1974): 54.

1524. Cushman, Kathleen. "Goddesses of Change." *National Observer*, 13 (Nov. 16, 1974): 27.

1525. Engel, Marian. "Women Also Have Dark Hearts." *New York Times Book Review*, 79 (Nov. 24, 1974): 7, 10.

1526. *New York Times Book Review*, 79 (Dec. 1, 1974): 68.

1527. Bartley, Edward. *Best Sellers*, 34 (Feb. 1, 1975): 483.

1528. Allen, Bruce. *Library Journal*, 100 (Feb. 1, 1975): 311.

1529. H[all], E[lizabeth]. *Psychology Today*, 8 (Mar. 1975): 96.

1530. *Booklist*, 71 (Mar. 15, 1975): 725.

1531. Avant, John Alfred. "New and Notable Fiction." *New Republic*, 172 (Mar. 29, 1975): 30-31.

1532. Lodge, David. "Under Compulsion." *Times Literary Supplement*, 3813 (Apr. 4, 1975): 353.

1533. Sage, Lorna. "The Edge of Hysteria." *Observer* (Apr. 6, 1975): 30.

1534. Phillips, Robert. *Commonweal*, 102 (Apr. 11, 1975): 55, 57-58.

1535. Bailey, Paul. "Muscular." *New Statesman*, 89 (Apr. 11, 1975): 488.

1536. Wordsworth, Christopher. "Cassandra Syndrome." *Guardian Weekly*, 112 (Apr. 12, 1975): 21.

1537. Mellors, John. "Americans and Others." *Listener*, 93 (May 22, 1975): 685-686.

1538. Eagle, Robert. "Being Beastly." *Books and Bookmen*, 21 (Jan. 1976): 56-57.

1539. *Publishers' Weekly*, 209 (Mar. 1, 1976): 97.

1540. Giles, James R. "Destructive and Redemptive 'Order': Joyce Carol Oates' 'Marriages and Infidelities' and 'The Goddess and Other Women.'" *Ball State University Forum*, 22, iii (1981): 58-70.

THE HOSTILE SUN: THE POETRY OF D.H. LAWRENCE (# 903)

1541. Gilbert, Sandra M. "Beyond the Walls of Light." *Nation*, 218 (Jan. 12, 1974): 58-60.

1542. Cushman, Keith. *Library Journal*, 99 (Mar. 1, 1974): 659.

1543. *British Book News* (Apr. 1980): 202.

HOW I CONTEMPLATED THE WORLD FROM THE DETROIT HOUSE OF CORRECTION AND BEGAN MY LIFE OVER AGAIN (# 175)

1544. Stevick, Philip. "Remembering, Knowing and Telling in Joyce Carol Oates" in *The Process of Fiction*, Barbara McKenzie, ed. New York: Harcourt Brace Jovanovich, 1974, pp. 490-499.

1545. Goetsch, Paul. "Joyce Carol Oates, 'How I Contemplated the World from the Detroit House of Correction and Began My Life over Again'", in *Die amerikanische Short Story der Gegenwart: Interpretationen*, Peter Freese, ed. Berlin: Schmidt, 1976, pp. 301-313.

1546. Park, Sue Simpson. "A Study in Counterpoint: Joyce Carol Oates's 'How I Contemplated the World from the Detroit House of Correction and Began My Life over Again.'" *Modern Fiction Studies*, 22, ii (Summer 1976): 213-224.

THE HUNGRY GHOSTS: SEVEN ALLUSIVE COMEDIES (# 179)

1547. Avant, John Alfred. *New Republic*, 171 (Aug. 31, 1974): 30-31.
Repr. in *Critical Essays on Joyce Carol Oates*, Linda W. Wagner. Boston, MA: G.K. Hall, 1979, pp. 36-37.

1548. *Booklist*, 71 (Sept. 1, 1974): 23.

1549. Hendin, Josephine. "Joyce Carol Oates Is Frankly Murderous." *New York Times Book Review*, 79 (Sept. 1, 1974): 5.

1550. Allen, Bruce. *Library Journal*, 99 (Sept. 15, 1974): 2176.

1551. *Choice*, 11 (Oct. 1974): 1139.

1552. H[all], E[lizabeth]. *Psychology Today*, 8 (Mar. 1975): 96.

IN THE REGION OF ICE (# 193)

1553. Liston, William T. "Her Brother's Keeper." *Southern Humanities Review*, 11, ii (Spring 1977): 195-203.

INVISIBLE WOMAN (# 600)

1554. *Publishers' Weekly*, 221 (Mar. 12, 1982): 74-75.

1555. Ratner, Rochelle. *Library Journal*, 107 (May 1, 1982): 892-893.

1556. *Booklist*, 78 (June 15, 1982): 1351.

1557. Murray, G.E. "Struck by Lightning: Four Distinct Modern Voices." *Michigan Quarterly Review*, 22, iv (Fall 1983): 646-648.

THE LAMB OF ABYSSALIA (# 206)

1558. Pinsker, Sanford. *Studies in Short Fiction*, 18, i (Winter 1981): 111.

LAST DAYS (# 208)

1559. *Publishers' Weekly*, 225 (June 8, 1984): 55-56.

1560. *Kirkus Reviews*, 52 (June 15, 1984): 544.

1561. Soete, Mary. *Library Journal*, 109 (Aug. 1984): 1468.

1562. Sternhell, Carol. *Vogue*, 174 (Aug. 1984): 212.

1563. Jong, Erica. *New York Times Book Review*, 89 (Aug. 5, 1984): 7.

1564. Timson, Judith. *Chatelaine*, 57 (Nov. 1984): 4.

LOVE AND ITS DERANGEMENTS: POEMS (# 624)

1565. *Publishers' Weekly*, 198 (Oct. 19, 1970): 52.

1566. Avant, John Alfred. *Library Journal*, 96 (Mar. 1, 1971): 839.

1567. Gregory, Hilda. "Love's Country." *Prairie Schooner*, 45, i (Spring 1971): 78-80.

1568. *Virginia Quarterly Review*, 47, iii (Summer 1971): cviii.

1569. Andersen, Sally. "The Poetry of Joyce Carol Oates." *Spirit*, 39, iii (Fall 1972): 24-29.

1570. McLellan, Joseph. *Washington Post Book World* (Aug. 25, 1974): 4.

MARRIAGES AND INFIDELITIES; SHORT STORIES (# 237)

1571. *Kirkus Reviews*, 40 (July 15, 1972): 821.

1572. *Publishers' Weekly*, 202 (Aug. 7, 1972): 40.

1573. Avant, John Alfred. *Library Journal*, 97 (Sept. 1, 1972): 2754.

1574. Oberbeck, S.K. "A Masterful Explorer in the Minefields of Emotion." *Washington Post Book World* (Sept. 17, 1972): 4, 10.

1575. *Christian Century*, 89 (Sept. 20, 1972): 928.

1576. Abrahams, William. "Stories of a Visionary." *Saturday Review*, 55 (Sept. 23, 1972): 76, 80.

1577. Wood, Michael. "Diminished People." *New York Times Book Review*, 77 (Oct. 1, 1972): 6, 43.

1578. Breslin, John B. *America*, 127 (Oct. 7, 1972): 265.

1579. Doyle, Paul A. *Best Sellers*, 32 (Oct. 15, 1972): 335-336.

1580. *Time*, 100 (Oct. 23, 1972): 109, 112.

1581. *Life*, 73 (Nov. 17, 1972): 26-27.

1582. De Feo, Ronald. "Only Prairie Dog Mounds." *National Review*, 24 (Nov. 24, 1972): 1307.
Repr. in *Critical Essays on Joyce Carol Oates*, Linda W. Wagner. Boston, MA: G.K. Hall, 1979, p. 31.

1583. *Saturday Review*, 55 (Dec. 2, 1972): 80.

1584. *New York Times Book Review*, 77 (Dec. 3, 1972): 76, 78.

1585. *Washington Post Book World* (Dec. 3, 1972): 5.

1586. Markmann, Charles Lam. "The Puzzle of People." *Nation*, 215 (Dec. 4, 1972): 566, 568.

1587. Kapp, Isa. "In Defense of Matrimony." *New Leader*, 55 (Dec. 11, 1972): 8-10.

1588. Doherty, Paul C. *America*, 130 (Feb. 9, 1974): 94.

1589. Sage, Lorna. "Coming Apart at the Seams." *Observer* (Aug. 18, 1974): 28.

1590. Straub, Peter. "Blood and Spinach." *New Statesman*, 88 (Aug. 23, 1974): 261.

1591. Mellors, John. "Kites and Aeroplanes." *Listener*, 92 (Sept. 26, 1974): 416-417.

1592. Alexander, John. "Occupational Hazards." *Times Literary Supplement*, 3792 (Nov. 8, 1974): 1249.

1593. Bender, Eileen T. "Autonomy and Influence: Joyce Carol Oates's 'Marriages and Infidelities.'" *Soundings*, 58, iii (Fall 1975): 390-406.

1594. Giles, James R. "Destructive and Redemptive 'Order': Joyce Carol Oates' 'Marriages and Infidelities' and 'The Goddess and Other Women.'" *Ball State University Forum*, 22, iii (1981): 58-70.

MIRACLE PLAY (# 841)

1595. Gussow, Mel. "Oates' 'Miracle Play' Depicts Violence," *New York Times*, 123 (Jan. 1, 1974): 12.

1596. Brukenfeld, Dick. "House Beautiful, Play Dull." *Village Voice*, 19 (Jan. 10, 1974): 52.

MYSTERIES OF WINTERTHURN (# 12)

1597. *Kirkus Reviews*, 51 (Dec. 1, 1983): 1221-1222.

1598. *Publishers' Weekly*, 224 (Dec. 23, 1983): 49-50.

1599. Mills, Beth Ann. *Library Journal*, 109 (Jan. 1984): 111.

1600. Salholz, Eloise. "Gothic Horrors." *Newsweek*, 103 (Feb. 6, 1984): 79A, 79C.

1601. Kakutani, Michiko. *New York Times*, 133 (Feb. 10, 1984), sect. 3: 25.

1602. Craig, Patricia. "Philosophical Tale of Gore." *New York Times Book Review*, 89 (Feb. 12, 1984): 7.

1603. Collins, Anne. "The Grotesque Face of Evil." *Maclean's*, 97 (Feb. 20, 1984): 60.

1604. *New Yorker*, 60 (Feb. 27, 1984): 133-134.

1605. Shafer, Ingrid H. "Oates's Hint of Light in Datum of Darkness." *National Catholic Reporter*, 21 (Nov. 16, 1984): 12.

NEW HEAVEN, NEW EARTH: THE VISIONARY EXPERIENCE IN LITERATURE (# 928)

1606. *Kirkus Reviews*, 42 (Aug. 1, 1974): 858.

1607. *Publishers' Weekly*, 206 (Aug. 12, 1974): 54.

1608. Staggs, Sammy. *Library Journal*, 99 (Oct. 1, 1974): 2481.

1609. Avant, John Alfred. "New and Notable Fiction." *New Republic*, 172 (Mar. 29, 1975): 30-31.

1610. *Booklist*, 71 (Apr. 1, 1975): 787.

1611. *Choice*, 12 (May 1975): 386-387.

1612. Allen, Bruce. "Intrusions of Consciousness." *Hudson Review*, 28, iv (Winter 1975-76): 611-615.

1613. Tanner, Tony. "Panic Stations." *New Statesman*, 91 (Mar. 12, 1976): 332.

1614. Carey, John. "Lucid Intervals." *Listener*, 95 (Mar. 25, 1976): 372-373.

1615. Chapman, Robert. *Books and Bookmen*, 21 (Sept. 1976): 61-62.

NIGHT-SIDE: EIGHTEEN TALES (# 260)

1616. *Kirkus Reviews*, 45 (Aug. 15, 1977): 875.

1617. *Publishers' Weekly*, 212 (Aug. 22, 1977): 60.

1618. Wiehe, Janet. *Library Journal*, 102 (Oct. 15, 1977): 2182.

1619. Romano, John. "A Way with Madness." *New York Times Book Review*, 82 (Oct. 23, 1977): 15, 18.

1620. Coslick, Linda. *Best Sellers*, 37 (Nov. 1977): 231.

1621. *Booklist*, 74 (Nov. 1, 1977): 463.

1622. Horn, Carole. "To the Edge of Consciousness." *Washington Post Book World* (Nov. 20, 1977): E7.

1623. Delbanco, Nicholas. *New Republic*, 177 (Nov. 26,
       1977): 44-45.

1624. Bator, Paul G. "Night-Side." *Virginia Woolf
       Quarterly*, 3, iii- iv (1978): 315-316.

1625. *Choice*, 14 (Feb. 1978): 1646.

1626. *Virginia Quarterly Review*, 54, ii (Spring 1978):
       67-68.

1627. Garrett, George. "Coming Out of Left Field: The
       Short Story Today." *Sewanee Review*, 86, iii
       (Summer 1978): 469.

1628. Phillips, Robert. "The Short Story--Four Collections."
       Commonweal, 105 (Sept. 15, 1978): 601.
       Repr. in *Critical Essays on Joyce Carol Oates*,
       Linda W. Wagner. Boston, MA: G.K. Hall, 1979,
       pp. 42-43.

1629. Cunningham, Valentine. "Going Places." *New States-
       man*, 97 (Jan. 12, 1979): 54.

1630. Thwaite, Anthony. "Politics in Paradise." *Observer*
       (Jan. 14, 1979): 35.

1631. Hope, Mary. *Spectator*, 242 (Jan. 27, 1979): 23.

1632. Mellors, John. "Psychic and Mental." *Listener*, 102
       (Aug. 23, 1979): 254.

1633. W[ilson], D. *Times Literary Supplement*, 4001
       (Nov. 23, 1979): 43.

1634. *New York Times Book Review*, 85 (Jan. 6, 1980): 31.

1635. *Kliatt Paperback Book Guide*, 14 (Spring 1980): 23.

NIGHT WALKS: A BEDSIDE COMPANION (# 848)

1636. *Publishers' Weekly*, 222 (Sept. 24, 1982): 61.

1637. Cox, Shelley. *Library Journal*, 107 (Nov. 15, 1982):
       2178.

1638. *Booklist*, 79 (Dec. 15, 1982): 549.

ONTOLOGICAL PROOF OF MY EXISTENCE (# 842)

1639. [Kroll, Jack.] "Action at the 'Cube.'" *Newsweek*, 79 (Feb. 21, 1972): 99.

PLOT (# 288)

1640. Walker, Carolyn. "Fear, Love, and Art in Oates' 'Plot.'" *Critique*, 15, i (1973): 59-70.

THE POISONED KISS AND OTHER STORIES FROM THE PORTUGUESE (Fernandes/Joyce Carol Oates) (# 292)

1641. *Kirkus Reviews*, 43 (June 15, 1975): 674-675.

1642. *Publishers' Weekly*, 207 (June 16, 1975): 74.

1643. McLellan, Joseph. *Washington Post Book World* (July 6, 1975): 2.

1644. Allen, Bruce. *Library Journal*, 100 (Aug. 1975): 1441.

1645. Cushman, Kathleen. "Oates: If She Was Not Besieged, Her Genius Is Indeed Immense." *National Observer*, 14 (Aug. 2, 1975): 19.

1646. Misurella, Fred. "Mary's Misery." *Village Voice*, 20 (Aug. 4, 1975): 36.

1647. Pochoda, Elizabeth. "Joyce Carol Oates Honoring the Complexities of the Real World." *New York Times Book Review*, 80 (Aug. 31, 1975): 6.

1648. Adams, Phoebe. *Atlantic*, 236 (Sept. 1975): 85.

1649. *Booklist*, 72 (Sept. 1, 1975): 25.

1650. *Choice*, 12 (Nov. 1975): 1171.

1651. Barnes, Julian. "No Picnic." *New Statesman*, 91 (May 21, 1976): 685.

1652. Dinnage, Rosemary. "Altered Egos." *Times Literary Supplement*, 3871 (May 21, 1976): 601.

1653. Fallowell, Duncan. "Trips." *Spectator*, 236 (May 29, 1976): 30.

1654. *Publishers' Weekly*, 212 (July 25, 1977): 70.

1655. Malin, Irving. "Possessive Material" in *Critical Essays on Joyce Carol Oates*, Linda W. Wagner. Boston, MA: G.K. Hall, 1979, pp. 39-41.

1656. Giles, James R. "Oates' 'The Poisoned Kiss.'" *Canadian Literature*, 80 (Spring 1979): 138-147.

THE PROFANE ART: ESSAYS AND REVIEWS (# 1039)

1657. *Kirkus Reviews*, 51 (Mar. 1, 1983): 290.

1658. *Publishers' Weekly*, 223 (Mar. 11, 1983): 73.

1659. *Booklist*, 79 (Apr. 15, 1983): 1070-1071.

1660. LaBarba, Barbara Susan. *Library Journal*, 108 (Apr. 15, 1983): 825.

1661. W[illiamson], C[hilton, Jr.]. *National Review*, 35 (Apr. 29, 1983): 505.

1662. Dawidoff, Robert. "Criticism: Human Conversation between Equals." *Los Angeles Times Book Review* (May 29, 1983): 2, 5.

THE SACRED MARRIAGE (# 314)

1663. Loeb, Monica. "Hieros Gamos, Analysis of a Short Story by Joyce Carol Oates" in *Vitterhetsnöjen, Festschrift for Magnus von Platen*. Umeå: Umeå Universitet, 1980, pp. 289-294.

SCENES FROM AMERICAN LIFE: CONTEMPORARY SHORT FICTION (Joyce Carol Oates, ed.) (# 849)

1664. *Washington Post Book World* (July 15, 1973): 15.

1665. *New York Times Book Review*, 78 (Oct. 7, 1973): 42.

THE SEDUCTION AND OTHER STORIES (# 326)

1666. Pochoda, Elizabeth. "Joyce Carol Oates Honoring the Complexities of the Real World." *New York Times Book Review*, 80 (Aug. 31, 1975): 6.

1667. Allen, Bruce. *Library Journal*, 100 (Sept. 15, 1975): 1653.

1668. *New York Times Book Review*, 80 (Dec. 7, 1975): 64.

1669. Baker, Jane. *Antioch Review*, 34, iii (Spring 1976): 377.

A SENTIMENTAL EDUCATION; STORIES (# 328)

1670. *Booklist*, 77 (Nov. 15, 1980): 422.

1671. *Kirkus Reviews*, 48 (Nov. 15, 1980): 1482.

1672. *Publishers' Weekly*, 218 (Nov. 28, 1980): 45.

1673. Soete, Mary. *Library Journal*, 105 (Dec. 1, 1980): 2516.

1674. Bell, David. *Saturday Review*, 8 (Jan. 1981): 72-73.

1675. Talmey, Allene. *Vogue*, 171 (Jan. 1981): 30, 32.

1676. Kiely, Robert. "An American Voice." *New York Times Book Review*, 86 (Jan. 4, 1981): 7, 21.

1677. P[rescott], P[eter] S. *Newsweek*, 97 (Jan. 26, 1981): 74A.

1678. Merkin, Daphne. *New Leader*, 64 (Feb. 9, 1981): 13.

1679. Wier, Allen. *Washington Post Book World* (Feb. 22, 1981): 10.

1680. Cooke, Judy. "Losing Innocence." *New Statesman*, 101 (Mar. 6, 1981): 22-23.

1681. Ackroyd, Peter. "A Family and Its Fortunes." *Sunday Times* (Mar. 8, 1981): 42.

1682. Sage, Lorna. "Across the Gothic Drawbridge." *Observer* (Mar. 15, 1981): 33.

1683. Cunningham, Valentine. "Counting up the Cost." *Times Literary Supplement*, 4068 (Mar. 20, 1981): 303.

1684. Parker, Dorothy. "Oates Stories Tread Precariously Close to Melodrama." *Christian Science Monitor*, 73 (Mar. 30, 1981): 19.

1685. Thompson, Kent. "New Dances for Dionysus." *Books in Canada*, 10 (Apr. 1981): 20.

1686. Wimsatt, Margaret. *America*, 144 (Apr. 4, 1981): 281.

1687. Kemp, Peter. "The Damaged Planet." *Listener*, 105 (Apr. 23, 1981): 549.

1688. van Boheemen, Christel. "Stormen van emoties." *Volkskrant*, 60 (9 mei 1981): 35.

1689. Phillips, Robert. "Overview of an Extraordinary Mind." *Commonweal*, 108 (Aug. 28, 1981): 475-476.

1690. Curran, Ronald. *World Literature Today*, 55, iv (Autumn 1981): 672-673.

1691. *Publishers' Weekly*, 222 (Aug. 6, 1982): 68.

1692. Pinsker, Sanford. *Studies in Short Fiction*, 19, i (Winter 1982): 94-96.

1693. *Virginia Quarterly Review*, 58, i (Winter 1982): 19.

SOLSTICE (# 13)

1694. Lehmann-Haupt, Christopher. *New York Times*, 134 (Jan. 10, 1985): C21.

1695. Sinkler, Rebecca Pepper. "Time and Her Sisters." *New York Times Book Review*, 90 (Jan. 20, 1985): 4.

1696. Prescott, Peter S. "The High Art of Melodrama." *Newsweek*, 105 (Jan. 21, 1985): 71.

1697. Maynard, Joyce. *Mademoiselle*, 91 (Feb. 1985): 84, 86.

1698. Jones, Robert. "Still Lost in the Maze." *Commonweal*, 112 (Mar. 8, 1985): 150-152.

1699. Petroski, Catherine. *Saturday Review*, 11 (Mar.-Apr. 1985): 61.

SON OF THE MORNING (# 14)

1700. *Kirkus Reviews*, 46 (June 1, 1978): 609.

1701. *Publishers' Weekly*, 213 (June 19, 1978): 92.

1702. *Village Voice*, 23 (June 19, 1978): 82.

1703. *Booklist*, 74 (July 15, 1978): 1719–1720.

1704. Wiehe, J[anet]. *Library Journal*, 103 (Aug. 1978):
    1532.

1705. Glendinning, Victoria. "In Touch with God." *New
    York Times*, 127 (Aug. 13, 1978): 281–282.

1706. Peer, Elizabeth. "Hound of Heaven." *Newsweek*, 92
    (Aug. 14, 1978): 65–66.

1707. *Critic* (Chicago), 37 (Oct. 15, 1978): 6.

1708. Rowan, Diana Newell. "Oates's Rousing Sermon
    without a Message." *Christian Science Monitor*,
    70 (Oct. 25, 1978): 19.

1709. Glendinning, Victoria. "Hungry for God." *New York
    Times Book Review*, 83 (Nov. 26, 1978): 11.
    Repr. in *Critical Essays on Joyce Carol Oates*,
    Linda W. Wagner. Boston, MA: G.K. Hall, 1979,
    pp. 44–45.

1710. Tyler, Anne. *Washington Post Book World* (Dec. 3,
    1978): 14.

1711. *Choice*, 15 (Jan. 1979): 1519.

1712. Smith, Julian. "Epiphanies." *Christian Century*, 96
    (Feb. 21, 1979): 190–191.

1713. Howard, Maureen V. "Eight Recent Novels." *Yale
    Review*, 68, iii (Spring 1979): 438.

1714. Gramm, Kent. *Theology Today*, 36, ii (July 1979):
    286–287.

1715. *New York Times Book Review*, 84 (July 22, 1979): 27.

1716. Lee, Hermione. "Backwoods Messiah." *Observer*
       (Aug. 19, 1979): 36.

1717. Miner, Valerie. *New Statesman*, 98 (Aug. 24, 1979):
       277.

1718. Kemp, Peter. "Manic Messianic." *Listener*, 102
       (Aug. 30, 1979): 286.

1719. Lee, Hermione. *Observer* (Dec. 9, 1979): 35.

1720. Johnson, Greg. "The Two Faces of God." *Southwest
       Review*, 64, i (Winter 1979): 93-95.

1721. Straumann, Heinrich. "Abrechnung mit dem
       Unfassbaren ? Hinweis auf den Roman 'Son of
       the Morning.'" *Neue Zürcher Zeitung*, 80
       (Apr. 5-6, 1980): 55.

1722. Schwartz, N. *Bonniers Litterära Magasin*, 51, iii
       (June 1982): 227.

1723. Coale, Samuel C. "Marriage in Contemporary American
       Literature: The Mismatched Marriages of Mani-
       chean Minds." *Thought*, 58 (Mar. 1983): 117.

SUNDAY DINNER (# 843)

1724. Barnes, Clive. "'Sunday Dinner' Begins Run: Play
       Provides a View of Unhappy Family." *New York
       Times*, 120 (Nov. 3, 1970): 28.

1725. Kerr, Walter. "Not a Breakthrough, but a Nice
       Evening." *New York Times*, 120 (Nov. 8, 1970),
       sect. 2: 1, 5.

1726. Clurman, Harold. *Nation*, 211 (Nov. 16, 1970): 508.

1727. Simon, John. *Uneasy Stages: A Chronicle of the New
       York Theater, 1963-73*. New York: Random
       House, 1976, pp. 284-285.

THE SWEET ENEMY (# 844)

1728. Taubman, Howard. "Theater: 'The Sweet Enemy'
       Opens." *New York Times*, 114 (Feb. 16, 1965):
       39.

1729. Sheed, Wilfrid. "The Stage: Absurd Reflections." *Commonweal*, 81 (Mar. 12, 1965): 764.

THEM (# 15)

1730. *Kirkus Reviews*, 37 (Aug. 1, 1969): 801.

1731. *Publishers' Weekly*, 196 (Aug. 11, 1969): 40.

1732. Adams, Robert M. "The Best Nightmares Are Retrospective." *New York Times Book Review*, 74 (Sept. 28, 1969): 4-5, 43.

1733. W[olff], G[eoffrey]. "Gothic City." *Newsweek*, 74 (Sept. 29, 1969): 120-122.

1734. L'Heureux, John. "Mirage-Seekers." *Atlantic*, 224 (Oct. 1969): 128-129.
      Repr. in *Critical Essays on Joyce Carol Oates*, Linda W. Wagner. Boston, MA: G.K. Hall, 1979, pp. 16-18.

1735. Curley, Dorothy. *Library Journal*, 94 (Oct. 1, 1969): 3469.

1736. Leonard, John. "We Are the Strangers in Our Mirrors." *New York Times*, 119 (Oct. 1, 1969): 45.

1737. "Urban Gothic." *Time*, 94 (Oct. 10, 1969): 106, 108.

1738. Leedom, Joanne. "Out of Riots--A Quest for Rebirth." *Christian Science Monitor*, 61 (Oct. 30, 1969): 10.

1739. DeMott, Benjamin. "The Necessity in Art of a Reflective Intelligence." *Saturday Review*, 52 (Nov. 22, 1969): 71-73, 89.
      Repr. in *Critical Essays on Joyce Carol Oates*, Linda W. Wagner. Boston, MA: G.K. Hall, 1979, pp. 19-23.

1740. Cassill, R[onald] V[erlin]. "Violence Can't Be Singled Out from an Ordinary Day." *Washington Post Book World* (Nov. 23, 1969): 13.

1741. *National Observer*, 8 (Nov. 24, 1969): 25.

1742. *Booklist*, 66 (Dec. 1, 1969): 439.

1743. Bedient, Calvin. "Vivid and Dazzling." *Nation*, 209
        (Dec. 1, 1969): 609-611.
        Repr. in *Critical Essays on Joyce Carol Oates*,
        Linda W. Wagner. Boston, MA: G.K. Hall, 1979,
        pp. 24-26.

1744. Sissman, L.E. "The Whole Truth." *New Yorker*, 45
        (Dec. 6, 1969): 238, 241-242.

1745. Wolff, Geoffrey. *Newsweek*, 74 (Dec. 22, 1969): 98.

1746. *American Libraries*, 1 (Jan. 1970): 91.

1747. Ricks, Christopher. "The Unignorable Real." *New
        York Review of Books*, 14 (Feb. 12, 1970):
        22-24.

1748. *American Libraries*, 1 (Mar. 1970): 277.

1749. Davenport, Guy. "C'est Magnifique, Mais Ce N'est Pas
        Daguerre." *Hudson Review*, 23, i (Spring 1970):
        154-155.

1750. *Virginia Quarterly Review*, 46, ii (Spring 1970): xl.

1751. Gray, Paul Edward. "New Books in Review." *Yale
        Review*, 59 (Spring 1970): 433-435.

1752. Hill, William B. *Best Sellers*, 30 (Apr. 1, 1970):
        14-15.

1753. Hill, William [B.]. *America*, 122 (May 2, 1970): 478.

1754. *Publishers' Weekly*, 198 (Sept. 7, 1970): 62.

1755. Petersen, Clarence. "Ladies' Day." *Washington Post
        Book World* (Oct. 18, 1970): 15.

1756. *Best Sellers*, 30 (Nov. 1, 1970): 332.

1757. *Saturday Review*, 53 (Dec. 26, 1970): 30.

1758. Kazin, Alfred. "Heroines." *New York Review of
        Books*, 16 (Feb. 11, 1971): 32-34.

1759. Sullivan, Mary. "Uninsistence." *Listener*, 85 (Mar. 18, 1971): 344-345.

1760. "Shooting Wars." *Times Literary Supplement*, 3603 (Mar. 19, 1971): 313.

1761. Wall, Stephen. "Californian Castaway." *Observer* (Mar. 21, 1971): 37.

1762. McGregor, Helen. *Books and Bookmen*, 16 (June 1971): 38.

1763. Harper, Howard M., Jr. "Trends in Recent American Fiction." *Contemporary Literature*, 12, iii (Summer 1971): 208.

1764. Kitchen, Paddy. "Love of Words." *New Statesman*, 84 (Oct. 6, 1972): 482.

1765. Terbille, Charles I. "Four Problems of a Classical Literature." *Michigan Quarterly Review*, 13, iii (Summer 1974): 209.

1766. Giles, James R. "Suffering, Transcendence, and Artistic 'Form': Joyce Carol Oates's 'them.'" *Arizona Quarterly*, 32, iii (Autumn 1976): 213-226.

1767. Giles, James R. "From Jimmy Gatz to Jules Wendall: A Study of 'Nothing Substantial.'" *Dalhousie Review*, 56, iv (Winter 1976-77): 718-724. [Formerly unpublished MLA Seminar Paper, 1973]

1768. Pinsker, Sanford. "The Blue Collar Apocalypse, or Detroit Bridge's Falling Down: Joyce Carol Oates's 'them.'" *Descant*, 23, iv (Summer 1979): 35-47.

1769. Decurtis, Anthony. "The Process of Fictionalization in Joyce Carol Oates's 'them.'" *International Fiction Review*, 6, ii (Summer 1979): 121-128.

1770. Karl, Frederick R. *American Fictions, 1940-1980*. New York: Harper & Row, 1983, pp. 298-302.

1771. Goodman, Charlotte. "The Lost Brother, the Twin: Women Novelists and the Male-Female Double Bildungsroman." *Novel: A Forum on Fiction*, 17, i (Fall 1983): 40-43.

THREE PLAYS (# 845)

1772.   Soete, George. *Library Journal*, 105 (Dec. 1, 1980):
         2512.

1773.   *Booklist*, 77 (Dec. 15, 1980): 554.

1774.   Phillips, Robert. "Overview of an Extraordinary
         Mind." *Commonweal*, 108 (Aug. 28, 1981):
         475-476.

THE TRIUMPH OF THE SPIDER MONKEY (# 374)

1775.   *Booklist*, 73 (Mar. 1, 1977): 992.

1776.   *Kliatt Paperback Book Guide*, 11 (Spring 1977): 7.

1777.   Wiehe, Janet. *Library Journal*, 102 (Apr. 1, 1977):
         834.

1778.   *Choice*, 14 (May 1977): 377.

1779.   Allen, Bruce. "Dream Journeys." *Sewanee Review*,
         85, iv (Fall 1977): 693.

UNHOLY LOVES (# 16)

1780.   *Kirkus Reviews*, 47 (Aug. 1, 1979): 883.

1781.   *Publishers' Weekly*, 216 (Sept. 3, 1979): 90.

1782.   Fremont-Smith, Eliot. "Making Book for Fall." *Village
         Voice*, 24 (Sept. 17, 1979): 44.

1783.   *Booklist*, 76 (Oct. 1, 1979): 219.

1784.   Wiehe, Janet. *Library Journal*, 104 (Oct. 1, 1979):
         2120.

1785.   Stone, Laurie. *Village Voice*, 24 (Oct. 1, 1979): 47.

1786.   Mojtabai, A.G. "Poet and Teachers." *New York Times
         Book Review*, 84 (Oct. 7, 1979): 9, 30.

1787.   Clemons, Walter. "Wild Oates in Academe." *Newsweek*,
         94 (Oct. 29, 1979): 99.

1788. Leedom-Ackerman, Joanne. "Rise and Fall of University Egos." *Christian Science Monitor*, 71 (Nov. 7, 1979): 17.

1789. *New York Times Book Review*, 84 (Nov. 25, 1979): 62.

1790. Grumbach, Doris. "Fictions for a Seasonal Feast." *Washington Post Book World* (Dec. 9, 1979): 8.

1791. Rule, Philip C. *America*, 141 (Dec. 29, 1979): 435.

1792. Guereschi, Edward. *Best Sellers*, 39 (Jan. 1980): 366.

1793. Kirby, David. "Sowing Their Oates." *Change*, 12 (Feb.-Mar. 1980): 58-59.

1794. Mellors, John. "Learning to Die." *Listener*, 104 (Aug. 28, 1980): 281.

1795. Sage, Lorna. "Havoc on the Campus." *Observer* (Sept. 7, 1980): 29.

1796. Wilce, Gillian. "Art & Craft." *New Statesman*, 100 (Sept. 12, 1980): 20-21.

1797. Duchêne, Anne. "Homer and Apollo on Campus." *Times Literary Supplement*, 4041 (Sept. 12, 1980): 983.

1798. van Boheemen, Christel. *Literair Paspoort*, 289 (maart-apr. 1981): 697-700.

1799. *Publishers' Weekly*, 220 (Sept. 25, 1981): 87.

1800. *New York Times Book Review*, 86 (Oct. 25, 1981): 51.

1801. *Contemporary Review*, 243 (Sept. 1983): 168.

1802. Barasch, Frances K. *College Literature*, 10, i (Winter 1983): 34-35.

UPON THE SWEEPING FLOOD AND OTHER STORIES (# 385)

1803. Kitching, J. *Publishers' Weekly*, 189 (Feb. 28, 1966): 90.

1804. *Kirkus Reviews*, 34 (Mar. 1, 1966): 265.

1805. Estok, Rita. *Library Journal*, 91 (Apr. 1, 1966): 1926.

1806. Bell, Millicent. "Her Own Rough Truth." *New York Times Book Review*, 71 (June 12, 1966): 4-5.

1807. Hall, Joan Joffe. "The Chaos of Men's Souls." *Saturday Review*, 49 (Aug. 6, 1966): 32-33.

1808. Madden, David. *Studies in Short Fiction*, 4, iv (Summer 1967): 369-373.
       Repr. under title "The Violent World of Joyce Carol Oates" In *The Poetic Image in Six Genres*, David Madden. Carbondale: Southern Illinois University Press, 1969, pp. 26-46.
       Repr. in *Critical Essays on Joyce Carol Oates*, Linda W. Wagner. Boston, MA: G.K. Hall, 1979, pp. 6-10.

1809. Hunter, Jim. "Engulfing." *Listener*, 89 (Mar. 1, 1973): 284.

1810. "Off the Map." *Times Literary Supplement*, 3705 (Mar. 9, 1973): 257.

1811. Tomalin, Claire. "Veldtschmerz." *Observer* (Mar. 18, 1973): 37.

1812. Donald, Miles. "Aversions." *New Statesman*, 85 (Mar. 30, 1973): 470.

1813. Mellor, Isha. *Books and Bookmen*, 18 (May 1973): 107.

1814. Dunn, Douglas. "Disturbing Stories." *Spectator*, 230 (May 19, 1973): 623.

1815. Keller, Karl. "A Modern Version of Edward Taylor." *Early American Literature*, 9, iii (Winter 1975): 321-324.

THE WHEEL OF LOVE AND OTHER STORIES (# 402)

1816. *Kirkus Reviews*, 38 (Aug. 1, 1970): 825.

1817. *Publishers' Weekly*, 198 (Aug. 10, 1970): 47.

1818. Avant, John Alfred. *Library Journal*, 95 (Sept. 1, 1970): 2829.

1819. Long, Robert Emmet. *Saturday Review*, 53 (Oct. 24, 1970): 36, 65.

1820. Gilman, Richard. "The Disasters of Love, Sexual and Otherwise." *New York Times Book Review*, 75 (Oct. 25, 1970): 4, 62.

1821. Stern, Daniel. "The Many Voices of Human Loneliness." *Washington Post Book World* (Oct. 25, 1970): 4-5.

1822. Sheppard, R.Z. "On the Rack." *Time*, 96 (Oct. 26, 1970): 119 (K5, K7).

1823. Bell, Pearl K. "A Time for Silence." *New Leader*, 53 (Nov. 16, 1970): 14-15.

1824. Darrach, Brad. "Consumed by a Piranha Complex." *Life*, 69 (Dec. 11, 1970): 14.

1825. Markmann, Charles Lam. "The Terror of Love." *Nation*, 211 (Dec. 14, 1970): 636-637.
        Repr. in *Critical Essays on Joyce Carol Oates*, Linda W. Wagner. Boston, MA: G.K. Hall, 1979, pp. 27-28.

1826. Perkins, Bill. "Similar They Are, but Miss Oates' Stories Still Stun." *National Observer*, 9 (Dec. 28, 1970): 17.

1827. Nardi, Marcia. "With No Heart." *Christian Science Monitor*, 63 (Dec. 31, 1970): 5.

1828. Crane, Lucille G. *Best Sellers*, 30 (Jan. 1, 1971): 429.

1829. *Booklist*, 67 (Jan. 15, 1971): 401.

1830. Sullivan, Mary. "Cranford in India." *Listener*, 86 (Oct. 21, 1971): 550.

1831. May, Derwent. "Never Knowingly Understated." *Observer* (Nov. 7, 1971): 34.

1832. *Virginia Quarterly Review*, 47, i (Winter 1971): xv.

1833. Hagopian, John V. *Studies in Short Fiction*, 9, iii
       (1972): 281-283.

1834. Gregory, Hilda. "Eros and Agape." *Prairie Schooner*,
       46, ii (Summer 1972): 177-178.

1835. Wildman, John Hazard. "Beyond Classification--Some
       Notes on Distinction." *Southern Review* (Baton
       Rouge), n.s., 9, i (Winter 1973): 235-237.

1836. Clerval, Alain. "L'érotisme dans une société puri-
       taine." *Quinzaine Littéraire*, 178 (1-15 janv.
       1974): 13-14.

1837. Creighton, Joanne V. "Joyce Carol Oates's Craftsman-
       ship in 'The Wheel of Love.'" *Studies in Short
       Fiction*, 15, iv (Fall 1978): 375-384.

WHERE ARE YOU GOING, WHERE HAVE YOU BEEN ? (# 403)

1838. Sullivan, Walter. "Where Have All the Flowers Gone ?:
       The Short Story in Search of Itself." *Sewanee
       Review*, 78, iii (Summer 1970): 535-537.

1839. Wegs, Joyce M. "Don't You Know Who I Am ?: The
       Grotesque in Oates's 'Where Are You Going,
       Where Have You Been ?'" *Journal of Narrative
       Technique*, 5, i (Jan. 1975): 66-72.
       Repr. in *Critical Essays on Joyce Carol Oates*,
       Linda W. Wagner. Boston, MA: G.K. Hall, 1979,
       pp. 87-92.
       [Formerly unpublished MLA Seminar Paper, 1973]

1840. Urbanski, Marie Mitchell Olesen. "Existential Allegory:
       Joyce Carol Oates's 'Where Are You Going,
       Where Have You Been ?'" *Studies in Short
       Fiction*, 15, ii (Spring 1978): 200-203.

1841. Schulz, Gretchen & Rockwood, R.J.R. "In Fairyland,
       without a Map: Connie's Exploration Inward in
       Joyce Carol Oates' 'Where Are You Going, Where
       Have You Been ?'" *Literature and Psychology*,
       30, iii-iv (1980): 155-167.

1842. Winslow, Joan D. "The Stranger Within: Two Stories
       by Oates and Hawthorne." *Studies in Short
       Fiction*, 17, iii (Summer 1980): 263-268.

1843. Harty, Kevin J. "Archetype and Popular Lyric in Joyce Carol Oates's 'Where Are You Going, Where Have You Been ?'" *Pennsylvania English*, 8, i (1980-81): 26-28.

1844. Quirk, Tom. "A Source for 'Where Are You Going, Where Have You Been ?'" *Studies in Short Fiction*, 18, iv (Fall 1981): 413-419.

1845. Gillis, Christian Marsden. "'Where Are You Going, Where Have You Been ?': Seduction, Space, and a Fictional Mode." *Studies in Short Fiction*, 18, i (Winter 1981): 65-70.

1846. Robson, Mark. *Explicator*, 40, iv (Summer 1982): 59-60.

1847. Healey, James. "Pop Music and Joyce Carol Oates' 'Where Are You Going, Where Have You Been ?'" *NMAL: Notes on Modern American Literature*, 7, i (Spring-Summer 1983): item 5.

WHERE ARE YOU GOING, WHERE HAVE YOU BEEN ?: STORIES OF YOUNG AMERICA (# 404)

1848. *Publishers' Weekly*, 205 (June 10, 1974): 42.

1849. McLellan, Joseph. *Washington Post Book World* (Aug. 25, 1974): 4.

1850. Bogart, Gary. "Elderly Books for Youngerly Readers." *Wilson Library Bulletin*, 49, ii (Oct. 1974): 140.

WHERE I LIVED, AND WHAT I LIVED FOR (# 406)

1851. Loeb, Monica. "Walden Revisited by Joyce Carol Oates." *American Studies in Scandinavia*, 14, ii (1982): 99-106.

WITH SHUDDERING FALL (# 17)

1852. Joseph, Ellen. "Growing up Assured." *Book Week* (Oct. 25, 1964): 21, 23.

1853. Knowles, John. "A Racing Car Is the Symbol of Violence." *New York Times Book Review*, 69 (Oct. 25, 1964): 5.

1854. Jackson, K.G. "Books in Brief." *Harper's*, 229 (Nov. 1964): 151.

1855. Barret, Mary L. *Library Journal*, 89 (Nov. 15, 1964): 4562.

1856. Pagones, Dorrie. "Price of Survival." *Saturday Review*, 47 (Nov. 28, 1964): 39.

1857. Kauffmann, Stanley. "O'Hara and Others." *New York Review of Books*, 3 (Dec. 17, 1964): 22.

1858. McConkey, James. "Joyce Carol Oates' 'With Shuddering Fall.'" *Epoch*, 14, ii (Winter 1965): 185-188.

1859. *Observer* (Jan. 9, 1966): 25.

1860. Hamilton, Ian. "Fatal Fascinations." *New Statesman*, 71 (Jan. 14, 1966): 55. Repr. in *Critical Essays on Joyce Carol Oates*, Linda W. Wagner. Boston, MA: G.K. Hall, 1979, p. 5.

1861. Scannell, Vernon. "Crackers." *Spectator*, 216 (Jan. 14, 1966): 50-51.

1862. *Times Literary Supplement*, 3336 (Feb. 3, 1966): 90.

1863. Worthy, Judith. "On Carnivals and Motor-Racing." *Books and Bookmen*, 11 (Mar. 1966): 46.

1864. *Publishers' Weekly*, 198 (Dec. 14, 1970): 40.

1865. *Best Sellers*, 30 (Feb. 1, 1971): 484.

1866. Nichols, Marianna da Vinci. "Women on Women: The Looking Glass Novel." *Denver Quarterly*, 11, iii (Autumn 1976): 2.

1867. Burwell, Rose Marie. "Joyce Carol Oates' First Novel." *Canadian Literature*, 73 (Summer 1977): 54-67.

WOMEN WHOSE LIVES ARE FOOD, MEN WHOSE LIVES ARE MONEY: POEMS (# 831)

1868. *Publishers' Weekly*, 213 (May 29, 1978): 47.

1869. *Kirkus Reviews*, 46 (July 1, 1978): 744.

1870. *Virginia Quarterly Review*, 54, iv (Autumn 1978): 145.

1871. Mitchell, Roger. *Library Journal*, 103 (Oct. 1, 1978): 1988.

1872. *Choice*, 15 (Dec. 1978): 1371.

1873. Cluysenaar, Anne. *Stand*, 20, iii (1979): 73.

1874. Zweig, Paul. "Violence, Madness and Description." *New York Times Book Review*, 84 (Apr. 29, 1979): 15, 59.

1875. Zinnes, H. *World Literature Today*, 53 (Summer 1979): 512.

WONDERLAND (# 18)

1876. Avant, John Alfred. *Library Journal*, 96 (Aug. 1971): 2545.

1877. *Kirkus Reviews*, 39 (Aug. 1, 1971): 831.

1878. *Publishers' Weekly*, 200 (Aug. 2, 1971): 62.

1879. Hayes, Brian P. *Saturday Review*, 54 (Oct. 9, 1971): 38.

1880. Oberbeck, S.K. "The Life Force Gone Wild." *Washington Post Book World* (Oct. 10, 1971): 4, 15.

1881. P[rescott], P[eter] S. "Everyday Monsters." *Newsweek*, 78 (Oct. 11, 1971): 96, 100, 101A, 102. Repr. in *Critical Essays on Joyce Carol Oates*, Linda W. Wagner. Boston, MA: G.K. Hall, 1979, pp. 29-30.

1882. Lask, Thomas. "The Child Is Father of the Man." *New York Times*, 121 (Oct. 16, 1971): 29.

1883. Sheppard, R.Z. "Wilder Oates." *Time*, 98 (Oct. 18, 1971): 89-90.

1884. Sale, Roger. "What Went Wrong ?" *New York Review of Books*, 17 (Oct. 21, 1971): 3-4, 6.

1885. Wolff, Geoffrey. "Miss Oates Loves to Splash Blood on Us." *New York Times Book Review*, 76 (Oct. 24, 1971): 5, 10.

1886. Weeks, Edward. "The Peripatetic Reviewer." *Atlantic*, 228 (Nov. 1971): 148-150.

1887. *Booklist*, 68 (Dec. 1, 1971): 319.

1888. Schott, Webster. "Joyce Carol Oates Reaches Her Limit." *Life*, 71 (Dec. 3, 1971): 18.

1889. *Washington Post Book World* (Dec. 5, 1971): 5.

1890. Godwin, Gail. "An Oates Scrapbook." *North American Review*, 256, iv (Winter 1971): 67-70.

1891. Zollman, Sol. "Propaganda for Theory of Human Nature in Current American Novels." *Literature and Ideology*, 12 (1972): 61-62, 65-66.

1892. Bedient, Calvin. "Blind Mouths." *Partisan Review*, 39, i (1972): 124-127.

1893. Gordon, Jan B. "Gothic Fiction and the Losing Battle to Contain Oneself." *Commonweal*, 95 (Feb. 11, 1972): 449-450.

1894. Spacks, Patricia Meyer. "A Chronicle of Women." *Hudson Review*, 25, i (Spring 1972): 168.

1895. Meyer, Ellen Hope. *Mediterranean Review*, 2, iii (Spring 1972): 50-54.

1896. Farrell, J.G. "Fat and Bloody." *Listener*, 87 (June 15, 1972): 797.

1897. Lurie, Alison. "The Enemy Within." *Observer* (June 18, 1972): 32.

1898. Shrapnel, Norman. "Intimations." *Guardian Weekly*, 106 (June 24, 1972): 23.

1899. "Bloody Weapons." *Times Literary Supplement*, 3671 (July 7, 1972): 765.

1900. Brown, F.J. *Books and Bookmen*, 17 (Aug. 1972): 72.

1901. *Best Sellers*, 32 (Mar. 1, 1973): 550.

1902. Taylor, Gordon O. "Joyce Carol Oates, Artist in 'Wonderland.'" *Southern Review* (Baton Rouge), n.s., 10, ii (Spring 1974): 490–503.

1903. Waller, G.F. "Joyce Carol Oates's 'Wonderland': An Introduction." *Dalhousie Review*, 54, iii (Autumn 1974): 480–490.

1904. *Observer* (Oct. 1974): 29.

1905. Key, James A. "Joyce Carol Oates's 'Wonderland' and the Idea of Control." *Arkansas Philological Association Publications*, 2, iii (1975): 15–21.

1906. Giles, James R. "The 'Marivaudian Being' Drowns His Children: Dehumanization in Donald Barthelme's 'Robert Kennedy Saved from Drowning' and Joyce Carol Oates's 'Wonderland.'" *Southern Humanities Review*, 9, i (Winter 1975): 63–75.

1907. Pinsker, Sanford. "Joyce Carol Oates's 'Wonderland': A Hungering for Personality." *Critique*, 20, ii (1978): 59–70.

1908. Higdon, David Leon. "'Suitable Conclusions': The Two Endings of Oates's 'Wonderland.'" *Studies in the Novel*, 10, iv (Winter 1978): 447–453.

1909. Friedman, Ellen G. "The Journey from the 'I' to the 'Eye': 'Wonderland'" in *Critical Essays on Joyce Carol Oates*, Linda W. Wagner. Boston, MA: G.K. Hall, 1979, pp. 102–116.
Repr. in *Studies in American Fiction*, 8, i (Spring 1980): 37–50.
and in *Joyce Carol Oates*, Ellen G. Friedman. New York: Ungar, 1980, pp. 95–115.

1910. Box, Patricia S. "Vision and Revision in 'Wonderland.'" *Notes on Contemporary Literature*, 9, i (1979): 3–6.

1911. Burwell, Rose Marie. "'Wonderland': Paradigm of the
       Psychohistorical Mode." *Mosaic*, 14, iii (Summer
       1981): 1-16.

1912. Karl, Frederick R. *American Fictions 1940-1980.* New
       York: Harper & Row, 1983, pp. 420-421.

DISSERTATIONS

1913. Allen, Mary Inez. *The Necessary Blankness: Women in Major American Fiction of the Sixties.* Ph.D., University of Maryland, 1973. 264p.

Dissertation Abstracts International, 34 (June 1974): 7736A.

1914. Wegs, Joyce Markert. *The Grotesque in Some American Novels of the Nineteen-Sixties: Ken Kesey, Joyce Carol Oates, Sylvia Plath.* Ph.D., University of Illinois at Urbana-Champaign, 1973. 302p.

Dissertation Abstracts International, 34 (June 1974): 7791A-7792A.

1915. Grant, Mary Kathryn. *The Tragic Vision of Joyce Carol Oates.* Ph.D., Indiana University, 1974. 189p.

Dissertation Abstracts International, 35 (Jan. 1975): 4520A-4521A.

1916. Hodge, Marion Cecil, Jr. *What Moment Is Not Terrible ?: An Introduction to the Work of Joyce Carol Oates.* Ph.D., University of Tennessee, 1974. 186p.

Dissertation Abstracts International, 35 (Feb. 1975): 5407A.

1917. Martin, Alice Conkright. *Toward a Higher Consciousness: A Study of the Novels of Joyce Carol Oates.* Ph.D., Northern Illinois University, 1974. 296p.

Dissertation Abstracts International, 35 (Feb. 1975): 5415A-5416A.

1918. Stevens, Cynthia Charlotte. *The Imprisoned Imagination: The Family in the Fiction of Joyce Carol Oates, 1960-1970.* Ph.D., University of Illinois at Urbana-Champaign, 1974. 212p.

Dissertation Abstracts International, 35 (July 1974): 479A.

1919. Rocco, Claire Joyce. *Flannery O'Connor and Joyce Carol Oates: Violence As Art.* Ph.D., University of Illinois at Urbana-Champaign, 1975. 336p.

Dissertation Abstracts International, 36 (Mar. 1976): 6090A.

1920. McLaughlin, Marilou Briggs. *The Love Dialectic.* Ph.D., State University of New York at Binghamton, 1976. 143p.

Dissertation Abstracts International, 36 (June 1976): 8035A.

1921. Petite, Joseph Michael. *The Interrelatedness of Marriage, Passion and Female Identity in the Fiction of Joyce Carol Oates.* Ph.D., Kansas State University, 1976. 138p.

Dissertation Abstracts International, 37 (Mar. 1977): 5831A.

1922. Bender, Eileen Teper. *The Artistic Vision: Theory and Practice of Joyce Carol Oates.* Ph.D., University of Notre Dame, 1977. 314p.

Dissertation Abstracts International, 38 (Sept. 1977): 1384A.

1923. Mesinger, Bonnie Martha. *Dissonance and Indeterminacy in the Critical Writings and Fiction of Joyce Carol Oates: Implications for the Interpreter.* Ph.D., Wayne State University, 1977. 259p.

Dissertation Abstracts International, 38 (May 1978): 6716A-6717A.

1924. Mistri, Zenobia. *Joyce Carol Oates: Transformation of 'Being' toward a Center.* Ph.D., Purdue University, 1977. 169p.

Dissertation Abstracts International, 38 (Apr. 1978): 6122A.

1925. Rozga, Margaret Groppi. *Development in the Short Stories of Joyce Carol Oates.* Ph.D., University of Wisconsin-Milwaukee, 1977. 273p.

Dissertation Abstracts International, 38 (Apr. 1978): 6124A.

1926. Scott, Phyllis Eva. *An Interpreter's Approach to the Language Behavior of Literary Speakers: A Sociolinguistic Analysis of Joyce Carol Oates' Poetry.* Ph.D., Southern Illinois University, 1977. 222p.

Dissertation Abstracts International, 38 (Aug. 1977): 549A.

1927. Wilson, Mary Ann. *The Image of Self in Selected Works of Joyce Carol Oates.* Ph.D., Louisiana State University and Agricultural and Mechanical College, 1977. 161p.

Dissertation Abstracts International, 38 (June 1978): 7340A.

1928. Friedman, Ellen. *'Dreaming America': The Fiction of Joyce Carol Oates.* Ph.D., New York University, 1978. 298p.

Dissertation Abstracts International, 39 (Dec. 1978): 3578A.

1929. Haneline, Douglas Latham. *The Swing of the Pendulum: Naturalism in Contemporary American Literature.* Ph.D., Ohio State University, 1978. 226p.

Dissertation Abstracts International, 39 (Oct. 1978): 2272A-2273A.

1930. Orenstein, Susan Beth. *Angel of Fire: Violence, Self and Grace in the Novels of Joyce Carol Oates.* Ph.D., New York University, 1978. 252p.

Dissertation Abstracts International, 39 (Dec. 1978): 3586A.

1931. Bloom, Kathleen Burke. *The Grotesque in the Fiction of Joyce Carol Oates.* Ph.D., Loyola University of Chicago, 1979. 201p.

Dissertation Abstracts International, 40 (Oct. 1979): 2059A.

1932. Ducas, Philomene C. *Determinism in Joyce Carol Oates's Novels, 1964–1975.* Ph.D., University of Wisconsin-Madison, 1979. 528p.

Dissertation Abstracts International, 40 (Feb. 1980): 4589A.

1933. Bliss, Corinne Demas. *The Short Story: Writer's Control/Reader's Response.* Ph.D., Columbia University, 1980. 208p.

Dissertation Abstracts International, 41 (Aug. 1980): 660A (Oates partim).

1934. Maney, Margaret Schaeffer. *The Urban Apocalypse in Contemporary American Novels.* Ph.D., University of Miami, 1980. 503p.

Dissertation Abstracts International, 41 (Nov. 1980): 2111A (Oates partim).

1935. Arrowood, Gayle F. *Execution, Obsession and Extinction: The Short Fiction of Joyce Carol Oates.* Ph.D., University of Maryland, 1981. 279p.

Dissertation Abstracts International, 43 (July 1982): 172A–173A.

1936. Parrott, Mary Lou Morrison. *Subversive Conformity: Feminism and Motherhood in Joyce Carol Oates.* Ph.D., University of Maryland, 1983. 366p.

Dissertation Abstracts International, 45 (Nov. 1984): 1399A.

1937. Norman, [K.] Torborg [M.]. *Isolation and Contact: A Study of Character Relationships in Joyce Carol Oates's Short Stories 1963–1980.* Ph.D., Göteborg University, 1984. 261p.

III. INDEXES

SUBJECT INDEX

OF JOYCE CAROL OATES'S CRITICAL WRITINGS